Writing for Computer Scienc

Springer
London
Berlin
Heidelberg
New York
Hong Kong
Milan
Paris
Tokyo

Justin Zobel

Writing for Computer Science

Second Edition

Springer

Justin Zobel
School of Computer Science and Information Technology, RMIT University, Melbourne, Australia

British Library Cataloguing in Publication Data
Zobel, Justin
Writing for computer science. - 2nd ed.
1. Technical writing 2. Computer science - Authorship
I. Title
808'.066004
ISBN 1852338024

Library of Congress Cataloging-in-Publication Data
Zobel, Justin, 1963-
Writing for computer science / Justin Zobel. -- 2nd ed.
p. cm.
Includes bibliographical references and index.
ISBN 1-85233-802-4 (soft cover: alk. paper)
1. Technical writing. 2. Communication of technical information. I. Title
T11.Z62 2004
808'.0666--dc22 2004042550

ISBN 1-85233-802-4 2nd edition Springer-Verlag London Berlin Heidelberg
ISBN 981-3083-22-0 1st edition
Springer-Verlag is part of Springer Science+Business Media GmbH
springeronline.com

Printed and bound in the United States of America
34/3830-543210 Printed on acid-free paper SPIN 10945148

Preface

Writing for Computer Science is an introduction to doing and describing research. For the most part the book is a discussion of good writing style and effective research strategies. Some of the material is accepted wisdom, some is controversial, and some is my opinions. Although the book is brief, it is designed to be comprehensive: some readers may be interested in exploring topics further, but for most readers this book should be sufficient.

The first edition of this book was almost entirely about writing. This edition, partly in response to reader feedback and partly in response to issues that arose in my own experiences as an advisor, researcher, and referee, is also about research methods. Indeed, the two topics—writing about and doing research—are not clearly separated. It is a small step from asking *how do I write?* to asking *what is it that I write about?*

As previously, the guidance on writing focuses on research, but much of the material is applicable to general technical and professional communication. Likewise, the guidance on the practice of research has broader lessons. A practitioner trying a new algorithm or explaining to colleagues why one solution is preferable to another should be confident that the arguments are built on robust foundations. And, while this edition has a stronger emphasis on research than did the first, nothing has been deleted; there is additional material on research, but the guidance on writing has not been taken away.

Since the first edition appeared, there have been many changes in the culture and environment of research. The web has become universal, whereas, for example, few papers were online. There are also more subtle changes. It now seems to be rare that a spoken presentation is truly unprofessional; a decade ago many talks were unendurably awful. The growth in the use of good tools for presentations has been a key factor in this development, and the use of overhead transparencies has become archaic.

On the other hand, it now seems common that a talk does not have a clear message and is merely a compilation of clever visuals. Writing style has become less stilted, which is a change for the better, but too many authors are submitting work too early. Today, algorithms are often poorly described; a well-described algorithm has become a welcome, rare exception. The web provides easy access to literature, but perhaps the necessity of using a library imposed discipline, as, increasingly, past work appears to be neglected.

The perspectives of all scientists are shaped by the research cultures in which they work. My research has involved some theoretical studies, but the bulk of my work has been experimental. I appreciate theoretical work for its elegance, yet find it sterile when it is too detached from practical value. While experimental work can be ad hoc, it can also be deeply satisfying, with the rewards of probing the space of possible algorithms and producing technology that can be applied to the things we do in practice. My perspective on research comes from this background, as does the use of experimental work as examples in this book (an approach that is also justified by the fact that such work is generally easier to outline than is a theoretical contribution). But that doesn't mean that my opinions are simply private biases. They are—I hope!—the considered views of a scientist with experience of different kinds of research.

Many people helped with this book in one way or another. For the first edition, thanks were due in particular to Alistair Moffat, who contributed to Chapters 6, 7, 8, 9, and 12; and to Philip Dart, who also contributed to Chapter 12. I remain grateful to both Alistair and Philip for our collaborations. Additionally, I thanked Isaac Balbin, Gill Dobbie, Evan Harris, Michael Fuller, Mary and Werner Pelz, Kotagiri Ramamohanarao, Ron Sacks-Davis, Ian Shelley, James Thom, Rodney Topor, Ross Wilkinson, and Hugh Williams. I also thanked my research students and the students who participated in my research methods lectures. To all these people—thanks again.

For this edition, I thank Timothy A.H. Bell, Bodo Billerbeck, Beverley Ford, Michael Fuller (again), Paul Gruba, Lin Padgham, Jenny Wolkowicki, and the many readers who pointed out mistakes or made helpful suggestions. My children showed remarkable patience and I thank them for their forbearance. The person I thank the most is my wife, Penny Tolhurst.

Justin Zobel
Melbourne, Australia
February 2004

Contents

1 Introduction

This writing seemeth to me ... not much better than the noise or sound which musicians make while they are in tuning their instruments.

Francis Bacon
The Advancement of Learning

No tale is so good that it can't be spoiled in the telling.

Proverb

A scientific paper presents new ideas and demonstrates their correctness. A paper can remain relevant for many years and, if published in a major journal or conference, may be read by thousands of students and scientists.

Unfortunately, many scientists do not write well. Bacon's remark was made four hundred years ago yet applies to much science writing today. Perhaps we should not always expect scientists to communicate well; surely the skills required for science and writing are different. Or are they? The best science is based on straightforward, logical thinking, and it isn't artistic prose that we expect in a research paper—we expect clarity. If the ideas are clearly expressed and well organized, the paper should be easy to read.

Scientists should not be content to write badly. Everyone whose work is affected by a poorly written paper will suffer: ambiguity leads to misunderstanding; omissions frustrate; obscurity makes readers struggle to reconstruct the author's intention. Effort used to understand the structure of a paper or the syntax of its sentences is effort not used to understand its content. And, as the proverb tells us, no tale is so good that it can't be spoiled in the telling. Irrespective of the importance and validity of a paper, it cannot be convincing if it is difficult to understand. The more important the results—or the more startling or unlikely they seem—the better the supporting arguments and their presentation should be.

It may seem unjust, but good writing and presentation can persuade readers that work is of value. Poorly presented material carries a strong subconscious message; for example, readers tend to judge statements to be wrong if they contain numerous spelling errors. Layout issues such as font and spacing are also important—if they weren't, we would be as comfortable reading fixed-width fonts on a computer screen as we are reading text in a book. A lazy presentation suggests to the reader that little care has been taken with the work.

Thus the ability to write well is a key skill of science. Like many aspects of research, writing can only be thoroughly learnt while working with other scientists. Too often, however, the only help a novice receives is an advisor's feedback on drafts of papers. Such interaction can be far from adequate: many scientists have little experience of writing extended documents, and may be confronting the difficulties of writing in English when it is not their first language. It is not surprising that some scientists struggle. Many are intimidated by writing, and avoid it because describing research is less entertaining than actually doing it. For some advisors, the task of helping a student to write well is not one that comes naturally, and it can be a distraction from the day-to-day work of research and teaching.

Few scientists are natural writers. Those who do write well have, largely, learnt through experience; their early papers are often embarrassingly poor. Yet it is not so difficult to become a good writer. Most scientists can produce competent papers simply by following elementary steps: create a logical organization, use concise sentences, revise against checklists of possible problems, seek feedback. Like many skills, writing improves through practice and a willingness to accept and learn from criticism.

Kinds of publication

Scientific results can be presented in a book, a thesis, a journal article, a complete paper or extended abstract in a conference or workshop proceedings, a technical report, or a manuscript. Each kind of publication has its own characteristics. Books are usually texts that tend not to contain new results or prove the correctness of the information they present. The main purpose of a textbook is to collect information and present it in an accessible, readable form, and thus textbooks are generally better written than are papers.

The other forms of publication are for describing the outcomes of new research. A thesis is usually a deep—or even definitive—exploration of a single problem. Journals and conference proceedings consist of contributions that range from substantial papers to extended abstracts. A journal paper is typically an end product of the research process, a careful presentation of new ideas that has been revised, sometimes over several iterations, according to referees' or advisors' suggestions and criticisms.

A paper or extended abstract in a conference proceedings can likewise be an end-product, but conferences are also used to report work in progress. Conference papers are usually refereed, but with more limited opportunities for iteration and revision, and may be constrained by strict length limits. There is no universal definition of "extended abstract", but a common meaning is that the detail of the work is omitted. That is, an extended abstract may review the results of a research program, but not in enough detail to make a solid argument for the hypothesis. It follows that refereeing of extended abstracts must be superficial.

In contrast to books—which can represent an author's opinions as well as established scientific knowledge—the content of a paper must be defended and justified. This is the purpose of refereeing: to attempt to ensure that papers published in a reputable journal or conference are trustworthy, high-quality work. Indeed, in a common usage a *published paper* is distinguished from a mere *paper* by having been refereed.

A typical research paper consists of the arguments, evidence, experiments, proofs, and background required to support and explain a central hypothesis. In contrast, the process of research that leads to a paper can include uninteresting failures, invalid hypotheses, misconceptions, and experimental mistakes. With few exceptions these do not belong in a paper. A paper should be an objective addition to scientific knowledge, not a description of the path you took to the result. Style is not just about how to write, but is also about what to say.

Writing, science, and skepticism

Science is a system for accumulating reliable knowledge. Broadly speaking, the process of science begins with speculation, observation, and a growing understanding of some idea or phenomenon. This understanding is used to develop hypotheses that can be tested by proof or experimentation. The results are described in a paper, which is then submitted for independent review before (hopefully) being published.

Writing underpins the research cycle. A key aspect of writing is that the discipline of stating ideas as organized text forces you to formulate and clarify your thoughts. Vague concepts become concrete, the act of writing suggests new concepts to consider, written material is easier to discuss and debate with colleagues, and the only effective way to develop complex arguments or threads of reasoning and evaluate whether they are sound is to write them down. That is, writing is not the end of the research process, but instead shapes it. Only the styling of a paper, the polishing process, truly follows the research.

It is writing, too, that defines what we consider to be knowledge. Scientific results are only accepted as correct once they are refereed and published; if they aren't published, they aren't confirmed. Each new contribution builds on a bed of existing concepts that are known and, within limits, trusted. New research may be wrong or misguided, but the process of refereeing eliminates some work of poor quality, while the scientific culture of questioning ideas and requiring convincing demonstrations of their correctness weeds out (perhaps gradually) published falsehoods.

A unifying principle for the scientific culture that determines the value of research is that of *skepticism*. Within science, skepticism is an open-minded approach to knowledge: a scientist should accept ideas provisionally given reasonable evidence and given agreement (or at least absence of contradiction) with other provisionally accepted ideas. A skeptic seeks the most accurate description or solution that fits the known facts, without concern for issues such as the need to seek favour with authorities, while suspending judgement until decisive information is available. Effective research programs are designed to seek the evidence needed to convince a reasonable skeptic. Absolute skepticism is unsustainable, but credulity—the willingness to believe anything—is pointless, as it means that it is impossible to learn anything new.

Skepticism is key to good science. For an idea to survive, other scientists must be persuaded of its relevance and correctness—not with rhetoric, but in the established framework of a scientific publication. New ideas must be explained clearly to give them the best possible chance of being understood, believed, remembered, and used. This begins with the task of explaining our ideas to the person at the next desk, or even to ourselves. It ends with publication, that is, an explanation of results to the research community. Thus good writing is a crucial part of the process of good science.

Using this book

There are many good books on writing style and research methods, but the conventions of style vary from discipline to discipline, and general guidance on science writing can be wrong or irrelevant for a specific subject. Some topics—such as algorithms, mathematics, and research methods for computer science—are not discussed in these books at all.

The role of this book is to help computer scientists with their writing and research. For novices, it introduces the elements of a scientific paper and reviews a wide range of issues that working scientists need to consider. For experienced researchers, it provides a reference point against which they can judge their own views and abilities, and is an exposure to wider cultures of research. This book is also intended to encourage reflection; the later chapters pose questions about research that a responsible scientist should address. Nobody can learn to write or become a scientist just by reading this book, or indeed any book. To become competent it is necessary to do research and write it up with other scientists. However, familiarity with the elements of writing and research is essential in scientific training.

Style is in some respects a matter of taste. The advice in this book is not a code of law to be rigidly obeyed; it is a collection of guidelines, not rules, and there are inevitably situations in which the "correct" style seems wrong. But generally there are good reasons for writing in a certain way. Almost certainly you will disagree with some of the points given in this book, but at least exposure to another's opinion should lead you to justify your own choice of style, rather than by habit continue with what may be poor writing. A good principle is: By all means break a rule, but have a good reason for doing so.

Most computer scientists can benefit from reading a book about writing and research. This book can be used as the principal text for a senior research methods subject, or for a series of lectures on the practice of research. Such a subject would not necessarily follow this book chapter by chapter, but instead use it as a resource. In my own teaching of research methods, lectures on writing style seem to work best as introductions to the key topics of good writing; talking students through the detailed advice given here is less effective than getting them to read the book while writing for themselves. Topics such as statistics, formal reasoning, or philosophies of science should be discussed in far more detail than they are here. However, for a range of topics—figures, algorithms, presentations, drafting a paper, ethics, and experimentation, for example—the relevant chapter can be used as the basis of one or two lectures.

This book includes material on the major facets of writing in computer science: writing style (Chapters 2, 3, and 4), mathematical style (Chapter 5), design of figures and graphs (Chapter 6), presentation of algorithms (Chapter 7), editing (Chapter 8), writing and organization of papers and theses (Chapter 9), and presentations (Chapter 14). A chapter on refereeing (Chapter 12) gives a perspective from the other side, by outlining what is expected of a completed paper. The quality of a paper rests on both the writing and the underlying work, and thus part of the book is about the doing of science: becoming a researcher, beginning a research project, and asking research questions (Chapter 10), experimentation (Chapter 11), and research ethics (Chapter 13). If you are new to research, Chapter 10 may be the right place to begin. There are also exercises to help develop writing and research skills.

This book has been written with the intention that it be browsed, not memorized or learnt by rote. Read through it once or twice, absorb whatever advice seems of value to you, then consult it for specific problems. Use the checklists as a reference for evaluating your work; for example, see pages 134, 155, 182, 204, 213, 224, and 237, as well as the many reference lists.

The book's website, `www.justinzobel.com`, has a range of supporting material. This includes an annotated bibliography (extended from the bibliography included in the print version of the first edition) and pointers to relevant material on the web.

Spelling and terminology

British spelling is used throughout this book, with just a couple of quirks, such as use of "program" rather than "programme". American readers: There is an "e" in "judgement" and a "u" in "rigour"—within these pages. Australian readers: There is a "z" in "customize". These are choices, not mistakes.

Choosing terminology is less straightforward. An undergraduate is an undergraduate, but the American graduate student is the British or Australian postgraduate. The generic "research student" is used throughout, and, making arbitrary choices, "thesis" rather than "dissertation" and "PhD" rather than "doctorate". The academic staff member (faculty in North America) who works with—"supervises"—a research student is, in this book, an "advisor" rather than a "supervisor". Researchers write articles, papers, reports, theses, extended abstracts, and reviews; in this book, the generic term for these forms of research writing is a "write-up", while "paper" is used for both refereed publications and for work submitted for refereeing.

Some of the examples are based on projects I've been involved in. Most of my research has been collaborative; rather than use circumlocutions such as "my colleagues and I", or "together with my students", the simple shorthand "we" is used to indicate that the work was not mine alone. Many of the examples of language use are drawn from other people's papers; in some cases, the text has been altered to disguise its origin.

2 Good style

Everything written with vitality expresses that vitality;
there are no dull subjects, only dull minds.

Raymond Chandler
The Simple Art of Murder

It is a golden rule always to use, if possible, a short old Saxon word. Such a sentence as "so purely dependent is the incipient plant on the specific morphological tendency" does not sound to my ears like good mother-English—it wants translating.

Charles Darwin
Letter to John Scott

There are many ways in which an idea can be expressed in English; writing can be verbose or cryptic, flowery or plain, poetic or literal. The manner of expression is the writing style. Style is not about correct use of grammar, but about how well you communicate with likely readers.

Conventions and styles are valuable because some forms of presentation are difficult to understand or are simply boring, and because conformity to commonly used styles reduces the effort required from readers. Flouting an established convention has the impact of this exclamation! It arrests attention and distracts from the message.

Science writing must by its nature be prosaic—the need for it to be accurate and clear makes poetry inappropriate. But this does not mean that science writing has to be dull. It can have style, and moreover the desire to communicate clearly is not the only reason to make good use of English. Lively writing suggests a lively mind with interesting ideas to discuss, while poor usage is distracting, suggests disorganized thinking, and prejudices readers against whatever is being presented.

This chapter, and Chapters 3 and 4, concern writing style, including issues that are specific to science and general issues that many scientists ignore. Good style for science is, ultimately, nothing more than writing that is easy to understand. Most of the points in these chapters are about the basic aims of science writing: to be clear, unambiguous, correct, interesting, and direct.

Economy

Text should be taut. The length of a paper should reflect its content—it is admirable to say much in a small space. Every sentence should be necessary. Papers are not made more important by padding with long-winded sentences; they are made less readable. In the following example, the italicized text can be discarded without affecting the intent.

> *The volume of information has been rapidly increasing in the past few decades. While computer technology has played a significant role in encouraging the information growth, the latter has also had a great impact on the evolution of computer technology in processing data throughout the years. Historically, many different kinds of databases have been developed to handle information, including the early hierarchical and network models, the relational model, as well as the latest object-oriented and deductive databases. However, no matter how much these databases have improved, they still have their deficiencies.* Much information is *in* textual *format*. This unstructured *style of* data, *in contrast to the old structured record format data,* cannot be managed properly by *the* traditional database models. Furthermore, *since so much information is available,* storage and indexing are not the only problems. We need to ensure that relevant information can be obtained upon querying *the database*.

Waffle, such as the italicized material above, is deadwood that readers must cut away before they can get to the meaning of the text.

Taut writing is a consequence of careful, frequent revision. Aim to delete superfluous words, simplify sentence structure, and establish a logical flow. That is, convey information without unnecessary dressing. Revise in a critical frame of mind, and avoid a sense of showing off or being clever. Be egoless—ready to dislike anything you have previously written. Expect to revise several times, perhaps many times.

If someone dislikes anything you have written, remember that it is readers you need to please, not yourself. Again, it helps to set aside your ego. For example, when you are making changes to a paper in response to comments from a reader, you may find that the reader has made a claim that is wrong or meaningless. However, rather than telling yourself "the reader is wrong", ask yourself "what did I write that led the reader astray?" Even misguided feedback tells you something about your writing.

Text can be condensed too far. Don't omit words that make the writing easier to understand.

✗ Bit-stream interpretation requires external description of stored structures. Stored descriptions are encoded, not external.

✓ Interpretation of bit-streams requires external information such as descriptions of stored structures. Such descriptions are themselves data, and if stored with the bit-stream become part of it, so that further external information is required.

Tone

Science writing should be objective and accurate. Many of the elements that give literature its strength—nuance, ambiguity, metaphor, sensuality—are inappropriate for technical work. In contrast to popular science writing, the primary objective is to inform, not entertain. On the other hand, use of turgid, convoluted language is perhaps the most common fault in scientific writing; a direct, simple style is appropriate. Aim for austerity, not pomposity.

Simple writing follows from a few simple rules:

- Have one idea per sentence or paragraph and one topic per section.
- Have a simple, logical organization.
- Use short words.
- Use short sentences with simple structure.
- Keep paragraphs short.
- Avoid buzzwords, clichés, and slang.
- Avoid excess, in length or style.
- Omit any unnecessary material.

- Be specific, not vague or abstract.
- Break these rules if there is a good reason to do so.

Sometimes a long word or a complex sentence is the best option. Use them when necessary, but not otherwise.

Another common fault in science writing is to overqualify, that is, to modify every claim with caveats and cautions. Such writing is a natural consequence of the scientist's desire to not make unfounded claims, but it can be taken too far.

✗ The results show that, for the given data, less memory is likely to be required by the new structure, depending on the magnitude of the numbers to be stored and the access pattern.

✓ The results show that less memory was required by the new structure. Whether this result holds for other data sets will depend on the magnitude of the numbers and the access pattern, but we expect that the new structure will usually require less memory than the old.

The first version is vague; the author has ventured an opinion that the new structure is likely to be better, but has buried it.

Use direct statements and expressions involving "we" or "I"—that is, the active voice—to make reading more pleasant and to help distinguish new results from old. (Voice is discussed on page 14.) There is nothing wrong with using a casual or conversational tone in technical writing, so long as it does not degenerate into slang.

Technical writing is not a good outlet for artistic impulses. The following is from a commercial software requirements document.

✗ The system should be developed with the end users clearly in view. It must therefore run the gamut from simplicity to sophistication, robustness to flexibility, all in the context of the individual user. From the first tentative familiarization steps, the consultation process has been used to refine the requirements by continued scrutiny and rigorous analysis until, by some alchemical process, those needs have been transmuted into specifications. These specifications distill the quintessence of the existing system.

The above extract has the excuse that it forms part of a sales pitch, but the following is from a scientific paper on concurrent database systems.

✗ We have already seen, in our consideration of *what is*, that the usual simplified assumptions lead inexorably to a representation that is desirable, because a solution is always desirable; but repugnant, because it is false. And we have presented *what should be*, assumptions whose nature is not susceptible to easy analysis but are the only tenable alternative to ignorance (absence of solution) or a false model (an incorrect solution). Our choice is then Hobson's choice, to make do with what material we have—viable assumptions—and to discover whether the intractable can be teased into a useful form.

Deciphering this paper was hard work. The following is a rough translation, with no guarantee that the intended meaning is preserved.

✓ We have seen that the usual assumptions lead to a tractable model, but this model is only a poor representation of real behaviour. We therefore proposed better assumptions, which however are difficult to analyze. Now we consider whether there is any way in which our assumptions can be usefully applied.

Novice writers can be tempted to imitate the style of, not science writing, but popular science writing.

✗ As each value is passed to the server, the "heart" of the system, it is checked to see whether it is in the appropriate range.

✓ Each value passed to the central server is checked to see whether it is in the appropriate range.

Don't dress up your ideas as if they were on sale. In the following I have changed the author's name to "Grimwade".

✗ Sometimes the local network stalls completely for a few seconds. This is what we call the "Grimwade effect", discovered serendipitously during an experiment to measure the impact of server configuration on network traffic.

✓ Sometimes the local network stalls for a few seconds. We first noticed this effect during an experimental measurement of the impact of server configuration on network traffic.

But consider the following extract from a paper on some pragmatics for indexing, which illustrates that it is not necessary to write in a literary or pedantic style. It is colloquial, poorly punctuated, and there were spelling errors (not reproduced here), but it is direct and frank.

✓ To improve the chance of a cache hit almost a complete recode was necessary to the data structure routines but no run with the new code showed any improvement. The cache may have been too small but more likely the problem was the operating system and instruction prefetch getting the cache dirty. Also after recoding a couple of extra machine instructions were needed for each access so the saving of having a few more hits was lost.

For researchers educated in an English-speaking country, it is easy to forget that English is not the first language of a great many readers. Simple writing allows these people to easily understand your work. Also, popular writing often uses shared cultural elements as references. Slang ("home run"), values ("cool"), analogies ("like turning left from the right lane"), and events ("the Northeastern power outage") may well be meaningless to people in other countries. Even dates can be confusing: in the United States, dates are often written month/day/year, but elsewhere this notation almost invariably means day/-month/year. Write for everybody.

Examples

Use an example whenever it adds clarification. A small example often means the difference between communication and confusion, particularly if the concept being illustrated is fundamental to understanding the paper. People learn by generalizing from concrete instances to abstractions, and examples can give substance to abstract concepts.

✓ In a semi-static model, each symbol has an associated probability representing its likelihood of occurrence. For example, if the symbols are characters in text, then a common character such as "e" might have an associated probability of 12%.

Each example should be an illustration of one concept; if you don't know what an example is illustrating, change it.

Examples can be blocks of text with a heading such as "Example 3.5" or detailed discussions of specific instances where a technique can be used, but often an informative example is just a few words.

✓ Large document collections, such as a repository of newspaper articles, can be managed with the same techniques.

✓ Special cases, such as the empty set, need to be handled separately.

✓ Algorithms that involve bit manipulation cannot be efficiently implemented in these languages. For example, Huffman coding is impractical because it involves processing a stream one bit at a time.

Motivation

Many authors take considerable trouble over the structure of their papers but don't make the structure obvious to the reader. Not only should the parts of a paper be ordered in a logical way, but this logic needs to be communicated.

The introduction usually gives some indication of the organization of the paper, by outlining the results and their context, and may include a list of the parts of the paper, but these measures by themselves are not sufficient. Brief summaries at the start and end of each section are helpful, as are sentences linking one section to the next; for example, a well-written section might conclude with:

✓ Together these results show that the hypothesis holds for linear coefficients. The difficulties presented by non-linear coefficients are considered in the next section.

Link text together as a narrative—each section should have a clear story to tell. The connection between one paragraph and the next should be obvious. This principle is sometimes expressed as: Tell the reader what you are going to say, then say it, and then tell the reader that you have said it.

A common error is to include material such as definitions or theorems without indicating why the material is useful. Usually the problem is lack of explanation; sometimes it is symptomatic of an ordering problem, such as including material before the need for it is obvious. Never assume that a series of definitions, theorems, or algorithms—or even the need for the series—is self-explanatory. Motivate the reader at each major step in the exposition: explain how a definition (theorem, lemma, whatever) is to be used, or why it is interesting, or how it fits into the overall plan.

The authors of a paper are almost always better informed than their readers. Even expert readers won't be familiar with some of the details of a problem, whereas the author has probably been studying the problem intimately for months or years and takes many difficult issues for granted. You should explain everything that is not common knowledge to the paper's readership; what constitutes common knowledge depends on the paper's subject and on where it is published. At each part of a paper you should consider what the reader has learnt so far, whether this knowledge is sufficient to allow understanding of what follows, and whether each part follows from what has already been said.

Balance

Within a paper, each topic should be discussed to a similar depth. A paragraph on a previous algorithm followed by seven pages on your refinements to it is unbalanced. If one relevant paper merits half a page, other papers of equal worth should not be dismissed in a line. An algorithm that is only sketched does not merit twenty graphs and tables; an algorithm that it is described in detail needs a substantial analysis or other justification. A four-page rambling introduction is unlikely to be readable.

The length of a paper is a consequence of how much material is included and of how much detail is given, that is, the depth to which each topic is discussed. When a paper must be kept within a length limit, some compromise is required. Some of the discussion must be omitted, or the graphs selected more carefully, or the text condensed. Perhaps it will even be necessary to omit a proof or a series of results. Such changes should not be used as an excuse for unbalancing the paper.

Voice

Avoid excessive use of indirect statements (or passive voice), particularly descriptions of actions that don't indicate who or what performs them.

✗ The following theorem can now be proved.

✓ We can now prove the following theorem.

The direct style (or active voice) is often less stilted and easier to read.

Another unpleasant indirect style is the artificial use of verbs like "perform" or "utilize", in the false belief that such writing is more precise or scientific. These words can often be removed.

✗ Tree structures can be utilized for dynamic storage of terms.

✓ Terms can be stored in dynamic tree structures.

✗ Local packet transmission was performed to test error rates.

✓ Error rates were tested by local packet transmission.

Other words often used in this way include "achieved", "carried out", "conducted", "done", "occurred", and "effected".

Change of voice sometimes changes meaning and often changes emphasis. If passive voice is necessary, use it. Complete absence of active voice is unpleasant, but that does not mean that all use of passive voice is poor.

Use of "we" is valuable when trying to distinguish between the contribution made in your paper and existing results in a field, particularly in an abstract or introduction. For example, in "it is shown that stable graphs are closed", the reader may have difficulty deciding who is doing the showing, and in "it is hypothesized that ... ", the reader will be unsure whether the hypothesis was posed in your paper or elsewhere. Use of "we" can allow some kinds of statements to be simplified—consider "we show" versus "in this paper it is shown that". "We" is preferable to pretentious expressions such as "the authors".

Some authors use phrases such as "this paper shows" and "this section argues". These phrases, with their implication that the paper is sentient, should not be used.

In some cases the use of "we" is wrong.

✗ When we conducted the experiment it showed that our conjecture was correct.

Here, the use of "we" suggests that if someone else ran the experiment it would behave differently.

✓ The experiment showed that our conjecture was correct.

I do not particularly like the use of "I" in scientific writing, except when it is used to indicate that what follows is the author's opinion. The use of "I" in place of "we" in papers with only one author is uncommon.

Use of personal pronouns has been a contentious issue in technical writing. Some people argue that it undermines objectivity by introducing the author's personality and is therefore unacceptable, even unscientific. Others argue that to suggest that a paper is not the work of individuals is intellectually dishonest, and that use of personal pronouns makes papers easier to read. Although opinions on this topic are divided, use of "we" is an accepted norm.

The upper hand

Some authors seem to have a superiority complex—a need to prove that they know more or are smarter than their readers. Perhaps the most appropriate word for this behaviour is swagger. One form of swagger is implying familiarity with material that most scientists will never read; an example is reference to philosophers such as Wittgenstein or Hegel, or statements such as "the argument proceeds on Voltarian principles". Another form is the unnecessary inclusion of difficult mathematics, or offhand remarks such as "analysis of this method is of course a straightforward application of tensor calculus". Yet another form is citation of obscure, inaccessible references.

This kind of showing off, of attempting to gain the upper hand over the reader, is snobbish and tiresome. Since the intention is to make statements the reader won't understand, the only information conveyed is an impression of the author's ego. Write for an ordinary reader, as your equal.

Obfuscation

Obfuscation is the making of statements in ambiguous or convoluted terms, with the intention of hiding meaning, or of appearing to say much while actually saying little. It can be used, for example, to give the impression of having done something without actually claiming to have done it.

✗ Experiments, with the improved version of the algorithm as we have described, are the step that confirms our speculation that performance would improve. The previous version of the algorithm is rather slow on our test data and improvements lead to better performance.

Note the use of bland statements such as "experiments ... are the step that confirms our speculation" (true, but not informative) and "improvements lead to better performance" (tautologous). The implication is that experiments were undertaken, but there is no direct claim that experiments actually took place.

In science writing, vague statements are common. It is always preferable to be specific: exceptions are or are not possible; data was transmitted at a certain rate; and so on. Stating that "there may be exceptions in some circumstances" or "data was transmitted fast" is not helpful.

✗ Amelioration can lead to large savings.

✓ Amelioration led to savings of 12%–33% in our experiments.

Obfuscation can arise in other ways: exaggeration, omission of relevant information, or bold statements of conclusions based on flimsy evidence. Use of stilted or long-winded sentences—often due to an unnecessary attempt to introduce formality—can obfuscate.

✗ The status of the system is such that a number of components are now able to be operated.

✓ Several of the system's components are working.

✗ In respect to the relative costs, the features of memory mean that with regard to systems today disk has greater associated expense for the elapsed time requirements of tasks involving access to stored data.

✓ Memory can be accessed more quickly than disk.

Some obfuscation arises because processes are unnecessarily complex, are presented in unnecessary detail, or are outright unnecessary. The following was written as part of a tender process.

✗ These draft guidelines are part of a process for seeking comments on the proposed stages for identifying the officers responsible for participating in the development of the initial specification.

Analogies

Analogies are curious things: what seems perfectly alike or parallel to one person may seem entirely unalike to another.

✗ Writing a program is like building a model with connector blocks.

What are "connector blocks"? How are they like programming? Even if the similarity is obvious to a programmer, is it obvious to a novice? This analogy (made in an introduction to computer science) seems to me to fail because it captures neither logic nor repetition. For an analogy to be worthwhile, it should significantly reduce the work of understanding the concept being described.

Another drawback to analogies is that they can take your reasoning astray—two situations with marked similarities may nonetheless have fundamental differences that the analogy leads you to ignore. I have seen more bad analogies than good in computing research papers; however, simple analogies can undoubtedly help illustrate unfamiliar concepts.

✓ Contrasting look-ahead graph traversal with standard approaches, look-ahead uses a bird's-eye view of the local neighbourhood to avoid dead ends, but at significant cost: it is necessary to feed the bird and wait for it to return after each observation.

Beware of analogies with situations that may be unfamiliar to the reader.

✗ One-sided protocols are like signals in football.

Straw men

A straw man is an indefensible hypothesis that an author describes for the sole purpose of criticizing it. A paraphrasing of an instance in a published paper is "it can be argued that databases do not require indexes", in which the author and reader are well aware that a database without an index is as practical as a library without a catalogue. Such writing says more about the author than it does about the subject.

Another form of straw man is the contrasting of a new idea with some impossibly bad alternative, to put the new idea in a favourable light. This form is obnoxious because it can lead the reader to believe that the impossibly bad idea might be worthwhile, and that the new idea is more important than is in fact the case. Contrasts should be between the new and the current, not the new and the fictitious.

✗ Query languages have changed over the years. For the first database systems there were no query languages and records were retrieved with programs. Before then data was kept in filing cabinets and indexes were printed on paper. Records were retrieved by getting them from the cabinets and queries were verbal, which led to many mistakes being made. Such mistakes are impossible with new query languages like QIL.

A more subtle form of straw man is comparison between the new and the ancient. For example, criticisms based on results in old papers are unreasonable because, in all likelihood, the state of the art has changed in the meanwhile.

A straw man is an example of rhetoric—of attempting to win an argument through presentation rather than reasoning. Other forms of rhetoric are appeal to authority, appeal to intuitively obvious truth, and presentation of received wisdom as fact.

✗ We did not investigate partial interpretation because it is known to be ineffective.

If there is evidence—a study or proof, not someone else's opinion—then cite it. Unsubstantiated claims should be clearly noted as such, not dressed up as accepted knowledge.

✗ Most users prefer the graphical style of interface.

✓ We believe that most users prefer the graphical style of interface.

✗ Another possibility would be a disk-based method, but this approach is unlikely to be successful.

✓ Another possibility would be a disk-based method, but our experience suggests that this approach is unlikely to be successful.

Reference and citation

You need to explain the relationship of your new work to existing work, showing how your work builds on previous knowledge and how it differs from contributions in other, relevant papers. The existing work is identified by reference to published theses, articles, books, and reports. All papers include a bibliography, that is, a list of such references in a standardized format, and embedded in each paper's text there are citations to the publications.

References, and discussion of them, serve three main purposes. They help demonstrate that work is new: claims of originality are much more convincing in the context of references to existing work that (from the reader's perspective) appears to be similar. They demonstrate your knowledge of the research area, which helps the reader to judge whether your statements are reliable. And they are pointers to background reading.

Before including a reference, consider whether it will be of service to the reader. A reference should be relevant, it should be up-to-date, it should be reasonably accessible, and it should be necessary. Don't add citations just to pad the bibliography. Refer to an original paper in preference to a secondary source; to well-written material in preference to bad; to a book or journal article in preference to a conference paper; to a conference paper in preference to a technical report or manuscript (which have the disadvantage of being unrefereed); and to printed documents rather than web pages. Avoid reference to private communications and information provided in forums such as seminars or talks—such information cannot be accessed or verified by the reader. In the rare circumstance that you must refer to such material, do so via a footnote, parenthetical remark, or acknowledgement.

If you discuss a paper in detail or note some particular contribution it makes, it must be cited. Otherwise, consider whether a reader needs the paper for knowledge in addition to that in the other papers you cite. If the answer is no, perhaps it should be omitted. At the same time, ensure that it is clear to the reader that you know all the pertinent background literature.

Don't cite to support common knowledge. For example, use of a binary tree in an algorithm doesn't require a reference to a data structures text. But claims, statements of fact, and discussion of previous work should be substantiated by reference if not substantiated within your write-up. This rule even applies to minor points. For some readers the minor points could be of major interest.

In many papers, some of the references are to previous papers by the same author. Such references establish the author's credentials as someone who understands the area, establish a research history for the paper, and allow the interested reader to gain a deeper understanding of the research by following it from its inception. Gratuitous self-reference, however, undermines these purposes; it is frustrating for readers to discover that references are not relevant. Technical reports in particular should not be self-referenced, unless they contain material that is genuinely important and not available elsewhere.

On rare occasions it is necessary to refer to a result in an inaccessible paper. For example, suppose that in 1981 Dawson wrote "Kelly (1959) shows that stable graphs are closed", but Kelly (1959) is inaccessible and Dawson (1981) does not give the details. In your write-up, do not refer directly to Kelly—after all, you can't check the details yourself, and Dawson may have made a mistake.

✓ According to Dawson (1981), stable graphs have been shown to be closed.

✓ According to Kelly (1959; as quoted by Dawson, 1981), stable graphs are closed.

The second form tells readers who originated the result without the effort of obtaining Dawson first. Kelly's entry in the bibliography should clearly show that the reference is second-hand.

Regardless of whether you have access to original sources, be careful to attribute work correctly. For example, some authors have referred to "Knuth's Soundex algorithm", although Knuth is not the author and the algorithm was at least fifty years old when Knuth discussed it.

Some readers of a paper will not have access to the publications it cites, and so may rely on the paper's description of them. For this reason alone you should describe results from other papers fairly and accurately. Any criticisms should be based on sound argument. That is, it is acceptable to make reasoned criticisms, and a careful assessment of past work is of great value because ultimately it is how a paper is regarded that determines its worth. However, only rarely is it acceptable to offer opinions, and it is never acceptable to use flattery or scorn. Neither belittle papers, regardless of your personal opinion of their merits, nor overstate their significance; and beware of statements that might be interpreted as pejorative.

✗ Robinson's theory suggests that a cycle of handshaking can be eliminated, but he did not perform experiments to confirm his results [22].

✓ Robinson's theory suggests that a cycle of handshaking can be eliminated [22], but as yet there is no experimental confirmation.

Careful wording is needed in these circumstances. When referring to the work of Robinson, you might write that "Robinson thinks that ...", but this implies that you believe he is wrong, and has a faint odour of insult; you might write that "Robinson has shown that ...", but this implies that he is incontrovertably right; or you might write that "Robinson has argued that ...", but then should make clear whether you agree.

A simple method of avoiding such pitfalls is to quote from the reference, particularly if it contains a short, memorable statement—one or two sentences, say—that is directly pertinent. Quotation also allows you to clearly distinguish between what you are saying and what others have said, and is far preferable to plagiarism.

Cited material often uses different terminology, spelling, or notation, or is written for an entirely different context. When you use results from other papers, be sure to show the relationship to your own work. For example, a reference might show a general case, but you use a special case; then you need to show that it is a special case. If you claim that concepts are equivalent, ensure that the equivalence is clear to the reader.

References that are discussed should not be anonymous.

✗ Other work [16] has used an approach in which ...

✓ Marsden [16] has used an approach in which ...
Other work (Marsden 1991) has used an approach in which ...

The modified versions provide more information to the reader, and "Marsden" is easier to remember than "[16]" if the same paper is discussed later on. Self-references should not be anonymous—it should be clear to the reader that references used to support your argument are your own papers, not independent authorities. Other references that are not discussed can just be listed.

✓ Better performance might be possible with string hashing techniques that do not use multiplication [11, 30].

Avoid unnecessary discussion of references.

✗ Several authors have considered the problem of unbounded delay. We cite, for example, Hong and Lu (1991) and Wesley (1987).

✓ Several authors have considered the problem of unbounded delay (Hong and Lu 1991; Wesley 1987).

Two styles of citation are illustrated above. One is the ordinal-number style, in which entries in the reference list are numbered and are cited by their number, as in "... is discussed elsewhere [16]". The other is the name-and-date or Harvard style—my preferred style—in which entries are cited by author name using either square or round brackets:

✓ ... is discussed by Whelks and Babb (1972).
... is discussed elsewhere (Whelks and Babb 1972).
... is discussed by Whelks and Babb [1972].
... is discussed elsewhere [Whelks and Babb 1972].

A third common style is to use superscripted ordinal numbers, as in "... is discussed elsewhere^{16}". Another style is use of uppercase abbreviations, where references are denoted by strings such as "[MAR91]". This is not a good style: the abbreviations seem encourage poor writing such as "... is discussed in [WHB72]" and, because uppercase characters stand out from text, they are rather distracting.

Note, however, that many publishers insist on a particular style. (Some also insist that bibliographic entries be ordered alphabetically, which is convenient for the reader, or that they appear by order of citation, which is convenient for typesetting.) Your writing should be designed to survive a change in the style of citation.

When discussing a reference with more than three authors, all but the first author's name can be replaced by "et al."

✓ Howers, Mann, Thompson, and Wills [9] provide another example.

✓ Howers et al. [9] provide another example.

In a variant of this style, the full list is given at the first citation, and the abbreviated form thereafter. Note the stop: "et al." is an abbreviation.

Each entry in the reference list should include enough detail to allow readers to find the paper. Other than in extreme cases, the names of all authors should be given—don't use "et al." in the reference list. An exception is the rare case in which the authors list themselves as "et al." (I have only seen one paper with such an author list: "The Story of O_2" by O. Deux et al.)

Format fields of the same type in the same way. For example, don't list one author as "Heinrich, J.", the next as "Peter Hurst", the next as "R. Johnson", and the next as "SL Klows". Capitalization, explained on pages 64–65, should be consistent. Don't use unfamiliar abbreviations of journal names. (One that has puzzled me is "*J. Comp.*")

Journal articles. The journal name should be given in full, and author names, paper title, year, volume, number, and pages must be provided. Consider also giving the month. Thus:

✗ T. Wendell, "Completeness of open negation in quasi-inductive programs", *J. Dd. Lang.*, 34.

is inadequate. Revise it to, say:

✓ T. Wendell, "Completeness of open negation in quasi-inductive programs", *ICSS Journal of Deductive Languages*, 34(3):217–222, November 1994.

Conference papers. The conference name should be complete, and authors, title, year, and pages must be provided. Information such as publisher, conference location, month, and editors should also be given.

Books. Give title, authors, publisher and publisher's address, year, and, where relevant, edition and volume. If the reference is to a specific part of the book, give page numbers; for example, write "(Howing 1994; pp. 22–31)" rather than just "(Howing 1994)". If the reference is to a chapter, give its title, pages, and, if applicable, authors.

Technical reports. In addition to title, authors, year, and report number you need to provide the address of the publisher (which is usually the authors' home institution). If the report is available online, say via the web, consider giving its electronic address.

Web pages. If you cite a web page, attempt to find a durable URL that is unlikely to change when, for example, a researcher changes institution. In addition to the usual details, give the URL and perhaps some search terms. URLs can include unusual characters; make sure you represent these correctly.

Obscure references. Take particular care to provide as much information as possible. If you must refer to the First Scandinavian Workshop on Backward Compatibility, consider explaining how to obtain the proceedings or a copy of the paper.

Punctuation of citations is considered on page 67, and ethical issues with regard to citations and references are discussed in Chapter 13.

Quotation

Quotations are text from another source, usually included in a paper to support an argument. The copied text, if short, is enclosed in double quotes (which are more visible than single quotes and cannot be confused with apostrophes). Longer quotes are set aside in an indented block.

✓ Computer security forensics is "the study of matching an intrusion event to an IP address, location, and individual" (Brinton 1997).

✓ As described by Kang [16], there are three stages:

> First, each distinct word is extracted from the data. During this phase, statistics are gathered about frequency of occurrence. Second, the set of words is analyzed, to decide which are to be discarded and what weights to allocate to those that remain. Third, the data is processed again to determine likely aliases for the remaining words.

The quoted material should be an exact transcription of the original text; some syntactic changes are permissible, so long as the meaning of the text is unaltered, but the changes should be held to a minimum. Changes of font, particularly addition of emphasis by changing words to italics, should be explicitly identified, as should changes of nomenclature.

The expression "[sic]" is used to indicate that an error is from the original quote, as in "Davis regards it as 'not worty [sic] of consideration' [11]". It is not polite to point out errors; avoid such use of "[sic]" and of quotes that seem to require it. More rarely "[sic]" is used to indicate that terminology or jargon is being used in a different way.

✗ Hamad and Quinn (1990) show that "similarity [sic] is functionally equivalent to identity"; note that similarity in this context means homology only, not the more general meaning used in this paper.

The long explanation renders the quote pointless.

✓ Hamad and Quinn (1990) show that homology "is functionally equivalent to identity".

For a short, natural statement of this kind the quotes are preferable but not essential.

✓ Hamad and Quinn (1990) show that homology is functionally equivalent to identity.

Other changes are insertions, replacements, or remarks, delimited by square brackets; and short omissions, represented by ellipses.

✓ They describe the methodology as "a hideous mess ... that somehow manages to work in the cases considered [but] shouldn't".

(Note that an ellipsis consists of three stops, neither more nor less.) Ellipses are unnecessary at the start of quotes, and at the end of quotes except where they imply "et cetera" or "and so on", or where the sentence is left hanging. For long omissions, don't use an ellipsis; separate the material into two quotations. Material in square brackets is used for comments or to make the quote parse when read in its new context.

Don't mutilate quotations.

✗ According to Fier and Byke such an approach is "simple and ... fast, [but] fairly crude and ... could be improved" [8].

It would be better to paraphrase.

✓ Fier and Byke describe the approach as simple and fast, but fairly crude and open to improvement [8].

Long quotations, and quotation in full of material such as algorithms or figures, require permission from the publisher and from the author of the original. (Plagiarism and inappropriate quotation are discussed in Chapter 13.)

Words can be quoted to show that they are inadequately defined.

✗ This language has more "power" than the functional form.

Here the author must assume that "power" will be understood in a consistent way by the reader. Such use of quotes indicates woolly thinking—that the author is not quite sure what "power" means, for example.

✓ This language allows simpler expression of queries than does the functional form.

More rarely, words can be quoted to indicate irony. The expression "in their 'methodology' " can be interpreted as *in their so-called methodology*, and is therefore insulting. This is not an appropriate use of quotes.

Acknowledgements

In the acknowledgements of a scientific paper you should thank everyone who made a contribution, whether advice, proofreading, or whatever: include research students, research assistants, technical support, and colleagues. Funding sources should also be acknowledged. It is usual to thank only those who contributed to the scientific content—don't thank your parents or your cat unless they really helped with the research. Books and theses often have broader acknowledgements, however, to include thanks for people who have helped in non-technical ways. Consider showing your acknowledgement to the people you wish to thank, in case they object to the wording or to the presence of their name in the paper.

There are two common forms of acknowledgement. One is to simply list the people who have helped with the paper.

✓ I am grateful to Dale Washman, Kim Micale, and Dong Wen. I thank the Foundation for Science and Development for financial support.

Even in this little example there is some scope for bruised egos—Kim might wonder why Dale was listed first, for example.

The other common form is to explain each person's contribution. On the one hand, don't make your thanks too broad; if Kim and Dong constructed the proof, why aren't they listed as authors? On the other hand, too much detail can damn with faint praise.

✗ I am grateful to Dale Washman for discussing aspects of the proof of Proposition 4.1, to Kim Micale for identifying some technical errors in Theorem 3, and to Dong Wen for helping with use of the debugging tools. I thank the Foundation for Science and Development for a year of financial support.

✓ I am grateful to Dale Washman and Kim Micale for our fruitful discussions, and to Dong Wen for programming assistance. I thank the Foundation for Science and Development for financial support.

This form has the advantage of identifying which of your colleagues contributed to the intellectual content.

Some authors write their thanks as "I would like to thank" or "I wish to thank". To me this seems to imply that *I wish to thank ... but for some reason I am unable to do so.* Consider instead using "I am grateful to" or simply "I thank" or "Thanks to".

Grammar

In this book I have not given advice on grammar, because the clarity of writing largely depends on whether it conforms to accepted usage. One aspect of grammar is, however, worth considering: that some people use traditional grammar to criticize other people's text, based on rules such as *don't split infinitives* or *don't begin a sentence with "and" or "but"*. I dislike this attitude to writing: grammatical rules should be observed, but not at the cost of clarity or meaning. However, be aware that an excess of sloppy grammar annoys some readers.

Beauty

Authors of style guides like to apply artistic judgements to text. This does not mean that scientific writing should be judged as literary prose; indeed, such prose would be inappropriate. But some authorities on writing style argue that everyone's text should be crystalline, transparent, and have good rhythm and cadence; and that one should dislike stuffy, soft, stodgy, and sagging sentences.

How useful such judgements are to most writers is not clear. Doubtless, well-crafted text is a pleasure to read, ill-written text can be hard going, and good rhythm in text helps us to parse. But appreciation of well-written text does not always help a novice to write it, nor is it evident that, to a poor writer, the argument that text should be elegant is meaningful. It is sufficient to aim for simplicity and clarity.

3 Style specifics

Those complicated sentences seemed to him very pearls . . .
"The reason for the unreason with which you treat my reason,
so weakens my reason that with reason I complain of your
beauty" . . . These writings drove the poor knight out of his wits.

Cervantes
Don Quixote

Underneath the knocker there was a notice that said:

PLES RING IF AN RNSER IS REQIRD

Underneath the bell-pull there was a notice that said:

PLEZ CNOKE IF AN RNSR IS NOT REQID

These notices had been written by Christopher Robin,
who was the only one in the forest who could spell.

A. A. Milne
Winnie the Pooh

Good style is about clear, easy-to-read writing, which can be achieved by following well-defined guidelines. These are not arbitrary rules, but are principles that have been observed by experienced writers to lead to good text. In the previous chapter, some of these principles were reviewed. This chapter concerns a range of specific problems that are common in technical writing.

Titles and headings

Titles of papers and sections should be concise and informative, have specific rather than general terms, and accurately describe the content. Complicated titles with long words are hard to swallow.

✗ A New Signature File Scheme Based on Multiple-Block Descriptor Files for Indexing Very Large Data Bases

✓ Signature File Indexes Based on Multiple-Block Descriptor Files

✗ An Investigation of the Effectiveness of Extensions to Standard Ranking Techniques for Large Text Collections

✓ Extensions to Ranking Techniques for Large Text Collections

Don't make the title so short that it is contentless. "Limited-Memory Huffman Coding for Databases of Textual and Numeric Data" is awkward, but it is superior to "Huffman Coding for Databases", which is far too general.

Accuracy is more important than catchiness—"Strong Modes Can Change the World!" is excessive, not to mention uninformative. The more interesting the title, however, the more likely that the text underneath it will be read. The title is the only part of your paper that most people see; if the title does not reflect the paper's contents, the paper will not be read by the right readership.

Titles and section headings do not have to be complete sentences; indeed, such titles can look rather odd.

✗ Duplication of Data Leads to Reduction in Network Traffic

✓ Duplicating Data to Reduce Network Traffic

Section headings should reflect the paper's structure. If a section is headed "Lists and Trees" and the first subsection is "Lists", another should be "Trees"; don't use, say, "Other Data Structures". If a section is headed "Index Organizations" the subsection heading should be "B-trees" rather than "B-tree indexes".

A paper (or thesis chapter) consists of sections and possibly subsections. There is rarely any need to break subsections into sub-subsections. Don't break text into small blocks; three headings on a page is too many. Headings below the level of subsections should be paragraph leads, not lines by themselves. Beware of having too few sections, because it is difficult to continue the logical flow of a section over more than a few pages.

Headings may or may not be numbered. In a paper, my preference is to use only two levels of headings, major and minor, and to only number major headings. In a thesis, numbered chapters, sections, and possibly subsections are appropriate. Deeper numbering allows more precise referencing, but often seems fussy. If all headings are unnumbered—as is required in some journals—make sure that major and minor headings are clearly distinguished by font, size, or placement.

The opening paragraphs

The opening paragraphs can set the reader's attitude to the whole paper, so begin well. All of a document should be created and edited with care, but take the most care with the opening, to create the best possible impression. The abstract should be written especially well, without an unnecessary word, and the opening sentence should be direct and straightforward.

✗ Trees, especially binary trees, are often applied—indeed indiscriminately applied—to management of dictionaries.

✓ Dictionaries are often managed by a data structure such as a tree, but trees are not always the best choice for this application.

The following example of how not to begin is the first sentence of a paper.

✗ This paper does not describe a general algorithm for transactions.

Only later does the reader discover than the paper describes an algorithm for a special case.

✓ General-purpose transaction algorithms guarantee freedom from deadlock but can be inefficient. In this paper we describe a new transaction algorithm that is particularly efficient for a special case, the class of linear queries.

The first paragraphs must be intelligible to any likely reader; save technicalities for later on, so that readers who can't understand the details of your paper are still able to understand your results and the importance of your work. That is, describe what you have done without the details of how it was done.

Starting an abstract or introduction with "This paper concerns" or "In this paper" often means that results are going to be stated out of context.

✗ In this paper we describe a new programming language with matrix manipulation operators.

✓ Most numerical computation is dedicated to manipulation of matrices, but matrix operations are difficult to implement efficiently in current high-level programming languages. In this paper we describe a new programming language with matrix manipulation operators.

The second version describes the context of the paper's contribution.

Beginning a paper by stating that a topic is popular or that a problem is important is flat and uninspiring.

✗ Use of digital libraries is increasingly common.

✗ It is important that the cost of disk accesses be reduced in query processing.

Such openings succeed in establishing context but fail in motivation, often because they are an assertion that a reasonable person might disagree with. A simpler or more specific statement may well be preferable.

✓ Digital libraries provide fast access to large numbers of documents.

✓ Query processing can involve many disk accesses.

A typical organization for the introduction of a paper is to use the first paragraphs to describe the context. It is these paragraphs that convince the reader that the paper is likely to be interesting. The opening sentences should clearly indicate the topic.

✗ Underutilization of main memory impairs the performance of operating systems.

✓ Operating systems are traditionally designed to use the least possible amount of main memory, but such design impairs their performance.

The second version is better for several reasons. It is clear; it states the context, which can be paraphrased as *operating systems don't use much memory*; and, in contrast to the first version, it is positive.

Take care to distinguish description of existing knowledge from the description of the paper's contribution.

✗ Many user interfaces are confusing and poorly arranged. Interfaces are superior if developed according to rigorous principles.

✓ Many user interfaces are confusing and poorly arranged. We demonstrate that interfaces are superior if developed according to rigorous principles.

In most papers, the introduction should not flow from the abstract, which is a summary of a paper rather than its opening. The paper should be complete even with the abstract removed. However, a few journals require otherwise.

Variation

Diversity—in organization, structure, length of sentences and paragraphs, and choice of words—is a useful device for keeping the reader's attention.

✗ The system of rational numbers is incomplete. This was discovered 2000 years ago by the Greeks. The problem arises in squares with sides of unit length. The length of the diagonals of these squares is irrational. This discovery was a serious blow to the Greek mathematicians.

✓ The Greeks discovered 2000 years ago that the system of rational numbers is incomplete. The problem is that some quantities, such as the length of the diagonal of a square with unit sides, are irrational. This discovery was a serious blow to the Greek mathematicians.

Note how, in the second version, the final statement is more effective although it hasn't been changed.

Paragraphing

A paragraph consists of discussion on a single topic or issue. The outline or the argument is typically captured in the first sentence of each paragraph, with the rest of the paragraph used for amplification or example. Every sentence in a paragraph should be on the topic announced in the opening. The last sentence has higher impact than those in the body, so pay attention to sentence order.

Long paragraphs can indicate that several lines of argument have not been sufficiently disentangled. If a long paragraph can be broken, break it. Lack of variation in paragraph length makes the page monotonous, however, so don't divide your text into paragraphs of uniform size.

Contextual information can be forgotten between paragraphs, and references between paragraphs can be difficult to follow. For example, if a paragraph discusses a fast sorting algorithm, the next paragraph should not begin "This algorithm" but rather "The fast sorting algorithm"; if one paragraph refers to Harvey, the next should not refer to "his" but rather to "Harvey's". Link paragraphs by re-use of key words or phrases, and by using expressions that connect the content of one paragraph to that of the next.

The use of formatted lists as an occasional alternative to paragraphs is common. Lists are useful for the following reasons:

- They highlight each main point clearly.
- The context remains obvious, whereas, in a long list of points made in a paragraph, it is hard to tell whether the later points are part of the original issue or belong to some subsequent discussion.
- An individual point can be considered in detail without confusing the main thread of narrative.
- They are easy to refer to.

List points can be numbered, named, or tagged. Use numbers only when ordering or reference is important. If it is necessary to refer to an individual point, use numbers or names. Otherwise use tags, as in the list above. Acceptable tags are bullets and dashes; fancy symbols such as $\hookrightarrow$, $\star$, or graphic icons look childish.

A disadvantage of lists is that they highlight rather too well: a list of trivia can be more attention-getting than a paragraph of crucial information. Reserve lists for material that is both significant and in need of enumeration.

Ambiguity

Check carefully for ambiguity. It is often hard to detect in your own text because you know what is intended.[1]

[1] A safe-sex guide issued by the Australian Government included "a table on which sexual practices are safe"; it transpired that this was not a piece of furniture. Government guidelines on planning for emergencies had a list of "events that emergency recovery agencies have assisted", including "destruction of homes ... toxic chemical spillage ... holding of hostages".

Newspaper headlines can be a rich source of ambiguity:

Enraged Cow Injures Farmer with Axe
Miners Refuse to Work After Death

✗ The compiler did not accept the program because it contained errors.

✓ The program did not compile because it contained errors.

The next example is from a manual.

✗ There is a new version of the operating system, so when using the "fetch" utility, the error messages can be ignored.

✓ There is a new version of the operating system, so the "fetch" utility's error messages can be ignored.

Part of the confusion comes from the redundant phrase "when using": there would be no error messages if the utility was not being used.

Ensure that pronouns such as "it", "this", and "they" have a clear referent.

✗ The next stage was the test of the complete system, but it failed.

What failed, the test or the system?

✗ In addition to skiplists we have tried trees. They are superior because they are slow in some circumstances but have lower asymptotic cost.

✓ In addition to skiplists we have tried trees. Skiplists are superior because, although slow in some circumstances, they have lower asymptotic cost.

Another problem with "it" is that it is overused.

✗ The machine crashed and it was necessary to reboot it.

✓ The machine crashed and a reboot was necessary.

The first sentence is not ambiguous, but "it" has been used in two senses. Use a more specific term whenever doing so doesn't make the text too clumsy.

Premature pronouns also lead to difficulties.

✗ When it was first developed, recursive compilation was impractically slow and required too much memory.

While not exactly ambiguous, the report that

the pilot of a plane that crashed killing six people was flying "out of his depth"

does convey the wrong impression.

✓ When recursive compilation was first developed, it was impractically slow and required too much memory.

A common source of confusion is between speed and time. Although not ambiguous, the phrase "increasing speed" is easily read as *increasing time*, which has quite the opposite meaning. There are similar problems with phrases such as "improving affordability".

A clumsy sentence is preferable to an ambiguous one. But remember that stilted sentences slow the reader, and it is difficult to entirely avoid ambiguity.[2]

Sentence structure

Sentences should have simple structure, which usually means that they will be no more than a line or two. Don't say too much all at once.[3]

---

[2]The following my-dog-has-no-nose joke, due to Andy Clews, is not ambiguous.

First circumlocutionist: I have in my possession a male animal belonging to the family Canidae, and it appears that he does not possess any extra-facial olfactory organs.

Second circumlocutionist: Could you therefore impart to me such knowledge as is necessary to describe how that animal circumvents the problem of satisfying his olfactory senses?

First circumlocutionist: Unfortunately the non-ambiguity of your enquiry does not easily permit me to provide a clever answer, but I am in fact thinking of referring the animal to an olfactologist. However, the animal does have an unpleasant body odour, should you be interested.

[3]The following quote is a single sentence from a version of the standard lease agreement of the Real Estate Institute of Victoria, Australia. It is 477 words long, but the punctuation amounts to only three pairs of parentheses, one comma, and one stop. This clause is an example of "the fine print"—for example, the holder of a lease containing this clause has agreed not to take action if, in circumstances such as failure to pay rent, assaulted by the property's owner.

> If the Lessee shall commit a breach or fails to observe or perform any of the covenants contained or implied in the Lease and on his part to be observed and performed or fails to pay the rent reserved as provided herein (whether expressly demanded or not) or if the Lessee or other person or persons in whom for the time being the term hereby created shall be vested, shall be found guilty of any indictable offence or felony or shall commit any act of bankruptcy or become bankrupt or make any assignment for the benefit of his her or their creditors or enter into an agreement or make any arrangement with his her or their creditors for liquidation of his her or their debts by composition or otherwise or being a company if proceedings shall be taken to wind up the same either voluntarily or compulsorily under any Act or Acts relating to Companies (except for the purposes of reconstruction or amalgamation) then and in any of the said cases the

✗ When the kernel process takes over, that is when in the default state, the time that is required for the kernel to deliver a message from a sending application process to another application process and to recompute the importance levels of these two application processes to determine which one has the higher priority is assumed to be randomly distributed with a constant service rate R.

✓ When the kernel process takes over, one of its activities is to deliver a message from a sending application process to another application process, and to then recompute the importance levels of these two application processes to determine which has the higher priority. The time required for this activity is assumed to be randomly distributed with a constant service rate R.

That the kernel process is the default state is irrelevant here, and should have been explained elsewhere.

This example also illustrates the consequence of having too many words between related phrases. The original version said that "the time that is required for *something* is assumed to be ...", where *something* was 34 words long. The main reason that the revision is clearer is that *something* has been reduced to two words; the structure of the sentence is much easier to see.

Lessor notwithstanding the waiver by the Lessor of any previous breach or default by the Lessee or the failure of the Lessor to have taken advantage of any previous breach or default at any time thereafter (in addition to its other power) may forthwith re-enter either by himself or by his agent upon the Premises or any part thereof in the name of the whole and the same have again repossess and enjoy as in their first and former estate and for that purpose may break open any inner or outer doorfastening or other obstruction to the Premises and forcibly eject and put out the Lessee or as permitted assigns any transferees and any other persons therefrom and any furniture property and other things found therein respectively without being liable for trespass assault or any other proceedings whatsoever for so doing but with liberty to plead the leave and licence which is hereby granted in bar of any such action or proceedings if any such be brought or otherwise and upon such re-entry this Lease and the said term shall absolutely determine but without prejudice to the right of action of the Lessor in respect of any antecedent breach of any of the Lessee's covenants herein contained provided that such right of re-entry for any breach of any covenant term agreement stipulation or condition herein contained or implied to which Section 146 of the Property Law Act 1958 extends shall not be exercisable unless and until the expiration of fourteen days after the Lessor has served on the Lessee the Notice required by Sub-section(1) of the said Section 146 specifying the particular breach complained of and if the breach is capable of remedy requiring the Lessee to remedy the breach and make reasonable compensation in money to the satisfaction of the Lessor for the breach.

It is likewise helpful to avoid nested sentences, that is, information embedded within a sentence that is not part of its main statement.

✗ In the first stage, the backtracking tokenizer with a two-element retry buffer, errors, including illegal adjacencies as well as unrecognized tokens, are stored on an error stack for collation into a complete report.

First, this is poor because crucial words are missing. The beginning should read "In the first stage, which is the backtracking tokenizer ...". Second, the main information—how errors are handled—is intermixed with definitions. Nested content, particularly if in parentheses, should be omitted. If such content really is required, then put it in a separate sentence.

✓ The first stage is the backtracking tokenizer with a two-element retry buffer. In this stage possible errors include illegal adjacencies as well as unrecognized tokens; when detected, errors are stored on a stack for collation into a complete report.

Watch out for fractured "if" expressions.

✗ If the machine is lightly loaded, then speed is acceptable whenever the data is on local disks.

✓ If the machine is lightly loaded and data is on local disks, then speed is acceptable.

✓ Speed is acceptable when the machine is lightly loaded and data is on local disks.

The first version is poor because the conditions of the "if" have been separated by the consequent.

It is easy to construct long, winding sentences by, for example, stating a principle, then qualifying it—a habit that is not necessarily bad, but does often lead to poor sentence structure—then explaining the qualification, the circumstances in which it applies, and in effect allowing the sentence to continue to another topic, such as the ideas underlying the principle, cases in which the qualification does or does not apply, or material which no longer belongs in the sentence at all, a property that is arguably true of most of this sentence, which should definitely be revised.

Sometimes longer sentences can be divided by, say, simply replacing an "and" or a semicolon with a period. If there is no particular reason to join two sentences, keep them separate.

Beware of misplaced modifiers.

✗ We collated the responses from the users, which were usually short, into the following table.

✓ The users' responses, most of which were short, were collated into the following table.

Double negatives are difficult to parse and are ambiguous.

✗ There do not seem to be any reasons not to adopt the new approach.

The impression here is of condemnation—*we don't like the new approach but we're not sure why*—but praise was intended; the quote is from a paper advocating the new approach. This is another example of the academic tendency to overqualification. The revision "There is no reason not to adopt the new approach" is punchier, but still negative. It is difficult to suggest further improvement with the same meaning, because the meaning was probably unintended; the following better reflects the original aims.

✓ The new approach is at least as good as the old and should be adopted.

Sing-song phrases are distracting, as are rhymes and alliteration.

✗ We propose that the principal procedure of proof be use of primary predicates.

✗ Semantics and phonetics are combined by heuristics to give a mix that is new for computational linguistics.

Organize your sentences so that they can be parsed without too much backtracking. Ambiguous words or phraseology, even if clear in the context of a whole sentence, can slow the reader down.

✗ Classifying handles can involve opening the files they represent.

The opening phrase can, without the context provided by the rest of the sentence, be interpreted as *handles for classifying*.

✓ Classification of handles can involve opening the files they represent.

Know your limits. Experienced writers can construct complex sentences that are easy to read, but don't make the mistake of believing that something is easy to understand because you—the author—understand it. Build your text from simple sentences and concise paragraphs.

Tense

In science writing, most text is in past or present tense. Present tense is used for eternal truths. Thus we write "the algorithm has complexity $O(n)$", not "the algorithm had complexity $O(n)$". Present tense is also used for statements about the text itself. It is better to write "related issues are discussed below" than to write "related issues will be discussed below".

Past tense is used for describing work and outcomes. Thus we write "the ideas were tested by experiment", not "the ideas are tested by experiment". It follows that occasionally it is correct to use past and present tense together.

✓ Although theory suggests that the Klein algorithm has asymptotic complexity $O(n^2)$, in our experiments the trend observed was $O(n)$.

Either past or present tense can be used for discussion of references. Present tense is preferable but past tense can be forced by context.

✓ Willert (1999) shows that the space is open.

✓ Haast (1986) postulated that the space is bounded, but Willert (1999) has since shown that it is open.

Other than in conclusions, future tense is rarely used in science writing.

Repetition and parallelism

Text that consists of the same form of sentence used again and again is monotonous. Watch out for sequences of sentences beginning with "however", "moreover", "therefore", "hence", "thus", "and", "but", "then", "so", "nevertheless", or "nonetheless". Likewise, don't overuse the pattern "First, ... Second, ... Last, ...".

Complementary concepts should be explained as parallels, or the reader will have difficulty seeing how the concepts relate.

✗ In SIMD, the same instructions are applied simultaneously to multiple data sets, whereas in MIMD different data sets are processed with different instructions.

✓ In SIMD, multiple data sets are processed simultaneously by the same instructions, whereas in MIMD multiple data sets are processed simultaneously by different instructions.

Parallels can be based on antonyms.

✗ Access is fast, but at the expense of slow update.

✓ Access is fast but update is slow.

Lack of parallel structure can result in ambiguity.

✗ The performance gains are the result of tuning the low-level code used for data access and improved interface design.

✓ The performance gains are the result of tuning the low-level code used for data access and of improved interface design.

This can be further improved. It is kinder to the reader to move the longer clauses in a list to the end.

✓ The performance gains are the result of improved interface design and of tuning the low-level code used for data access.

There are some standard forms of parallel. The phrase "on the one hand" should have a matching "on the other hand". A sentence beginning "One ..." suggests that a sentence beginning "Another ..." is imminent. If you flag a point with "First" then every following point should have a similar flag, such as "Second", "Next", or "Last".

Parallel structures should be used in lists.

✗ For real-time response there should be sufficient memory, parallel disk arrays should be used, and fast processors.

The syntax can be fixed by adding "should be used" at the end but the result is clumsy. A complete revision is preferable.

✓ Real-time response requires sufficient memory, parallel disk arrays, and fast processors.

Comparisons and relative statements should be complete. If "the Entity-Relationship model is a better method for developing schema", then it is better than something else. Say what that something is.

Emphasis

The structure of a sentence places implicit emphasis, or stress, on some words. Reorganizing a sentence changes the emphasis.

✗ A static model is appropriate because each item is written once and read often.

It is not clear what makes the model's behaviour appropriate; the emphasis should be on the last two words, not the last five.

✓ A static model is appropriate because each item is only written once but is read often.

Inappropriate stress can lead to ambiguity.

✗ Additional memory can lead to faster response, but user surveys have indicated that it is not required.

✓ Faster response is possible with additional memory, but user surveys have indicated that it is not required.

The first version, which has the stress on "additional memory", incorrectly implies that users had commented on memory rather than response. Since the sentence is about "response", that is where the stress should be.

Explicit stress can be provided with italics, but is almost never necessary. Don't italicize words *unnecessarily*—let sentence structure provide the emphasis. Few papers require explicit stress more than once or twice. DON'T use capitals for emphasis. Some authors use the word "emphatic" to provide emphasis, as in "which are emphatically not equivalent". Other words used in this way are "certainly" and "indeed". The resulting wordiness weakens rather than strengthens; use of this form of emphasis should be rare.

Italicized passages of any length are hard to read. Rather than italicize a whole sentence, say, stress it in some other way: italicize one or two words only, or make it the opening sentence of a paragraph.

When a key word is used for the first time, consider placing it in italics.

✓ The data structure has two components, a *vocabulary* containing all of the distinct words and, for each word, a *hit list* of references.

Definitions

Terminology, variables, abbreviations, and acronyms should be defined or explained the first time they are used. Definitions should be specific and concrete. Don't create questions by defining in terms of concepts that are unknown or uncertain.

Use a consistent format for introducing new terminology. Implicit or explicit emphasis on the first occurrence of a new word is often helpful, because it stresses what is being introduced.

✗ We use homogeneous sets to represent these events.

The reader has not been told that "homogeneous" is a new term that is about to be defined, and may look back for an explanation.

✓ We use *homogeneous* sets to represent these events.

✓ To represent these events we use homogeneous sets, whose members are all of the same type.

It can be helpful to give multiple explanations or illustrations of unfamiliar concepts.

✓ Compaction, in contrast to compression, does not preserve information; that is, compacted data cannot be exactly restored to the original form.

Sometimes a discursion—a discussion that is not part of the main thread of argument—is needed to motivate a definition. The discursion might consider negative examples, showing what happens in the absence of the definition, or it might lead the reader by steps to agree that the definition is necessary.

Choice of words

Use short, direct words rather than long, circumlocutionary ones; the result is vigorous, emphatic writing. For example, use "begin" rather than "initiate", "first" and "second" rather than "firstly" and "secondly", "part" rather than "component", and "use" rather than "utilize". Use short words in preference to long, but use an exact long word rather than an approximate short one.

The words you choose should be specific and familiar. Abstract, vague, or broad terms have different meanings for different readers and lead to confusion.

X The analysis derives information about programs.

The "information" could be anything: optimizations, function-point descriptions, bug reports, or complexity.

✓ The analysis estimates the resource costs of programs.

Other abstract terms that are overused include "important", "intelligent", "method", "paradigm", "performance", and "semantic". "Difficult" is often used when a better term is available: if something is "difficult to compute", does that mean that it is slow, or memory-hungry, or requires double precision, or something else altogether? "Efficient" is another word that is often vague. Use the most precise term available.

A common reason for using vague terms is that some authors feel they are writing badly if they use the same word twice in a sentence or paragraph, and thus substitute a synonym, which is usually less specific.

X The database executes on a remote machine to provide better security for the system and insulation from network difficulties.

✓ The database executes on a remote machine to provide better security for the database and insulation from network difficulties.

The "don't repeat words" rule might apply to creative writing, but not to technical terms that must be clearly understood.

Some sequences of words are awkward because they can be run together to form another, valid word.

X There are some times that appear inconsistent.

✓ Some of the times appear inconsistent.

This form is awkward for another reason—"some of the time" is a common phrase.

✓ Several of the times appear inconsistent.

Language is not static. Words enter the language, or go out of vogue, or change in meaning. A word whose meaning has changed—at least, some people still use the old meaning, but most use the new—is "data". Since "data" is by etymology a plural, expressions such as "the data is stored on disk" have been regarded as grammatically incorrect, but "the data are stored on disk" simply seems wrong. Correspondingly, "datum" is now rare. "Data" is appropriate for both singular and plural. On the other hand, use "automaton" rather than "automata" for the singular case.

Use a word only if you are sure that you know the meaning and can apply it correctly. Some words are familiar because of their use in a certain context—perhaps in a saying such as "hoist by his own petard" or a cliché such as "critical juncture"—but have otherwise lost their meaning. Other words, such as "notwithstanding", "whilst", and "amongst", have an archaic feel and are out of place in new writing. Some words have acquired meanings in computing that are distinct from their meaning elsewhere. Besides re-use of nouns such as "bus" there are more subtle cases. For example, "iterate" in computing means *to loop*, but in other writing it can mean *to do again*.

If you are unsure about a word, check it in a dictionary. For technical writing, I use the Collins English dictionary, which gives both British and American spelling and, in contrast to some other dictionaries, for technical terms often gives the meaning appropriate to computing or mathematics. But there are many reasons for choosing a particular dictionary and you should make your own decision. A rule of thumb is that a dictionary small enough to conveniently carry around is unlikely to be satisfactory. Check the dictionary whenever you are not sure that you are using a word correctly. A thesaurus is useful too. Sometimes it can help you to find the right word; more often, it can help to illustrate the meaning of a word that is unfamiliar, giving a broader context than is common in a dictionary.

Slang should not be used in technical writing. Nor should the choice of words suggest that the writing is careless; avoid sloppy-looking abbreviations and contractions. Use "cannot" in preference to "can't", for example.

Don't make excessive claims about your own work. Phrases such as "our method is an ideal solution to these problems" or "our work is remarkable" are not acceptable. Claims about your own work should be unarguable.

Qualifiers

Don't pile qualifiers on top of one another. Within a sentence, use at most one qualifier such as "might", "may", "perhaps", "possibly", "likely", "likelihood", or "could". Overuse of qualifiers results in text that is lame and timid.

✗ It is perhaps possible that the algorithm might fail on unusual input.

✓ The algorithm might fail on unusual input.

✓ It is possible that the algorithm would fail on unusual input.

Here is another example, from the conclusions of a paper.

✗ We are planning to consider possible options for extending our results.

✓ We are considering how to extend our results.

Double negatives are a form of qualifier; they are commonly used to express uncertainty.

✗ Merten's algorithm is not dissimilar to ours.

Such statements tell the reader little.

Qualifiers such as "very" and "quite" should be avoided altogether, because they are in effect meaningless. If an algorithm is "very fast", is an algorithm that is merely "fast" deficient in some way? Writing is invariably more forceful without "very".

✗ There is very little advantage to the networked approach.

✓ There is little advantage to the networked approach.

Likewise, "simply" can often be deleted.

✗ The standard method is simply too slow.

✓ The standard method is too slow.

Other words of this kind are "totally", "completely", "truly", "highly", "usually", "accordingly", "certainly", "necessarily", and "somewhat".

Misused words

The upper table on page 48 lists words that are often used incorrectly because of confusion with another word of similar form or sound. The "usually correct" form is shown on the left; the form with which each word gets confused is shown on the right. Some other problem words are as follows.

Which, that, the. Many writers use "which" when they mean "that". Use "that" in preference to "which"; use "which" only when it cannot be replaced by "that".

× There is one method which is acceptable.

✓ There is one method that is acceptable.

✓ There are three options, of which only one is tractable.

The word "that" is often underused. Use of "that" can make a sentence seem stilted, but its absence can make the sentence unclear.

× It is true the result is hard to generalize.

✓ It is true that the result is hard to generalize.

On the other hand, "the" is often used unnecessarily; delete it where doing so does not change the meaning.

Less, fewer. Use "less" for continuous quantities ("it used less space") and "fewer" for discrete quantities ("there were fewer errors").

Affect, effect. The "effect", or *consequence*, of an action is to "affect", or *influence*, outcomes.

Alternate, alternative, choice. The word "alternate" means *other* or *switch between*, whereas an "alternative" is something that can be chosen. If there is but one alternative, there is no choice; "alternative" and "choice" are not synonyms.

Assume, presume. "Assume" means *for now, take as being true*, while "presume" means *take for granted*. A fact is assumed as the basis of an argument, an event is presumed to have occurred.

May, might, can. Many writers use "may" or "might" when they mean "can". Use "may" to indicate personal choice, and "can" to indicate capability.

✓ Users can access this facility, but may not wish to do so.

Misused words

Usual	*Other*	*Usual*	*Other*
alternative	alternate	foregoing	forgoing
comparable	comparative	further	farther
complement	compliment	elusive	illusive
dependent	dependant	manyfold	manifold
descendant	descendent	omit	emit
discrete	discreet	partly	partially
emit	omit	principle	principal
ensure	insure	simple	simplistic
ensure	assure	solvable	soluble
excerpt	exert	stationary	stationery

Misspelt words

Right	*Wrong*	*Right*	*Wrong*
adaptation	adaption	miniature	minature
apparent	apparant	occasional	occaisional
argument	arguement	occurred	occured
comparison	comparision	participate	participate
consistent	consistant	primitive	primative
definite	definate	propagate	propogate
existence	existance	pronunciation	pronounciation
foreign	foriegn	pseudo	psuedo
grammar	grammer	referred	refered
heterogeneous	heterogenous	repository	repositery
homogeneous	homogenous	separate	seperate
independent	independant	supersede	supercede
insoluble	insolvable	transparent	transparant

Basic, fundamental. Some writers confuse "basic" with "fundamental": the former means *elementary* as well as *a foundation*. A result should only be described as "basic" if *elementary* is meant, or readers may get the wrong idea.

Novel, complex, sophisticated. "Sophisticated" does not mean *new* or *novel*, but either *advanced* or *complex*. Use "novel" or "complex" if these meanings are intended.

Will, shall. The word "shall" can seem archaic and is rarely preferable to "will". Both "will" and "shall" are often used unnecessarily and in many cases can be deleted.

Compile, compose. In general usage, "compile" means *assemble*, *gather*, or *collect*, but it has such a strong specific meaning in computing that it should not be used for other purposes. To "compose" is to *invent* or perhaps *prepare*; it is not a synonym of "compile", even though "composed of" means *made up of*.

Conflate, merge, confuse. The word "conflate" means *regard distinct things as similar*, while "merge" means *join distinct things to form one new thing*. If two things are "confused", then one has been mistaken for the other. These three terms are not equivalent.

Continual, continuous. "Continual" is not equivalent to "continuous". The former means *ceaselessly*; the latter means *unbroken*.

Conversely, inversely, similarly, likewise. Only use "conversely" if the statement that follows really is the opposite of the preceding material. Don't use "similarly" or "likewise" unless whatever follows has a strong parallel to the preceding material. Some authors use "inversely", but the meaning is rarely clear; avoid it.

Fast, quickly, presently, timely, currently. A process is "fast" if it *runs quickly*; "quickly" means *fast*, but does not necessarily mean *in the near future*. Something is "timely" if it is *opportune*; timeliness has nothing to do with rapidity. Also on the subject of time, "presently" means *soon*, whereas "currently" means *at present*.

Optimize, minimize, maximize. Absolute terms are often misused. One such word is "optimize", which means *find an optimum* or *find the best solution*, but is often used to mean *improve*. The latter usage is now so common that it could be argued that the meaning of "optimize" has changed, but as there is no synonym for "optimize" such a change would be unfortunate. Other absolute terms that are misused are "maximize" and "minimize".

Overlook, oversee. To "overlook" is to fail to notice, or to *ignore*. To "oversee" is to *manage* or look after. They are not synonyms!

Spelling conventions

The lower table on page 48 lists some words that are often spelt incorrectly in science writing. Use a spell checker to locate such mistakes, but learn to recognize them by yourself—studies have found that writers who depend on spell checkers have more errors in their work. A problem word with regard to spelling is "disk"; both this spelling and "disc" are so common that either is acceptable, but be consistent. However, "hard disk" is more common than "hard disc", and "compact disk" is incorrect. Other words that don't have a stable spelling include "enquire" ("inquire"), "biased" ("biassed"), and "dispatch" ("despatch"). Note that "ae" is obsolete in many words: "encyclopaedia" has become "encyclopedia", for example.

The English-speaking countries have different spelling conventions. For example, the American "traveler" becomes the British "traveller" while "fulfill" becomes "fulfil". In Britain it is incorrect to spell "-our" words as "-or", but, for example, "vigour" and "vigorous" are both correct.[4] The American "center" is the British "centre", "program" is "programme" (except for *computer program*), "catalog" is "catalogue", and "judgment" is "judgement". Perhaps the greatest confusion is with regard to the suffixes "-ize" and "-yze", which have the same recommended spelling in both countries, but are often spelt as "-ise" and "-yse" outside the United States.[5] As discussed in Chapter 1, British spelling has been used throughout this book.

Science is international—technical writing is usually for a readership that is accustomed to reading text from around the world—and it is accepted that a national of one country won't necessarily use the spelling of another. The most

[4] An editor of the first edition of this book suggested that the material should have "an international flavor".

[5] However, these problems are overrated. Of the 6000 or so distinct words used to write this book, for example, other than "-ize" words only 20 or so have a nationality-specific spelling.

important thing is to spell consistently and to be consistent with suffixes such as "-ize" without introducing errors such as "expertize" or "otherwize". Note that many journals insist on their own standards for spelling and presentation, or insist that the spelling be consistently of one nationality or another, and thus may choose to modify anything they publish.

The best authority for national spelling is a respectable dictionary written for that country. However, dictionaries are primarily a record of current non-technical spelling; the presence of a particular spelling in a dictionary does not prove that it is used in your discipline. The choice of spelling for a technical term may be dictated by the usage in other papers, not by your nationality.

Jargon

The word "jargon" means *terms used in a specialized vocabulary* or *mode of speech familiar only to a group or profession.*[6] As such, the use of jargon is an important part of scientific communication—how convenient it is to be able to say "CPU" rather than "the part of the computer that executes instructions". Some use of technical language, which inevitably makes the writing inaccessible to a wider readership, is essential for communication with specialists. But the more technical the language in a paper, the smaller the audience will be.

In mathematical writing, formal notation is a commonly used jargon. Mathematics is often unavoidable, but that doesn't mean that it must be impenetrable.

✗ **Theorem.** Let $\delta_1, \ldots, \delta_n, n > 2$ be such that $\delta_1 \mapsto_{\Omega_1} \delta_2, \ldots, \delta_{n-1} \mapsto_{\Omega_{n-1}} \delta_n$. Let $\eta', \eta'' \in \mathscr{R}$ be such that $\Omega_1 \models \eta'$ and $\Omega_{n-1} \models \eta''$. Then

$$\exists(\eta', \eta_1)(\eta_1, \eta_2) \cdots (\eta_{r-1}, \eta_r)(\eta_r, \eta'') \in L$$

such that $\forall \eta_i$, $1 \leq i \leq r$, $\exists \Omega_j$, $1 \leq j < n$, such that $\Omega_j \models \eta_i$.

Mathematics as jargon is discussed further on page 73.

Jargon does not have to consist of obscure terms; indeed, it can be at its most confusing when words in common use are given a new meaning; and some words have multiple meanings even within computing.

✗ The transaction log is a record of changes to the database.

✓ The transaction log is a history of changes to the database.

---

[6] From the Oxford Shorter Dictionary, which also lists *unintelligible or meaningless talk or writing; nonsense; gibberish; twittering.*

The first version is confusing because databases consist of records. Likewise, consider "the program's function". Synonyms also cause such problems.

✗ Hughes describes an array of algorithms for list processing.

✓ Hughes describes several algorithms for list processing.

New jargon inevitably arises during research, as ideas are debated and simple labels are attached to new concepts. Consider whether your terminology conveys the intended meaning (or any meaning at all) to likely readers.

The need to name variants of existing ideas or systems presents a dilemma, because if the new name is dissimilar to the old then the relationship is not obvious, but prefixing a modifier to the old name—for example, to obtain "binary tree" from "tree"—can result in ridiculous constructs such as the "variable-length bitstring multiple-descriptor floating bucket extensible hashing scheme". If you need to qualify a name, choose a meaningful adjective. There are already too many "intelligent" algorithms, for example.

Where new terminology or jargon is introduced, use it consistently. Existing terminology or notation should only be changed with good reason. Sometimes your problem requires new terminology that is inconsistent with the terminology already being used, thus making change essential; but remember that any change is likely to make your paper harder to read.

Cliché and idiom

Some expressions are clichés, that is, stock phrases whose meaning has little relationship to their words. Many readers, especially those from other cultures, may misunderstand such phrases. Examples include "follow suit", "up to scratch", "reinvent the wheel", "go through with a fine-tooth comb", "flat out", "cut and dried", and "bells and whistles". Idiomatic phrases are also poor, for similar reasons. Examples include "crop up", "lose track", "come to grips with", "it turned out that", "play up", and "right out". Do not use such phrases.

Foreign words

If you use a foreign word that you feel needs to go in italics, consider instead using an English equivalent. Some writers feel that use of foreign words is *de rigueur* because it lends the work a certain *je ne sais quoi* and shows *savoir-vivre*, but such writing is hard to understand.

Latin expressions are occasionally used—but more often misused—in technical writing. Examples include *mutatis mutandis*, *prima facie*, *circa*, *mea culpa*, and *vice versa*. Such phrases are not universally understood, and should only be used if you are confident of the meaning.

It is polite to use appropriate characters for foreign names. Don't write "Børstëdt" as "Borstedt", for example.

Overuse of words

Repetition of a word is annoying when it makes the reader feel they have read the same phrase twice, or have read a phrase and an inversion of it.

✗ Ada was used for this project because the underlying operating system is implemented in Ada.

✓ Ada was used for this project because it is the language used for implementation of the underlying operating system.

Repetition should be eliminated when the same word is used in different senses, or when a word and a synonym of it are used together.

✗ Values are stored in a set of accumulators, each initially set to zero.

✓ Values are stored in a set of accumulators, each initialized to zero.

Some words grate when they are used too frequently. Common offenders include "this", "very", and "case". Other words are even more memorable—unusual words, other than technical terms, should only be used once or twice in a paper. Watch out for tics: excessive use of some stock word or phrase. Typical tics include "so", "also", "hence", "note that", and "thus".

There are cases in which repetition is useful. In the phrase "discrete quantities and continuous quantities", the first "quantities" can be omitted, but such omissions are ambiguous surprisingly often and can result in text that is difficult to parse. What, for example, is intended by "from two to four hundred"? A common error relating to this form of expression is to shorten phrases by deleting adjectives, such as the second "long" in the expression "long lists and long arrays". Overuse of a word can lead to ambiguity,[7] but technical concepts should always be described in the same way, not by a series of synonyms.

---

[7]The following requirement was once in the Australian Tax Act.

> Where the amount of an annuity derived by the taxpayer during a year of income is more than, or less than, the amount payable for a whole year, the amount to be excluded

Some phrases are worn out from overuse and, like clichés and the words listed earlier, should be avoided. Examples include "vicious circle", "as a matter of fact", "tip of the iceberg", "knotty problem", "in the final analysis", "every effort was made", and "vexed question".

Padding

Padding is the use of pedantic phrases such as "the fact that" or "in general", which should be deleted, not least because they are irritating. The phrase "of course" can be patronizing or even insulting—"*of course* it is now clear that that the order is stable". The phrase "note that" is not padding, but is typically used to introduce something that readers should be able to deduce for themselves.

Phrases involving the word "case" ("in any case", "it is perhaps the case") are also suspect. There is no reason to use "it is frequently the case that ..." instead of "often ...", for example. Unnecessary introduction of quantities, or the concept of quantities, is a form of padding. For example, the phrase "a number of" can be replaced by "several", and "a large number of" by "many".

Adjectives are another form of padding.

✗ A well-known method such as the venerable quicksort is a potential practical alternative in instances of this kind.

In all likelihood, the context has made clear that impractical alternatives are not being discussed.

✓ A method such as quicksort is a potential alternative.

Use the minimum number of words, of minimum length, in your writing. The table on page 55 lists common redundant or wordy expressions and possible substitutes for them. The list is illustrative rather than exhaustive; there are some typical forms of redundancy, such as "completely unique" for "unique", for which there are hundreds of examples. Sometimes a wordy expression is the right choice—to emphasise a key point, for example, or to lend the writing a conversational style—but in most cases a concise form is preferable.

---

from the amount so derived is the amount which bears to the amount which, but for this sub-section, would be the amount to be so excluded the same proportion as the amount so derived bears to the amount payable for a whole year.

Examples of redundant or wordy expressions

Wordy	*Concise*
adding together	adding
after the end of	after
in the region of	approximately
cancel out	cancel
conflated together	conflated
let us now consider	consider
cooperate together	cooperate
currently ... today	currently ...
divided up	divided
give a description of	describe
during the course of	during
totally eliminated	eliminated
of fast speed	fast
first of all	first
for the purpose of	for
free up	free
in view of the fact	given
joined up	joined
of large size	large
semantic meaning	meaning
merged together	merged
the vast majority of	most
it is frequently the case that	often
completely optimized	optimized
separate into partitions	partition
at a fast rate	quickly
completely random	random
reason why	reason
a number of	several
such as ... etc.	such as ...
completely unique	unique
in the majority of cases	usually
whether or not	whether
the fact that	—
it can be seen that	—
it is a fact that	—

Plurals

A common problem in English for writers educated in another language is agreement of plurals—a plural noun can require a differently formed verb to that required by a singular noun. For example, "a parser checks syntax" whereas "compilers check programs". Simple errors such as "the instructions is" are easy to identify, but care needs to be taken with complex sentence constructions. A particular problem is with collectives.

✗ The set of positive matches are then discarded.
The range of numbers that must be considered are easy to identify.

✓ The set of positive matches is then discarded.
The range of numbers that must be considered is easy to identify.

Consider proofreading your paper just to check for plural agreement.

When describing classes of things, excessive use of plurals can be confusing. The following is from a paper on minimum redundancy codes.

✗ Packets that contain an error are automatically corrected.

✗ Packets that contain errors are automatically corrected.

The first version implies that packets with a particular error are corrected, the second that packets with multiple errors are corrected. Both of these interpretations are wrong. Whenever it is reasonable to do so, convert plurals to singular.

✓ A packet that contains an error is automatically corrected.

Classes may not need a plural.

✗ These kinds of algorithms are irrelevant.

✓ These kinds of algorithm are irrelevant.
Algorithms of this kind are irrelevant.

The use of variant plurals is becoming less common. Where once it was thought correct to base the plural form on that of the language of the root of the word, now it is almost always acceptable to use "-s" or "-es". Thus "schemata" can be "schemas", "formulae" can be "formulas", and "indices" can be "indexes"; but, while "indices" is used in the context of arrays, it is almost never used in the context of databases. However, "radii" is not yet "radiuses", and "matrices" is not yet "matrixes". Special cases remain, in particular where the plural form has replaced the singular as in "data", and in old-English forms such as "children".

Abbreviations

It is often tempting to use abbreviations such as "no.", "i.e.", "e.g.", "c.f.", and "w.r.t." These save a little space on the page, but slow readers down. It is almost always desirable to expand these abbreviations, to "number", "that is", "for example", "compared with" (or more accurately "in contrast to", since that is the sense in which "c.f." should be used), and "with respect to", or synonyms of these expressions. Where such abbreviations are used, the punctuation should be as if the expanded form were used. Also consider expanding abbreviations such as "Fig." and "Alg." and don't use concoctions such as "1st" or "2nd". Months should not be abbreviated. Make sure that all abbreviations and acronyms are explained when they are first used.

Avoid use of "etc." and "and so on". They are clumsy, and sometimes patronizing, as they can imply that the reader ought to be able to complete the list without the author's help.

✗ Methods available are random probing, extrapolation, etc.

✓ Methods available include random probing and extrapolation.
Methods such as random probing and extrapolation can be used.

Never write "etc., etc." or "etc. . . . ".

The ellipsis is a useful notation for indicating that text has been omitted. It should, therefore, only be used in quotations.

A slash, also known as a virgule or solidus, is often used for abbreviation, as in "save time and/or space" or "used for list/tree processing". Use of slashes betrays confusion, since it is often not clear whether the intended meaning is *or* (in the usual English sense of *either but not both*), *or* (in the usual computing sense of *either or both*), *and*, or *also*. If you want to be clear, don't use slashes.

An exception is "I/O", meaning *input and output*. There was once a variety of forms for this expression; now, all forms other than "I/O" are rare.

Acronyms

In technical documents with many compound terms it can be helpful to use acronyms, but as with abbreviations they can confuse the reader. An acronym is desirable if it replaces an otherwise indigestible name such as "pneumonoultramicroscopicsilicovolcanoconiosis" (miner's black lung disease), in which case the acronym becomes the name—as has happened with DNA for "deoxyribonucleic acid". Frequently used sequences of ordinary words, such as "central processing unit", are usually more convenient as acronyms; in a paper about a "dynamic multiprocessing operating system", it is probably best to introduce the DMOS right at the start. However, a surfeit of acronyms will force readers to flip back and forth through the paper to search for definitions. Don't introduce an acronym unless it is to be used frequently.

Acronyms can be fashionable. It was once common to write "WWW" to denote the World Wide Web, but today it is most often denoted by "the web"—it isn't even capitalized. And watch out for redundant acronyms, such as "the CPU unit". How, exactly, does a "local area LAN network" differ from a "LAN"?

Abbreviations end with a stop but it is unusual to put stops in acronyms. Thus "CPU" is correct, "C.P.U." is acceptable, and "CPU." is incorrect.

Sexism

Forms of expression that unnecessarily specify gender are widely regarded as sexist. In technical writing, sexist usage is easy to avoid.

✗ A user may be disconnected when he makes a mistake.

✓ A user may be disconnected when they make a mistake.

✓ Users may be disconnected when they make a mistake.

The first use of "they", as a singular pronoun, is acceptable but, to some readers, jarring. The second use, as a plural, removes sexism at the cost of clarity. It is preferable to recast the sentence.

✓ A user who makes a mistake may be disconnected.

Don't use ugly constructs such as "s/he" or engage in reverse sexism by using "she" unless it is absolutely impossible to avoid a generic reference. Remember that some readers find use of "he" or "his" for a generic case offensive and dislike writing that employs such usage.

4 Punctuation

Taste and common sense are more important than any rules; you put in stops to help your readers to understand you, not to please grammarians.

Ernest Gowers
The Complete Plain Words

Punctuation is a fundamental skill. Anyone reading this book is familiar with the functions of spaces, commas, stops, and capital letters. Stylistic issues of punctuation and common punctuation errors in science writing are the topic of this chapter.

Fonts and formatting

There is no obligation to use fancy typesetting just because a word processor provides it. Most computing or mathematical writing uses three fonts (plain, italic, and bold) or four (if, say, a fixed-width font is used for the text of programs) but use of more is likely to be annoying, and all but the plain font should be used sparingly. Overuse of fonts results in messy-looking text. Some authors prefer **bold** to *italic* for emphasis, but bold print is distracting. Use of underlining for emphasis, once common because of the limitations of typewriters as typesetting devices, is obsolete.

Use standard fonts for the text of papers. This book is set in Times Roman. An alternative is Computer Modern, the default font in LaTeX. Fonts such as Helvetica and `Courier` are awkward and hard to read; sans-serif fonts are widely used in advertising and create the wrong impression. An elaborate or unfamiliar font is almost always inappropriate. A font that is too similar to the main text has no effect other than to look untidy.

Visual clutter of any kind is distracting and should be eliminated unless there is a clear need for it. Emphasis is one kind of clutter. Another is the use of graphic devices such as boxes around important points or icons next to results. Yet another kind of clutter is punctuation: excessive use of parentheses, quotes, italics, hyphens, semicolons, and uppercase letters.

Indentation is an important tool of layout, used primarily to indicate the start of a new paragraph. Some authors prefer to use a blank line instead, a decision that is often unwise; the meaning is unclear at a page break, for example. In literature, a blank line can be used to signal the start of a new topic, but this convention has not been adopted by technical writers. Changes of topic should be signalled by headings.

Indentation is also used to offset material that is not part of the textual flow, such as quotes, programs, and displayed mathematics. The indentation is useful because it allows easier scanning of the page.

In papers submitted for review, use wide margins, a decent font size, and don't cram lines together; referees need space for red ink. Text looks tidier if it is right-justified as well as left-justified (although it is not always easier to read). Consider using a running header, of say the authors' surnames or the paper's title, so that the paper can be reconstructed if the pages become separated. Pages should be numbered. For some journals and conferences the author information needs be on a separate face sheet, and many venues have specific formatting guidelines in their "Information for Authors".

Stops

Stops (or full-stops or periods) end sentences. Some writers don't use any other punctuation. Sentences should usually be short but commas and other marks give text variety. Lack of other marks makes text telegrammatic. Such text can be tiring to read.

Stops are also used in abbreviations, acronyms, and ellipses. When these occur at the end of sentence, the sentence's stop is omitted. Problems with stops are a good reason to avoid abbreviations.

✗ The process required less than a second (except when the machine was heavily loaded, the network was saturated, etc.).

✓ The process required less than a second (unless, for example, the machine was heavily loaded or the network was saturated).

It is not usual to put a stop at the end of a heading.

✗ 3. Neural Nets for Image Classification.

✓ 3. Neural Nets for Image Classification

Commas

The primary uses of commas are to mark pauses, indicate the correct parsing, form lists, and indicate that a phrase is a parenthetical remark (that is, a comment) rather than a qualifier. Thus "the four processes that use the network are almost never idle" means *of the processes, the four that use the network are almost never idle*, while "the four processes, which use the network, are almost never idle" means *the four processes use the network and are almost never idle*. Incorrect use of commas in parenthetical remarks, in particular omission of the first of a pair of commas, is a frequent error.

✗ The process may be waiting for a signal, or even if processing input, may be delayed by network interrupts.

✓ The process may be waiting for a signal, or, even if processing input, may be delayed by network interrupts.

Use the minimum number of commas needed to avoid ambiguity. Sentences with many commas often have strangulated syntax; if the commas seem necessary, consider breaking the sentence into shorter ones or rewriting it altogether. But don't omit too many commas.

✗ When using disk tree algorithms were found to be particularly poor.

✓ When using disk, tree algorithms were found to be particularly poor.

Here is another example.

✗ One node was allocated for each of the states, but of the nine seven were not used.

✓ One node was allocated for each of the states, but, of the nine, seven were not used.

✓ Nine nodes were allocated, one for each of the states, but seven were not used.

Another exception to the minimal-commas rule is in lists. A simple example of a list is "the structures were arrays, trees, and hash tables". Many authors (and editors) prefer to omit the last comma from a list, a process that rarely adds clarity and often does it serious damage.

Commas can be used to give the reader time to breathe.

✗ As illustrated by the techniques listed at the end of the section there are recent advances in parallel algorithms and multiprocessor hardware that indicate the possibility of optimal use of shared disk arrays by indexing algorithms such as those of interest here.

✓ As illustrated by the techniques listed at the end of the section, recent advances in parallel algorithms and multiprocessor hardware may allow optimal use of shared disk arrays by some algorithms, including indexing algorithms such as those of interest here.

Cutting this into several sentences would undoubtedly improve it further.

Colons and semicolons

Colons are used to join related statements.

✓ These small additional structures allow a large saving: the worst case is reduced from $O(n)$ to $O(\log n)$.

Colons are also used to introduce lists.

✓ There are three phases: accumulation of distinct symbols, construction of the tree, and the compression itself.

The elements in a list can be separated by semicolons, allowing commas or other marks within each element.

✓ There are three phases: accumulation of distinct symbols in a hash table; construction of the tree, using a temporary array to hold the symbols for sorting; and the compression itself.

A semicolon can also be used to divide a long sentence, or to set off part of a sentence for emphasis.

✓ In theory the algorithm would be more efficient with an array; but in practice a tree is preferable.

Colons and semicolons are valuable but should not be overused.

Apostrophes

Many people seem to have trouble with apostrophes. Even professional writers get them wrong now and again. But the rules are quite simple.

- Singular possessives such as “the student’s algorithm”, “Brandt’s book”, and “Su and Ling’s method” require an apostrophe and an “s”. (Some people would write “Su’s and Ling’s method”, which is fine too.) For some names ending in “-s”, such as in “Williams’s book”, you can optionally omit the “s” after the apostrophe. If you are unsure, then the “s” should be given.
- Plural possessives such as “students’ passwords” require an apostrophe but no “s”.
- Pronoun possessives such as “its” (as in “its speed”) and “hers” do not require an apostrophe.
- Contractions such as “it’s” (as in “it is blue”) and “can’t” require an apostrophe; but note that contractions should be avoided in technical writing.

Other than in the cases above, apostrophes are not required. The uses “in the 1980’s”, “each of the CPU’s”, “the computers’s power supplies”, and “Goss’ approach” are all incorrect.

Exclamations

Avoid exclamation marks! Never use more than one!!

The proper place for an exclamation mark is after an exclamation (such as “Oh!”—not a common expression in technical writing), or, rarely, after a genuine surprise.

✓ Performance deteriorated after addition of resources!

This is acceptable but not particularly desirable. It would be better to omit the exclamation and add emphasis some other way.

✓ Remarkably, performance deteriorated after addition of resources.

Hyphenation

Many compound words, such as "website", would originally have been written as two separate words, "web site". When the combination becomes common, it is hyphenated, "web-site", then eventually the hyphen is dropped to give the final form. Some words are in a state of transition from one form to another. In the database literature, for example, all three of "data base", "data-base", and "database" are used, and in general writing both "co-ordinate" and "coordinate" are common. Make sure that you are consistent.

Hyphens are also used to override right associativity. By default we parse phrases such as "randomized data structure" into *randomized data-structure*, and thus realize that the topic is not a structure for randomized data. In some phrases that are not right-associative, such as "skew-data hashing", we need the hyphen to disambiguate (although in this case it might be better to write "hashing for skew data").[8] Sometimes there is no correct hyphenation and the sentence has to be rewritten. The phrase "array based data structure" should be written "array-based data structure", but "binary tree based data structure" should probably be written, albeit awkwardly, as "data structure based on binary trees".

Good word-processors hyphenate words when they run over the end of a line, to preserve right-justification. Automatic hyphenation is not always correct and should be checked, to ensure that none of the syllables are broken or that the break is not too close to the word's end. For example, the hyphenations "mac-hine" and "availab-le" should be changed (to "mach-ine" and "avail-able"), and "edited" should probably not be hyphenated at all.

Note that there are three different "dash" symbols: the hyphen "-" used for joining words, the minus sign or en-dash "–" used in arithmetic and for ranges such as "pages 101–127", and the em-dash "—" used for punctuation.

Capitalization

Capital letters were once used more liberally than they are now; in the eighteenth century writers commonly used capitalization (that is, an initial capital letter) to denote nouns. Today, only proper names are capitalized, and even these can be in lowercase if the name is in common use; for example, the capitals in the phrase "the Extensible Hashing method" should be in lowercase.

Some names are not consistently capitalized, particularly those of program-

[8] There is a hyphen missing in the headline "Squad helps dog bite victim".

ming languages. Acronyms that cannot be sounded, such as "APL", should always be written that way, but the only general rule for other cases is to follow other authors. For example, both of the names "FORTRAN" and "Prolog" are abbreviations derived from truncated words. These are however proper names and should always have an initial capital; "lisp" and "pascal" are incorrect.

In technical writing it is usual to capitalize names such as "Theorem 3.1", "Figure 4", and "Section 11". In other writing, lowercase is preferred, but in technical writing lowercase looks sloppy to some readers.

Headings can be either minimally or maximally capitalized. In the former, words are capitalized as they would be in normal text, except that the word following a colon is capitalized.

✓ The use of jump statements: Advice for Prolog programmers

In the latter, words other than articles, conjunctions, or prepositions are capitalized; even these may be capitalized if they are over three letters long.

✓ The Use of Jump Statements: Advice for Prolog Programmers

The same rules apply to captions and titles of references.

Be consistent in your style of capitalization. It is acceptable to use maximum capitalization for sections and minimum capitalization for subsections, but not the other way around.

Quotations

One convention for quotations is that some punctuation marks are placed inside the quotation even when they are not part of the original material. An alternative is to place a punctuation mark within the quotation only if it was used in the original text—such as when a complete sentence is being quoted—as is done throughout this book.

✓ Crosley [2000] argues that "open sets are of insufficient power", but Davies [2002] disagrees: "If a concept is interesting, open sets can express it."

(But note that it is not essential to quote such a dull statement as "open sets are of insufficient power"; paraphrase, or even simply omitting the quote symbols, would be more appropriate. Omission of quotation marks in this case is acceptable—that is, not plagiarism—because Crosley's statement is a natural way to express the concept.)

If the material in the quotation marks is a literal string, the punctuation must go outside. Since most punctuation symbols have meaning in programming languages, when programming statements are quoted the matter in the quote will be syntactically incorrect if the punctuation is in the wrong place.

× One of the reserved words in C is "for."

✓ One of the reserved words in C is "for".

Some editors change this to the wrong form. You may prefer to avoid the problem altogether.

✓ One of the reserved words in C is `for`.

Note that the angled or smart quotation symbols (“ and ”) are not the same as the straight ASCII double-quote symbol (").

Parentheses

A sentence containing a statement in parentheses should be punctuated exactly as if the parenthetical statement was not there.

× Most quantities are small (but there are exceptions.)

✓ Most quantities are small (but there are exceptions).

× (Note that outlying points have been omitted).

✓ (Note that outlying points have been omitted.)

Parenthetical remarks should be asides that the reader can ignore—important text should not be in parentheses. The same rule applies to footnotes. If you think some text should be relegated to a footnote, perhaps it can be deleted.

Overuse of parentheses looks crowded. Avoid having more than one parenthesized remark per paragraph, or more than a couple per page. Parentheses within parentheses are hard to read and look like typing errors. Get rid of them.

The use of "(s)" to denote the possibility of a plural, as in "any observed error(s)", is ugly and unnecessary; omit the parentheses or recast the sentence.

Citations

Citations should be punctuated as if they were parenthetical remarks.

✗ In [2] such cases are shown to be rare.
In (Wilson 1984) such cases are shown to be rare.

Some journals typeset citation numbers as superscripts, in which case this example becomes "In[2] such cases are shown to be rare". Never treat a bracketed expression, whether a citation or otherwise, as a word.

✓ Such cases have been shown to be rare [2].
Such cases have been shown to be rare (Wilson 1984).
Wilson [2] has shown that such cases are rare.
Wilson has shown that such cases are rare [2].
Wilson (1984) has shown that such cases are rare.

The cite should be close to the material it relates to—poor placement of cites can be ambiguous.

✗ The original algorithm has asymptotic complexity $O(n^2)$ but low memory usage, so it is not entirely superseded by Ahlberg's approach, which although of complexity $O(n \log n)$ requires a large in-memory array (Ahlberg 1996, Keele 1989).

Since Ahlberg did not recognize the array as a problem and does not describe the old approach, this sentence is misleading.

✓ The original algorithm has asymptotic complexity $O(n^2)$ but low memory usage (Keele 1989). Thus it is not entirely superseded by Ahlberg's approach (Ahlberg 1996), which, although of complexity $O(n \log n)$, requires a large in-memory array.

The placement of citations depends partly on the citation style used. With the superscript style, for example, it is usual to try and place citations at the end of the sentence.

5 Mathematics

Mathematics is no more than a symbolism. But it is the only symbolism invented by the human mind which steadfastly resists the constant attempts of the mind to shift and smudge the meaning . . . . Our confidence in any science is roughly proportional to the amount of mathematics it employs—that is, to its ability to formulate its concepts with enough precision to allow them to be handled mathematically.

Jacob Bronowski and Bruce Mazlish
The Western Intellectual Tradition

Mathematics gives solidity to abstract concepts. As for writing in general, there are well-established conventions of presentation for mathematics and mathematical concepts. Reading of mathematics is difficult work at the best of times, unpleasant work if the mathematics is badly presented, and pointless if the mathematics does not make sense.

The use of mathematics for expressing ideas is often the difference between a vague paper and a clear one. Mathematical notation can be used to describe algorithms, data structures, automata, or just about any of the objects that computer scientists study. The discipline of describing work in a mathematical form can expose inconsistencies and gaps, and provides a basis for making formal statements about the ideas being studied. While mathematics should not be used unnecessarily—to dress up uninteresting ideas, for example—ultimately a great deal of computer science has a mathematical foundation.

Clarity

In mathematical writing it is essential to be precise. For example, an ambiguous statement of a theorem can make its proof incomprehensible. The principles of mathematical writing can be applied to technical writing in general, and many discussions can be clarified through the use of mathematical notation.

× An inverted list for a given term is a sequence of pairs, where the first element in each pair is a document identifier and the second is the frequency of the term in the document to which the identifier corresponds.

✓ An inverted list for a term t is a sequence of pairs of the form $\langle d, f \rangle$, where each d is a document identifier and f is the frequency of t in d.

In the first version, the author has had to struggle to avoid ambiguity.

Many terms have well-defined mathematical meanings and are confusing if used in another way.

Normal, usual. The word "normal" has several mathematical meanings; it is often best to use, say, "usual" if a non-mathematical meaning is intended.

Definite, strict, proper, all, some. Avoid "definite", "strict", and "proper" in their non-mathematical meanings, and be careful with "all" and "some".

Intractable. An algorithm or problem is "intractable" only if it is NP-hard, that is, the computational complexity is worse than polynomial. "Intractable" is sometimes used to mean *hard to do*, which is acceptable if there is no possibility of confusion.

Formula, equation. A "formula" is not necessarily an "equation"; the latter involves an equality.

Equivalent, similar. Two things are "equivalent" if they are indistinguishable with regard to some criteria. If they are not indistinguishable, they are at best "similar".

Element, partition. An "element" is a member of a set (or list or array) and should not be used to refer to a subpart of an expression. If a set is "partitioned" into subsets, the subsets are disjoint and form the original set under union.

Average, mean. "Average" is used loosely to mean *typical*. Only use it in the formal sense—of *arithmetic mean*—if it is clear to the reader that the formal sense is intended. Otherwise use "mean" or even "arithmetic mean".

Subset, strict. "Subset" should not be used to mean *subproblem*. Orderings (or partial orderings) specified in writing are assumed to be non-strict. For example, "A is a subset of B" means that $A \subseteq B$; to specify $A \subset B$ use "A is a strict subset of B". The same rule applies to "less than", "greater than", and "monotonic".

Metric, measure. "Metric" is sometimes used informally to mean *measure*, but has specific meanings in mathematics. Use "measure" if that is the meaning intended.

Theorems

When you submit a paper containing a proof of a theorem, always be satisfied that the proof is correct. However, the details of the proof may not be important to the reader and can often be omitted. Steps in the logic of a proof should be simple enough that the gaps can be completed by a reader mechanically, without too much invention. A common mistake is to unnecessarily include mechanical algebraic transformations; you need to work through these to check the proof, but the reader is unlikely to find them valuable.

Theorems, definitions, lemmas, and propositions should be numbered, even if there are only two or three of each in the paper, and you could consider numbering key examples. Not only does numbering allow reference within the paper, but it simplifies discussion of the paper later on. It is much easier for a correspondent to refer to "Definition 4.2" than "the definition towards the bottom of page 6". Many readers skim papers to find theorems (or other results such as illustrations or tables). For this reason, and because they may be quoted verbatim in other papers, theorems should be stated as completely as possible.

Some presentation problems are not easily resolved. For a theorem with a complex proof, if the lemmas are proved early they appear irrelevant, and if they are proved late the main proof is harder to understand. One approach is to state the main theorem first, then state and prove the lemmas before giving the main proof, but in other cases all that can be done is to take extra care in the motivation and make liberal use of examples. Explain the structure of long proofs before getting to the detail, and explain how each part of the proof relates to the structure.

Proof by contradiction is overused. By all means use contradiction to develop your understanding of the problem, if it helps you to get the details right, but it is always worthwhile exploring how to achieve the result directly instead of by contradiction.

When stating your proof in a paper—that is, making it comprehensible to a reader—remember that you are presenting a reasoned argument. Use any available means to convey your argument with the greatest possible clarity; a diagram, for example, is perfectly acceptable. The end of each proof, example, or definition can be marked with a symbol such as a box. Alternatively, proofs and so on can be indented to set them apart from the running text.

Readability

Mathematics is usually presented in italics, to distinguish it from other text. For example, in the expression "of length n" it is clear that n is a variable of some kind. The main exception is names such as log or sin, which are written in an upright font. Always use the same font for the same variable, and use the same font for all variables unless there is a good reason not to.

Brackets or square brackets ([,]), parentheses ((,)), and braces ({, }) are all used to delimit subexpressions, but braces can be confusing because they are also used to denote sets. Angle brackets ($\langle$, $\rangle$) can also be used; these are not the same symbols as the relational operators ($<$, $>$). Use parentheses of appropriate size; they should stand out from the expressions they enclose.

✗ $(p \cdot (\sum_{i=0}^{n} A_i))$

✓ $\big(p \cdot (\sum_{i=0}^{n} A_i) \big)$

Sentences with embedded mathematics should be structured as if each formula was a simple phrase. Phrases indicate how the following text will be structured, but mathematics does not, and so should not be used at the start of a sentence.

✗ $p \leftarrow q_1 \wedge \cdots \wedge q_n$ is a conditional dependency.

✓ The dependency $p \leftarrow q_1 \wedge \cdots \wedge q_n$ is conditional.

Give the type of each variable every time it is used, so that the reader doesn't have to remember as many details and can concentrate on understanding the content. Watch out for misplaced types or variables.

✗ The values are represented as a list of numbers L.

✓ The values are represented as a list L of numbers.

The former version is ambiguous—the symbol L might denote an individual member of the set.

Mathematics should not take the place of text: readers quickly get lost if they need to decipher a stream of complex expressions.

✗ Let $\langle S \rangle = \{ \sum_{i=1}^{n} \alpha_i x_i \mid \alpha_i \in F, 1 \leq i \leq n \}$. For $x = \sum_{i=1}^{n} \alpha_i x_i$ and $y = \sum_{i=1}^{n} \beta_i x_i$, so that $x, y \in \langle S \rangle$, we have $\alpha x + \beta y = \alpha (\sum_{i=1}^{n} \alpha_i x_i) + \beta (\sum_{i=1}^{n} \beta_i x_i) = \sum_{i=1}^{n} (\alpha \alpha_i + \beta \beta_i) x_i \in \langle S \rangle$.

Although the mathematics in this example is straightforward, there is no motivation, and the thicket of symbols is daunting.

✓ Let $\langle S \rangle$ be a vector space defined by

$$\langle S \rangle = \left\{ \sum_{i=1}^{n} \alpha_i x_i \mid \alpha_i \in F, 1 \leq i \leq n \right\}.$$

We now show that $\langle S \rangle$ is closed under addition. Consider any two vectors $x, y \in \langle S \rangle$. Then $x = \sum_{i=1}^{n} \alpha_i x_i$ and $y = \sum_{i=1}^{n} \beta_i x_i$. For any constants $\alpha, \beta \in F$, we have

$$\begin{aligned} \alpha x + \beta y &= \alpha (\textstyle\sum_{i=1}^{n} \alpha_i x_i) + \beta (\textstyle\sum_{i=1}^{n} \beta_i x_i) \\ &= \sum_{i=1}^{n} (\alpha \alpha_i + \beta \beta_i) x_i , \end{aligned}$$

so that $\alpha x + \beta y \in \langle S \rangle$.

Note the vertical alignment of the equality symbols.

Mathematical expressions should not run together.

✗ For each x_i, $1 \leq i \leq n$, x_i is positive.

✓ Each x_i, where $1 \leq i \leq n$, is positive.

If a formula is complex, or is a key result, it should be displayed. In such displays, the formula can be either centred or indented; choose either, but be consistent. However, if part of the display is an algorithm or program, centering can look peculiar. Displayed formulas (or graphs or diagrams) should be positive results, not counter-examples, so that readers who skim through the paper won't be misled. If a displayed formula is sufficiently important it should be numbered, to allow discussion of it elsewhere in the paper and for reference once the paper is published. As in the example above, a displayed formula should be treated as a phrase.

Mathematical symbols should, if possible, be the same font size as other characters. For example, the expression $(n(n+1)+1)/2$ is more legible than $\frac{n(n+1)+1}{2}$ even though the former uses more characters; but take care with potentially ambiguous expressions such as $a/b+c$. Font sizes should be consistent (though not necessarily identical) in text and displayed equations; large symbols are ugly and tiny symbols are illegible.

Consider breaking down expressions to make them more readable, especially if doing so enlarges small symbols.

$$\times \quad f(x) = e^{2^{-\frac{b}{a}x\sqrt{1-\frac{a^2}{x^2}}}}$$

$$\checkmark \quad f(x) = e^{2^{g(x)}} \quad \text{where} \quad g(x) = -\tfrac{b}{a}x\sqrt{1-\tfrac{a^2}{x^2}}$$

Avoid unnecessary subscripts: use x and y rather than x_1 and x_2. Also, don't nest subscripts on top of each other: the symbol i is legible in x_i, barely acceptable in x_{j_i}, and ridiculous in $x_{k_{j_i}}$. Mix subscripts and superscripts with caution: the expression $x_{j'}^{p_k}$ is a mess. Be careful with choice of letters for subscripts: in some small fonts, the letters i, j, and l are not easy to distinguish.

The presence of subscripts may be due to poor use of notation. For example, if $W = \{w_1, \ldots, w_k\}$ then you might write $\sum_{i=1}^{k} f_{w_i}$, but the equivalent expression $\sum_{w \in W} f_w$ is easier to read.

As illustrated in these examples, even simple mathematical expressions require competent typesetting. Such typesetting may involve use of advanced word-processing facilities, but failure to learn such facilities is no excuse for sloppy presentation.

Notation

Ensure that the symbols you use will be correctly understood by, and familiar to, the reader. For example, there are several symbols (including $\Rightarrow$, $\mapsto$, $\vdash$, $\supset$, $\sqsupset$, $\models$, and probably others) that are used in one context or another for logical implication. These symbols also have other meanings, so there is plenty of scope for confusion. The symbols $\sim$, $\simeq$, and $\approx$ are all used to mean *approximately equal to*, but $\sim$ is also used in other contexts. The symbol $\cong$ means *is congruent to*, not *approximately equal*. Don't be lazy; use $\leq$, not $<=$, for *less than or equal to*.

The symbols for *floor* ($\lfloor, \rfloor$) and *ceiling* ($\lceil, \rceil$) seem to cause particular problems in typesetting. In more than one of my papers the typesetters changed these to square brackets ([,]), and in the process utterly destroyed the meaning of the equations. Similarly, mistakes in placement are common with subscripts. Watch out for such errors.

Symbols such as $\forall$, $\exists$, $<$, $>$, $=$, and $\Rightarrow$, and abbreviations such as "iff", should not be used as substitutes for words. These symbols may be compact but they are hard for readers to digest. But don't replace symbols by words unnecessarily; for example, write "$a \leq b$" rather than "a is less than or equal to b". Concocted or amusing symbols are not a good idea; don't use $\clubsuit$ as an operator, for example. Use each operator for one purpose only. Compilers may understand overloading, but people do not.

Don't re-use notation: an excellent way of confusing readers is to use N for one quantity on page 6 and for another on page 13. But expressions with similar meaning should have similar notation that follows consistent rules. Adhere to conventions such as using i and j for integer subscripts and calligraphic letters for classes. And don't vary an existing notation without good reason.

Take care with accents. Don't use $\hat{a}$, $\tilde{a}$, $\bar{a}$, and $\vec{a}$ together, and don't pile up primes: the symbol a'' may be clear, but what about $D_{i'}^{l'\prime}$? Some authors put powers on primes, as in a'^4 to represent a'''', but this notation is often unclear. If you have such deep primes, consider reworking your notation to get rid of them.

Ranges and sequences

The closed range of real numbers r where $a \leq r \leq b$ is represented by "$[a,b]$"; the open range $a < r < b$ is represented by "(a,b)"; the range $a \leq r < b$ is represented by "$[a,b)$"; and the range $a < r \leq b$ is represented by "$(a,b]$".

It is common practice to use an ellipsis to describe a sequence of integers; thus $m,\ldots,n$ represents all integers between m and n inclusive. An infinite sequence is usually represented by $m_1,m_2,\ldots$, where it is assumed that the reader can extrapolate from the initial values to the other members of the sequence. Thus "$2,4,8,\ldots$" would be assumed to be the sequence of positive powers of 2. Always state both the lower and the upper bound if the sequence is finite and ensure that the intended sequence is clear.

An expression such as $1 \leq i \leq 6$ should be replaced by $i = 1,\ldots,6$ if it is not clear that i should be an integer.

Alphabets

Use of characters from the Greek alphabet to denote variables and quantities can add clarity to mathematical writing, because these characters cannot be confused with English text.

Most readers are familiar with only a few Greek letters, so use of unfamiliar letters should be minimized, if only because use of any new notation should be minimized. Most people find it easier to remember that a letter denotes a certain quantity if they know the name of the letter; if they do not know the name they invent one, but this invention is generally not as effective a label as a real name. For example, reading the statement "sets are denoted by α" might result in the thought *sets are denoted by alpha* while reading "sets are denoted by ρ" (a form of rho) might result in the thought *sets are denoted by a squiggle-that-looks-like-a-backwards-g*. Other characters that have this effect are the Greek letters ζ (zeta), ξ and Ξ (xi), and symbols such as $\aleph$, $\Re$, and $\Im$.

Some mathematical symbols and characters from other alphabets have a superficial resemblance to more familiar symbols. Some pairs that can cause confusion, particularly after imperfect reproduction, are as follows.

Symbol		Confused with	
ε	epsilon	e	
η	eta	n	
ι	iota	i	
μ	mu	u	
ρ	rho	p	
υ	upsilon	v	
ω	omega	w	
$\vee$	or	v	
$\propto$	proportional	α	alpha
$\emptyset$	empty set	ϕ	phi

Never use handwritten symbols. If you can't print the symbol you want to use, change it.

Line breaks

Avoid letting a number, symbol, or abbreviation appear at the start of the line, particularly if it is the end of a sentence.

✗ We have therefore introduced an additional variable, denoted by x. It allows ...

✓ We therefore introduce an additional variable, denoted by x. It allows ...

✗ Accesses to the new kind of disk typically require about 12 ms using our techniques.

✓ Accesses to the new kind of disk typically require about 12 ms using our techniques.

Most word processors provide an unbreakable-space character that prevents this behaviour. However, some word processors insist on breaking lines at awkward places in mathematical expressions.

✗ The problem can be simplified by using the term $f(x_1, \ldots,$ $x_n)$ as a descriptor.

Sometimes the only solution is to rewrite the surrounding text.

✓ The problem is simplified if the term $f(x_1, \ldots, x_n)$ is used as a descriptor.

Numbers

In technical writing, numbers should usually be written as figures, not spelt out. The common exceptions are approximate numbers; numbers up to twenty, unless they are literal values or part of an expression of measurement; and numbers at the start of a sentence, although it is generally better to recast the sentence so that the number is elsewhere. Percentages should always be in figures.

✗ 1024 computers were linked into the ring.
Partial compilation gave a 4-fold improvement.
The increase was over five per cent.
The method requires 2 passes.

✓ There were 1024 computers linked into the ring.
Partial compilation gave a four-fold improvement.
The increase was over 5 per cent.
The increase was over 5%.

Method 2 is illustrated in Figure 1.
The leftmost 2 in the sequence was changed to a 1.
The method requires two passes.

Don't mix modes.

✗ There were between four and 32 processors in each machine.

✓ There were between 4 and 32 processors in each machine.

In English-speaking countries, the traditional method for separating long sequences of digits into groups of three is to use commas, as in "1,897,600". This method has two disadvantages: it can be confusing if the numbers are part of a comma-separated list, and decimal points are denoted by commas in many countries, so a number such as "1,375" could be misinterpreted. It is for these reasons that the alternative of using thin spaces was introduced, as in "1 897 600" or "73 802". But the comma-separated style remains popular and the use of thin spaces has not become established in computer science papers. Comma separation is used throughout this book.

Fractions are only rarely used for values, and should not be used as abbreviations.

✗ About 1/3 of the data was noise.

✓ About one-third of the data was noise.

As for mathematical symbols in general, numbers should not be used to start a sentence. Nor should they be adjacent.

✗ There were 14 512-Kb sets.

✓ There were fourteen 512-Kb sets.

Never omit the leading 0 in numbers whose magnitude is less than 1; write "the size was 0.3 Kb", not "the size was .3 Kb".

Avoid the phrase "orders of magnitude".

✗ The new algorithm is at least two orders of magnitude faster.

In this example, is the unit of magnitude binary or decimal? It would be better to be explicit.

✓ The new algorithm is at least a hundred times faster.

Be clear about which base a number is in.[9]

Numbers of the same units should, for consistency, be represented to the same precision. In physical experiments, it is usual to represent numbers to the same relative precision, that is, the same number of digits. In computer science, in which values are usually measured to the same absolute precision, it is more logical to represent numbers to the same units.

✗ The sizes were 7.31 Kb and 181 Kb, respectively.

✓ The sizes were 7.3 Kb and 181.4 Kb, respectively.

A paper gave the same figure in different places as "almost 200,000", "about 170,000", "173,000", and "173,255"—an entirely unnecessary inconsistency.

Be realistic about accuracy and error. Your system may report that a process required 13.271844 CPU seconds, but in all likelihood the last four or five digits are meaningless. You should not imply accuracy by including spurious numbers. For example, "0.5 second" is not equivalent to "half a second", since the former implies that careful measurements were taken. Guesses and approximations should be clearly indicated as such, with words such as "roughly", "nearly", "approximately", "about", "almost", or "over"; but don't use wordy phrases such as "in the region of".

Percentages

Use percentages with caution.

✗ The error rate grew by 4%.

This example is ambiguous because an error rate is presumably a percentage. It is better to be explicit, and to avoid mixing kinds of percentages.

✗ The error rate grew by 4%, from 52% to 54%.

✓ The error rate grew by 2%, from 52% to 54%.

When stating a percentage, ensure that the reader knows what is a percentage of what. If you write that "the capacity decreased by 30%", is this 30% of the old figure or the new? The convention is to use 100% as the starting point, but in a series of statements of percentages it is easy to get lost. Use percentages rather than odds to express probabilities.

[9] I'm told that there are 10 kinds of people in the world, those that understand binary and those that don't. (And how true it is. A reader suggested that "10" be changed to "ten".)

✗ The likelihood of failure is 2:1.

✓ The likelihood of failure is one in three.

✓ The likelihood of failure is about 30%.

Don't use probabilities to describe small sets of observations. Success in two of five cases does not mean that the method "works 40% of the time". The percentage gives the result an authority it does not deserve.

Units of measurement

Two quantities are commonly measured in computer science: space and time. For time, the basic units are the second (sec), minute (min) and hour (hr); note that it is unusual to give the abbreviated forms of these units. For the divisions of the second—the millisecond (ms or msec), microsecond (μs or μsec), and nanosecond (ns or nsec)—some readers may be unsure of the notation. For example, "ms" might be interpreted as *microsecond*. State such units in unabbreviated form at least once. When writing about hours or minutes use a colon rather than a stop to separate the components of the time. That is, write "3:30 minutes" rather than "3.30 minutes".

For space, the basic units are bit and byte. These are combined in tenth powers of 2 rather than third powers of 10.

Unit	value (bytes)	denotation
kilobyte	$2^{10} \approx 10^3$	Kb, Kbyte
megabyte	$2^{20} \approx 10^6$	Mb, Mbyte
gigabyte	$2^{30} \approx 10^9$	Gb, Gbyte
terabyte	$2^{40} \approx 10^{12}$	Tb, Tbyte
petabyte	$2^{50} \approx 10^{15}$	Pb, Pbyte
exabyte	$2^{60} \approx 10^{18}$	Eb, Ebyte
zettabyte	$2^{70} \approx 10^{21}$	Zb, Zbyte
yottabyte	$2^{80} \approx 10^{24}$	Yb, Ybyte

If there is any likelihood that, for example, a reader could interpret "Mb" as *megabit*, use "Mbyte" or "megabyte" instead. The larger units, especially "Pb", "Eb", "Zb", and "Yb", are unfamiliar to most readers and should be written in full at least once, preferably with an explanation.

There are few derived units in computing other than the transfer rate of bytes per second, as in "18 Mb/sec". It was surprising to see "millibits" in a paper on arithmetic coding (in which symbols can be represented in a fraction of a bit). The unit is so unusual that "thousandths of a bit" is preferable.

Choose units that are easy to understand. For example, seconds can be preferable to minutes because fractions of a minute can be confusing: does "1.50 minutes" mean *one and a half minutes* or *one minute and fifty seconds*? (This problem can be avoided by using colons instead of stops, as discussed above.) Also, as values such as clock speeds and transfer rates are quoted in seconds, use of minutes makes comparison more difficult. On the other hand, "13:21 hours" is perhaps kinder to the reader than "47.8×10^3 seconds".

Some units, although in general use, are not well-defined. For example, MIPS (a million instructions per second) and gigaflops (a billion instructions per second) are increasingly meaningless; they cannot be used to compare machines of different architectures, in particular asynchronous processors without a central clock. Also, "gigaflops" strictly means a billion floating point operations per second, but is widely used to mean a billion instructions of any kind. Architecture-independent measures such as benchmarks may be more appropriate.

For quantities greater than 1, the unit is plural. For smaller quantities, the convention is that the unit is singular, but in computer science this convention is often not observed.

✓ The average run took 1.3 seconds, and the fastest took 0.8 second.
The average run took 1.3 seconds, and the fastest took 0.8 seconds.

Units should be typeset in the font used in the paper for text, even when they are part of a mathematical expression.

✗ The volume is r^p *Kb* in total.

✓ The volume is r^p Kb in total.

Put white space between values and units. Write "11.2 Kbytes" rather than "11.2Kbytes"; the second form may be common, but it is much harder to read. Numbers and their units should be hyphenated when used as an adjective.

✓ We also tried the method on the 2.7-Kb input.

6 Graphs, figures, and tables

"And what is the use of a book", thought Alice,
"without pictures or conversations?"

Lewis Carroll
Alice in Wonderland

Well-chosen illustrations breathe life into a paper, giving the reader interesting visual elements to browse and highlighting the central results and ideas. A typical figure is of visual matter such as a graph or diagram, or of textual matter such as a table, algorithm, or, less commonly, complex mathematics. Some information is best presented in a pictorial form, such as a graph or figure, to show trends and relationships. Other information is best as a table, to show regularities. This chapter concerns style issues related to such material.

Graphs

Graphs are usually the best way to present numerical results. Numbers should be used sparingly. Instead, use graphs wherever appropriate, to elegantly summarize numbers so that the behaviour under discussion is obvious. If you must list the numbers as well, put a detailed table of results in an appendix, but in many cases the trend is the interesting outcome; the numbers are only of transient significance and can be omitted.

Don't flood your paper with statistics, even in graphical form, and avoid repetition; each graph should convey interesting new information. It is all too easy to generate reams of numbers by running software with different combinations of parameters, but, even though these numbers may contribute to your analysis and understanding of the phenomena being observed, they are unlikely to be of value to a reader. You should present information because it is supporting evidence for a hypothesis, not because it is an output of some program.

Graphs should be simple, with no more than a few plotted lines and a minimum of clutter. The horizontal or x-axis should be used for the parameter being varied, or the input; the vertical or y-axis is for the function of the parameter, or the output. Plotted lines of discrete data should always have points marked by distinctive marks such as circles, boxes, or triangles. Ticks or crosses are acceptable if they are easy to see.

Consider using greys and line thickness rather than dots and dashes to distinguish between lines. If you use shades of grey to distinguish different elements in the graph, ensure that the shades are sufficiently distinct; lines in lighter grey sometimes need to be a little thicker than other lines. Greys are preferable to cross-hatching, which can create the optical illusion of shimmering and does not photocopy well. Only use colour in a write-up if colour printing is used to produce the final version.

Minimize use of unnecessary elements and remove all decoration. Are the secondary ticks on the axes useful? If not, discard them. Is a legend necessary? If not, remove it, and label the lines directly. Do the captions have to be in a large font? If not, diminish them. Axes should be inconspicuous; ink should be used for data, not dressing. Gridlines and boxing are other forms of unnecessary ornamentation. Secondary marks, such as axis ticks, should be a little lighter than the other elements. The lines and other elements should be of similar weight—don't mix a large, bold font with lightly drawn lines, for example.

Many of the commonly used graphing tools provide features that are only rarely of value; worse, some of these features are invoked by default. Poor versions of a graph are shown on page 86, with revisions of it on page 87. A slightly more complex graph is shown on page 88. See also the graphs on pages 89–92 and 95–98.

Note the shape of these graphs: rectangular rather than square, with the legends placed in spare space within the body of the graph. The legend needs to be placed where it can't be confused with other material; default placement may mean that the legend obscures part of a curve. The emphasis is on creating as much space as possible for presentation of data, while other elements are held to a minimum.

You may need a little imagination to allow the desired picture to emerge. Logarithmic axes are useful because they show behaviour at different orders of magnitude. An example of changing to a logarithmic axis is shown on page 89. Graphs with logarithmic axes are also useful when plotting problem size against algorithm running time, as different asymptotic growth rates give straight lines of different slope. If the relationship is more complex, some sort of transformation on the data may yield a straight line or some other simple curve.

Log scaling is not always appropriate. If one algorithm is 30% faster than another at all scales, then their performance will be almost indistinguishable on a log-log graph. Even if one algorithm is twice as fast as the other, a log-log graph will show one line just a little below the other.

In some cases data that seems innately tabular can be represented as a graph. Often a bar graph is suitable because the items being compared are not ordered, as illustrated in the graph on page 90. (Such data should not be represented by joined points, which would imply that the axes were related by a function.) A more complex example is shown on page 91. Another example of how to represent tabular data as a graph, for the more complex problem of comparing space and time simultaneously, is the graph on page 92.

Graph-drawing tools allow bar graphs to be three-dimensional, but the addition of depth is deceptive; if one bar is twice the height of another, the use of depth exaggerates the difference.

Graphs are used to illustrate change in one parameter as another is varied. In some cases more than two parameters can interact in complex ways. If two parameters, say A and B, depend on a third, C, then a good solution is to plot C on the x-axis and have two y axes, one for each of A and B, as illustrated in the graph on page 88. If two parameters, say D and E, jointly determine a third, F, in some complex way—thus describing a three-dimensional space—the problem is more difficult. A three-dimensional representation can be used, but these are rarely clear. The best solution is to experimentally graph D against F for several fixed values of E, and use these results to choose an E value that yields a representative graph; and similarly vary E for several fixed D, to choose a representative D.

Where several methods of achieving the same aim are being illustrated, the axes in each graph should have the same scale. For example, if you are comparing different data structures and a separate graph is used for each one, the axes should be consistent from one graph to the next. That is, if y, say, ranges from 0 to 80 on one graph, it should also range from 0 to 80 on the other, to allow direct comparison between the methods. Comparison is easier with several (but not too many) lines on one graph.

Beware of using graphs to make unsupported claims. For example, consider the "space wastage" line in the graph on page 88: it would not be possible to identify the slope of this line with any confidence, nor identify it as a particular kind of curve. The only reasonable inference would be that increasing list length increases space wastage.

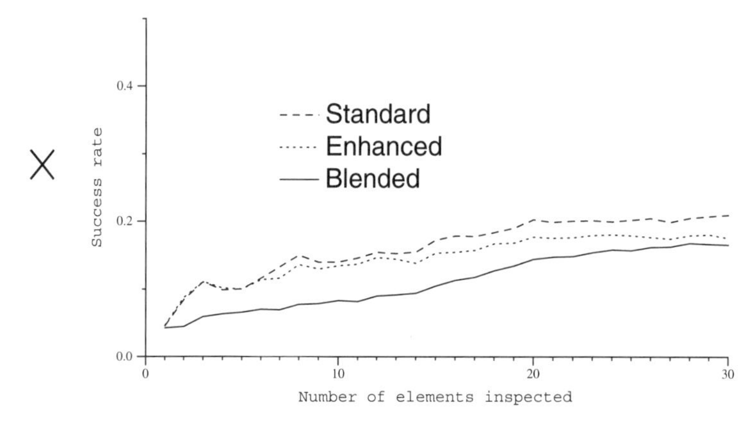

FIGURE 7. *Success rate as the number of inspected items is increased. It is clear that blending is not effective.*

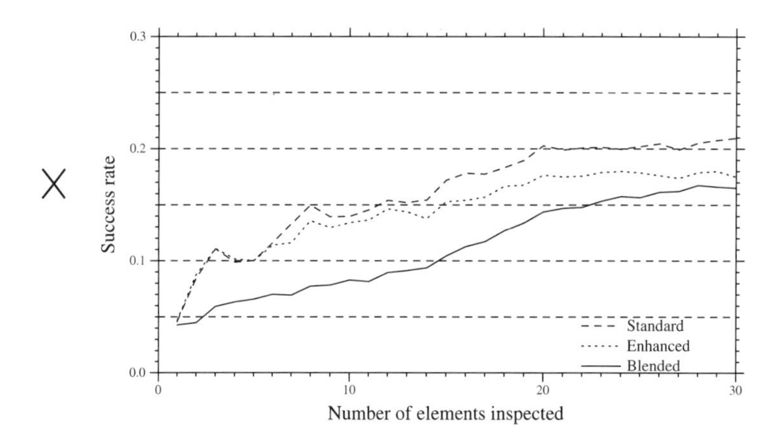

FIGURE 7. *Success rate as the number of inspected items is increased. It is clear that blending is not effective.*

Badly designed graphs. These graphs show the same data. In the upper version, poor use has been made of the vertical space available, and the legend is awkwardly placed. Fonts and size are changed unnecessarily, and are inconsistent with the main text. In the lower version, the vertical scaling and fonts have been corrected, but unnecessary ornamentation has been introduced. The grid lines and heavy border now greatly outweigh the data being presented.

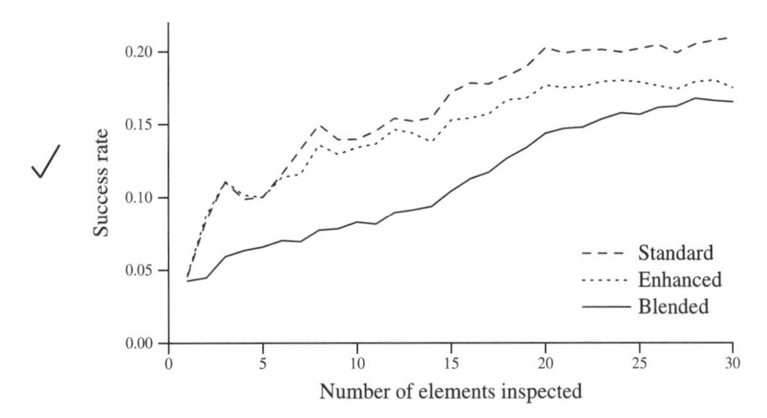

FIGURE 7. *Success rate as the number of inspected items is increased. It is clear that blending is not effective.*

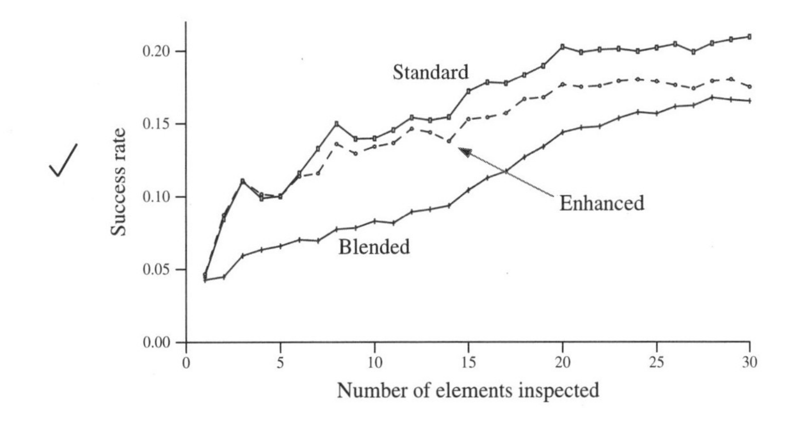

FIGURE 7. *Success rate as the number of inspected items is increased. It is clear that blending is not effective.*

Graphs reconsidered. These graphs show the same data as those on the previous page. Vertical scale is now completely corrected, and unnecessary tick marks have been removed. In the lower version, the data lines are stronger and the legend has been replaced with direct labelling. Line ticks have been introduced to reflect the fact that the data is discrete, that is, non-integer values are not meaningful.

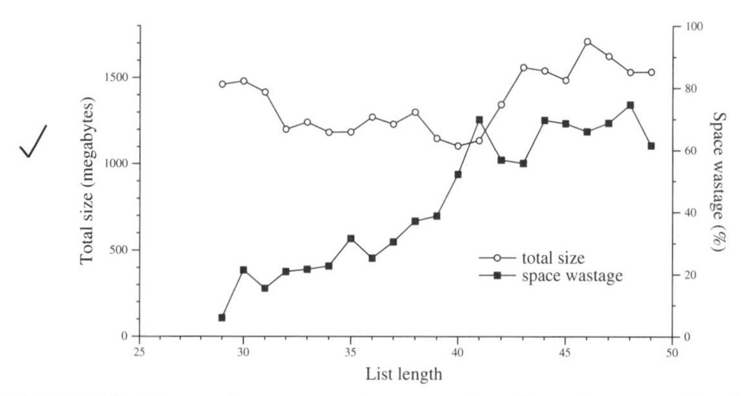

FIGURE 2. *Size and space wastage as a function of average list length.*

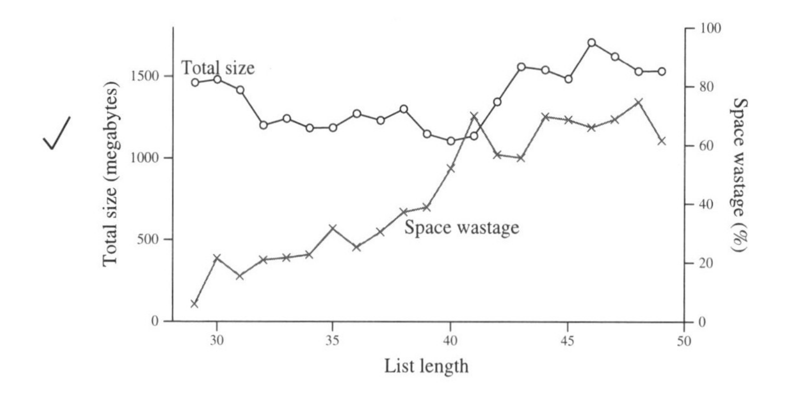

FIGURE 2. *Size and space wastage as a function of average list length.*

Two functions plotted on one graph. It is necessary to label the axes to correspond with the curves; otherwise it would be difficult to identify which curve matched which axis. The upper version is (almost) as in the first edition of this book; the lower version is a revision with distracting elements removed or de-emphasised and several other minor alterations.

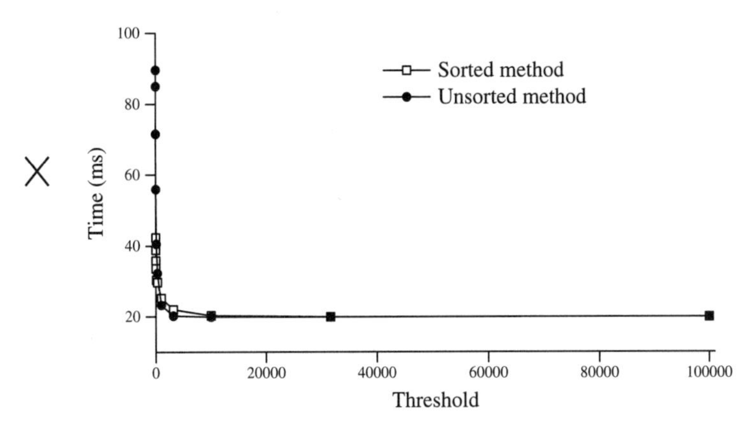

FIGURE 6. *Evaluation time (in milliseconds) for bulk insertion methods as threshold is varied.*

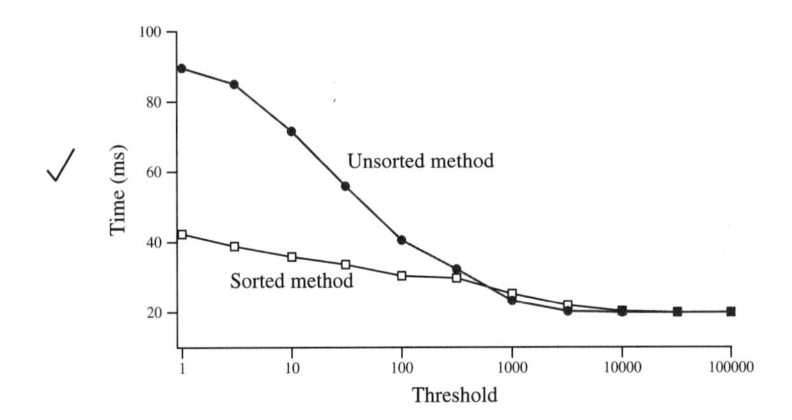

FIGURE 6. *Evaluation time (in milliseconds) for bulk insertion methods as threshold is varied.*

Choice of axis scaling. For these graphs showing the same data, in the lower graph the logarithmic scaling on the x-axis allows the behaviour for small thresholds to be seen.

Data set	Method	
	A	B
Small, random	11.5	11.6
Large, random	27.9	17.1
Small, clustered	9.7	8.2
Large, clustered	24.0	13.5
All documents	49.4	60.1
First 1000	21.1	35.4
Last 1000	1.0	5.5

TABLE 2. *Elapsed time (milliseconds) for methods A and B applied to data sets 1–7.*

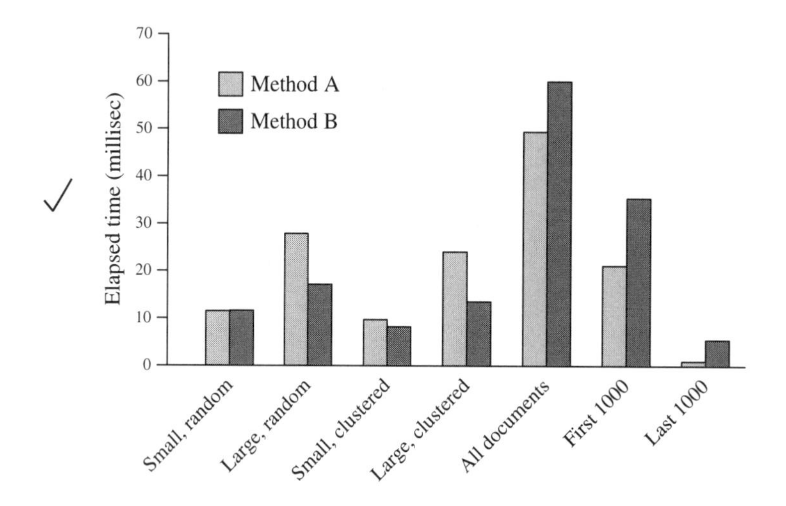

FIGURE 2. *Elapsed time (milliseconds) for methods A and B applied to data sets 1–7.*

A table compared to a graph. The data shows how two methods compare over seven experiments. The graph is a better choice for this data because the pattern is more obvious.

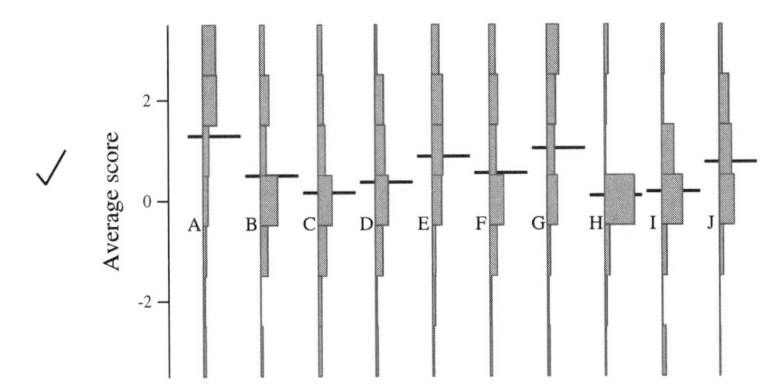

FIGURE 2. *Average score in each category. There were 75 responses overall. The proportion of responses in each category, for the possible scores of* -3, -2, -1, 0, 1, 2, *and* 3, *is shown as a vertical histogram. The solid bar is the mean in each case.*

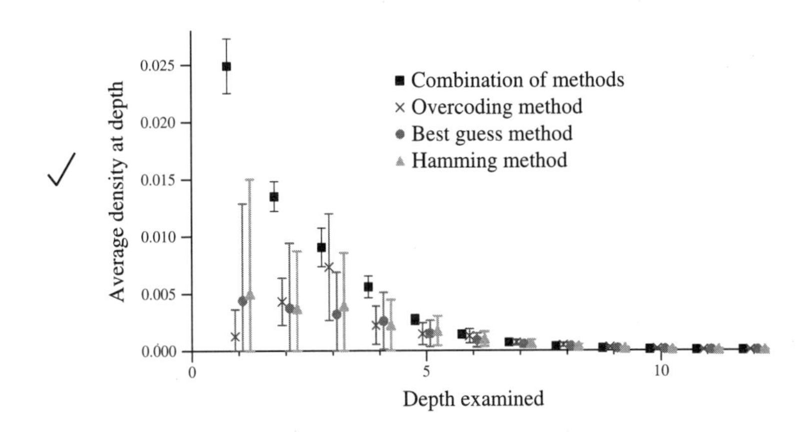

FIGURE 9. *Range of scores with each method, at each depth. The principle mark in each range is the average score. As can be seen, each method returns results within a reasonably narrow band, but they are surprisingly different from each other. Combination is highly effective in this case.*

Further bargraphs. The upper graph shows an approach to comparing distributions across a set of related statistics. The lower graph has error bars to show range and scale.

Method	Space (%)	Time (ms)
A	1.0	7,564.5
B	31.7	895.6
C	44.7	458.4
D	97.8	71.8
E	158.1	18.9
F	173.7	1.4
G	300.0	0.9

TABLE 8.4. *Tradeoff of space against time for methods A to G.*

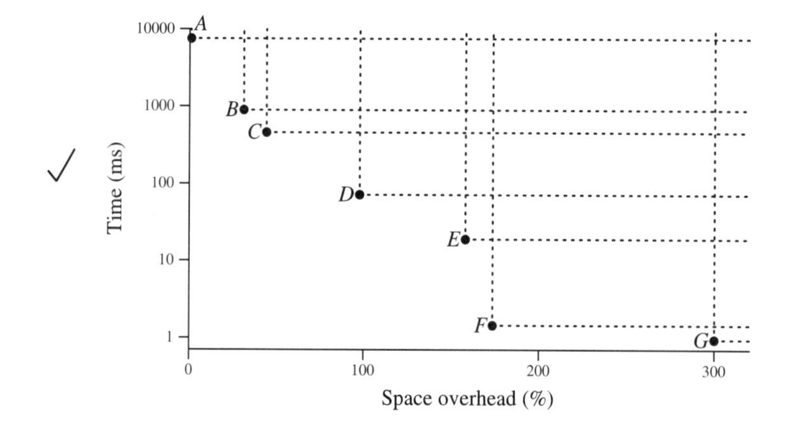

FIGURE 8.4. *Tradeoff of space against time for methods A to G. The boxed area to the right and above each point is of unacceptable performance: any method in that area will be less efficient with respect to both space and time than the point at the box's corner.*

Another table compared to a graph. The data shows how different methods compare with respect to space and time. The table is difficult to interpret.

There are several good software packages for drawing graphs. Valuable features include:

- Placing of several lines on one graph.
- A range of symbols (such as crosses, squares, and triangles) for marking points.
- The ability to create custom symbols of custom size for marking points.
- Optional connection of points with solid, dotted, or dashed lines, and optional omission of the point marks.
- The ability to place text at specified places in the graph.
- Multiple font sizes and line thicknesses.
- Availability of greys and colours.
- Optional logarithmic or exponential scaling on both axes.
- Axis editing, to specify where the ticks are placed, how many digits of precision to use, and what range to cover.
- The ability to move and rotate the legend or key, line labels, axis labels, and the graph label.
- The ability to apply simple functions or external programs to (x, y) values.

Most of these features were used in the example graphs in this chapter.

Graphs and diagrams attract the attention of readers, so should be reserved for material that is central to the paper.

Visualization of results

We use computers to produce results, and can also use computers to digest them. One approach is to apply statistics. Another approach is to use visualization. For example, curve fitting can be used to summarize data; and a graph showing the fitted curve can give a strong sense of whether the fitting was accurate. Graphs can also be used to interpret data from a variety of perspectives.

The upper graph on page 95 shows the number of events observed as a parameter "depth" is increased. (This is real data from an experiment in information retrieval.) The crosses, joined by a jagged line, show the actual number of events. This graph illustrates that the number of events declines with increasing depth, but inconsistently; the long-term trend is unclear. A line has been used to connect the crosses to indicate overall behaviour. However, including the jagged line in such a graph is a mistake, especially if the number of points is small, as it wrongly suggests that there is a trend from point to point. A line is an interpolation between two points; if no data can be validly said to lie in that space, omit the line.

The lower graph on page 95 shows the same events, without the jagged line. It instead shows, as a solid line, a linear regression on $\log(depth)$ and $\log(events)$ that has been used to find parameters C and p for the equation

$$events = C \cdot depth^{p} - 1\,.$$

The computation of linear regression returns a measure of error, but what this value means in practice is difficult to interpret. However, the visualization of the fit is striking: the line rides neatly between the points.

The quality of the fit is further illustrated in the graphs on page 96, where two additional curves have been added. In the upper graph, the first line is a fit determined from points 1–50 and the second line is a fit determined from points 1–20. What this graph demonstrates is that the first 50 or even 20 points are an excellent predictor of the remainder. The lower graph expands the detail in the upper graph, further confirming the closeness of the fit.

Another use for visualization is shown in the graphs on page 97, where two systems are being compared by their ability to respond to 50 events (the score is a human-assigned value for quality of response; again, this is data from a real experiment). In the upper graph, System 1, with the crosses, often appears to be better than System 2, with the triangles; but in a reasonable number of cases the reverse is observed.

Which is better? Wilcoxon's signed rank hypothesis test reports that, for a specified level of 99% confidence, System 1 is superior. This can be confirmed through visualization. One possible visualization is shown in the lower graph on page 97, where the events have been sorted by the performance on System 1. The crosses now form a clear line; while a few of the triangles are above, the majority are below. It is a simple transformation, but highly informative.

Another example of visualization is shown on page 98. In the upper figure, a dot plot has been used to capture the relationship between the effectiveness of a baseline query evaluation technique and the improvement available through an alternative method. The hypothesis was that queries that were originally successful would be less amenable to further improvement than queries that originally were poor. Original effectiveness and new effectiveness are strongly correlated: a query that can be resolved with one method can also be resolved with the other. However, as the figure illustrates, there is no clear indication that poor queries can be improved more than others.

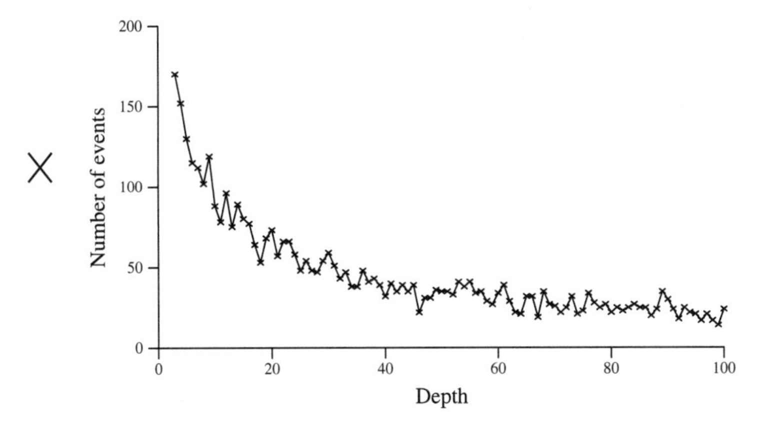

FIGURE 7. *The number of events observed at each depth; depths 1 and 2 have been omitted for reasons of scale.*

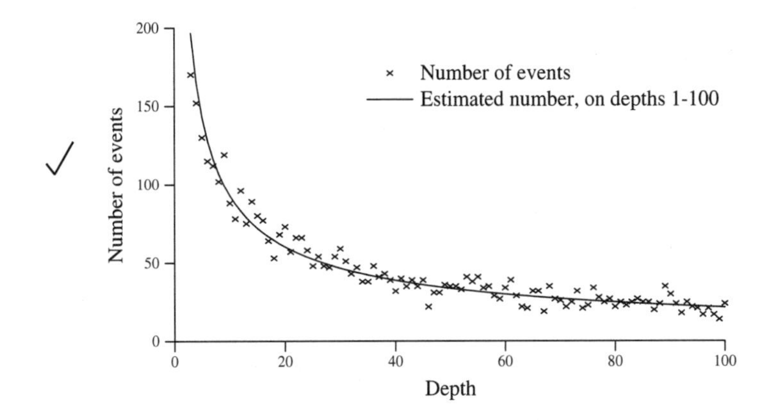

FIGURE 7. *The number of events observed at each depth; depths 1 and 2 have been omitted for reasons of scale. The solid line shows a best-fit to the points.*

Curve fitting. In the upper graph, it is an error to show a line that implicitly interpolates the points, as such interpolation is not meaningful. The lower graph shows the quality of the fitted line, visualizing information that would not otherwise be intuitive.

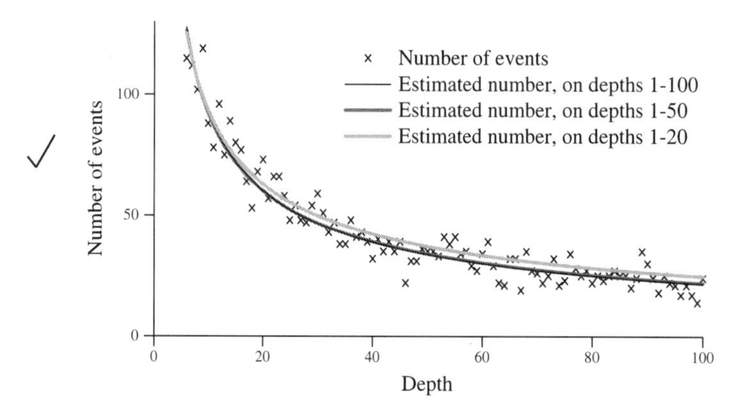

FIGURE 7. *The number of events observed at each depth; depths 1 and 2 have been omitted for reasons of scale. The first solid line shows a best-fit to all 100 points. The other lines show a fit based on the first 50 and 20 points respectively.*

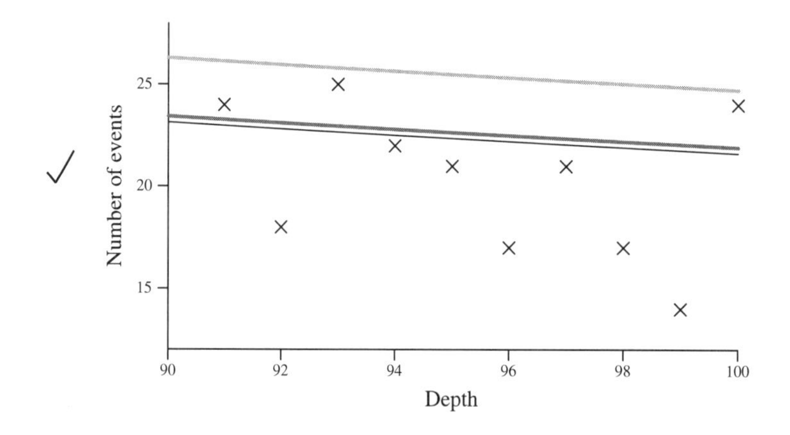

FIGURE 8. *Ten-fold magnification of the right-hand side of Figure 7. Even at this resolution, the fit based on 50 points is extremely close to the fit based on 100 points.*

Curve fitting continued. The upper graph shows that a fit based on the first 50 or 20 points is highly consistent with a fit based on all of the points. The lower graph shows the right-hand end of the upper graph in more detail, thus confirming that the fits are indeed very close.

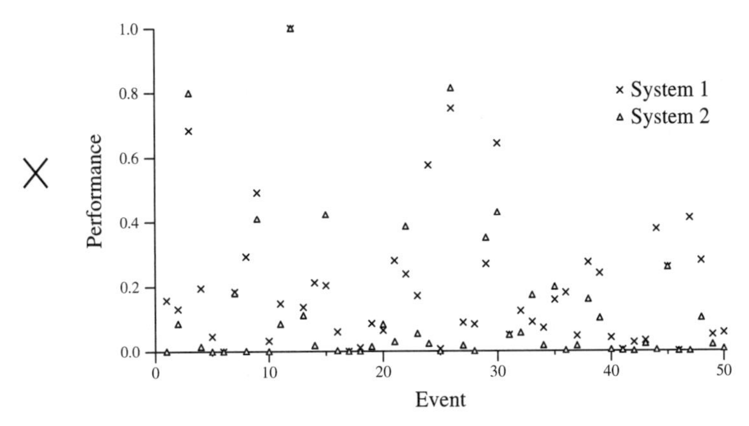

FIGURE 3.3. *The ability of each system to respond to an event, for each of 50 events.*

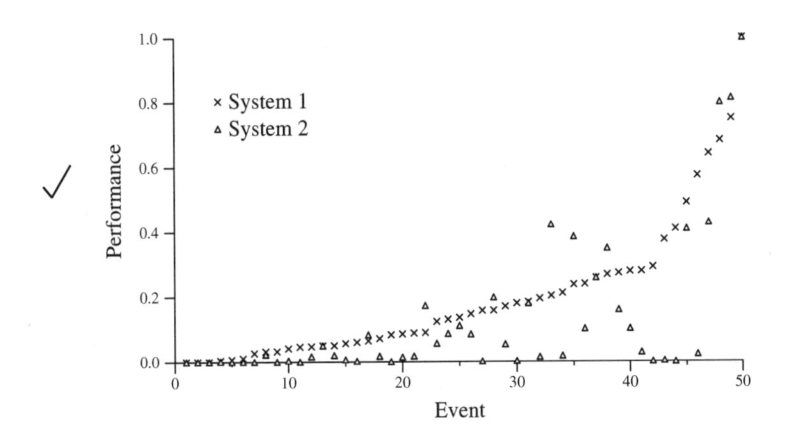

FIGURE 3.3. *The ability of each system to respond to an event, for each of 50 events. The events have been sorted on the score allocated to System 1, demonstrating that in most cases it has outperformed System 2.*

Revisualization. The simple action of sorting the points according to score achieved by one of the systems shows how the performance of the systems compares. Even though System 2 is occasionally superior, the lower graph clearly shows that System 1 is better in most cases.

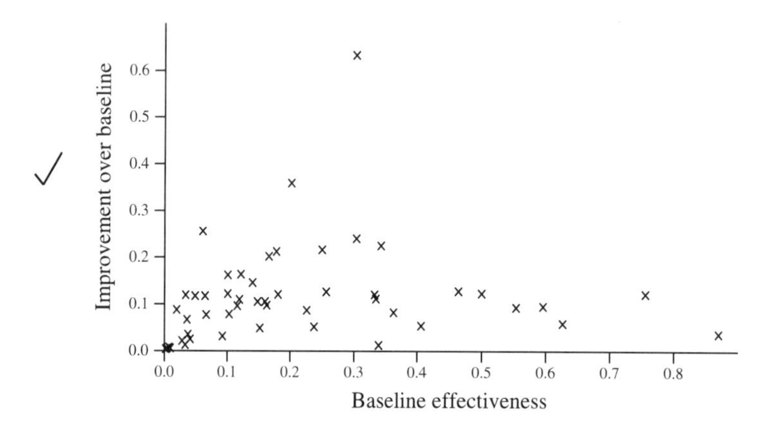

FIGURE 3. *For each query on the* FINNEGAN *data, original effectiveness versus improvement.*

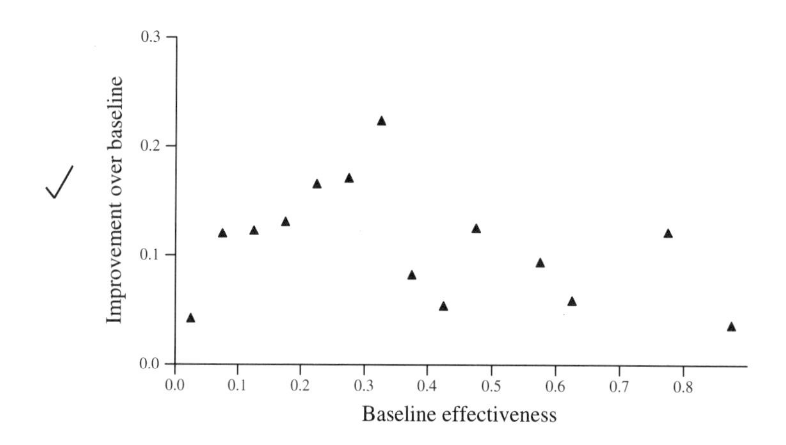

FIGURE 3. *Average improvement against original effectiveness, for queries on the* FINNEGAN *data. Each triangle is the average over a range of 0.05. Thus, for example, the average improvement for queries with effectiveness in the range 0.20 to 0.25 is 0.166.*

Correlation. In the upper figure, no clear correlation can be seen between the two variables. In the lower figure, the same data is revisualized by plotting the average improvement in each of 20 sub-ranges. In this figure, averaging has removed the extreme data points and the trend is clear—there is no correlation.

An alternative view is presented in the lower figure, where the effectiveness values on the horizontal axis have been averaged across subranges of width 0.05. This graph shows that the improvements are more or less the same, independent of the original effectiveness of each query, and thus shows that there is no correlation.

Good visualization requires inventiveness and care, but it is time well spent. Such analysis is often the best way to explore and explain data.

Diagrams

Diagrams are put to many uses in papers about computing. They illustrate processes or architectures, explain data structures and algorithms, present relationships, and show examples of interfaces. There are areas of computer science in which the diagrams are, in some sense, the result being presented in the paper: entity-relationship models are diagrams conforming to a well-defined notation, for example, and automata are often described by diagrams. Many areas of research have highly developed conventions and standards for diagrams. Browsing a few relevant papers in the same area as your work should you give a good idea of what elements a diagram should incorporate and of how it should be presented.

Broadly speaking, diagrams are used to show either a structure, a process, or a state. Although these are high-level distinctions, they are valuable because a common mistake in design of diagrams is to attempt to combine these purposes inappropriately. For example, a schematic showing data flow in an architecture is likely to be unclear if control flow is also illustrated.

Use preliminary hand sketches to develop the diagram. This early stage is the appropriate time to balance the diagram, by checking that it is well-proportioned, that it makes good use of the space, that it is laid out well and doesn't have the elements bunched to one side, and that the relative sizes of the elements look reasonable. However, never submit a paper with a hand-drawn diagram unless it has been prepared by a professional; almost any diagram can be drawn well with the tools available on a typical computer.

A diagram should not be too dark; keep it as open as possible. This is best achieved by eliminating all clutter. A diagram does not have to be too faithful to every detail of the concept being illustrated; fine details can always be clarified in the supporting text and even the best diagram requires some explanation. Use meaningful labels, which should be displayed horizontally, and make the point size and font of the labels similar to that of the other text. As for text in general, there should be no more than two or three fonts and font sizes.

Lines should not be too heavy, but at most a little thicker than the lines used to draw the text font. Shades of grey can be used to distinguish between solids but are not as effective for distinguishing between lines, and don't use shades that are too light or too similar. Pictorial elements should be used consistently, so that, for example, arrows and lines of the same kind have the same meaning. Use shading rather than cross-hatching. As for graphs, do not use colour if the paper will ultimately be printed in black-and-white. If arrows are used to show arcs as well as to point at features, distinguish them by, say, using dashed lines in one case and solid lines in another. Lines should not touch each other unless separating them would create an unnatural break. Thus, for example, there should usually be a small gap between an arrowhead and the thing the arrow is pointing at.

Diagrams, like graphs, can add greatly to the clarity of a paper. But be aware that the design of good diagrams is not easy. Expect to revise your pictures as often as you would your writing. Some simple diagrams are shown on pages 101, 112, and 119. A weak diagram is shown on page 102 and a revision of it is on page 103.

Diagrams illustrating system structure often seem to be poor. In too many of these pictures the symbolism is used inconsistently: boxes have different meanings in different places, lines represent both control flow and data flow, objects of primary interest are not distinguished from minor components, and so on. Unnecessary elements are included, such as cheesy clip-art or computer components that are irrelevant to the system. A poor structural diagram is shown on page 104, with a revision on page 105.

Illustrations are covered by copyright; figures from another source can only be re-used with permission of the author and the publisher of the original. If you re-use a figure, get permission to do so and identify the original author and source, preferably in the caption. You may also need to include the original copyright statement.

Tables

Tables are used for presentation of information that is unsuitable for graphs or figures, such as the properties of each of a series of datasets or data where the exact values are important. The tables on pages 107–110 have appropriate content, although two are poorly laid out. The table on page 90 is of debatable value, as the graph explains the data well and the precise timings may not be interesting. The table on page 92 is much less informative than the graph; in this case the table should not be used.

√

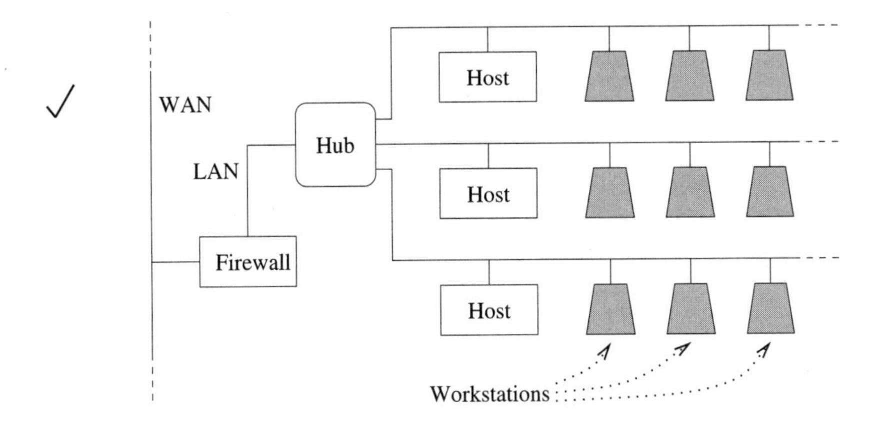

FIGURE C. *Revised network, incorporating firewall and hub with hosts and workstations on separate cables.*

√

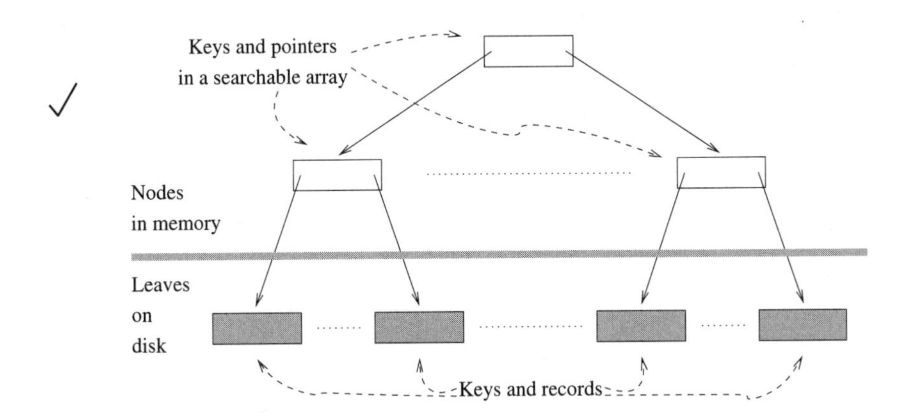

FIGURE 1.3. *Tree data structure, showing internal nodes in memory and external leaves on disk; omitted nodes are indicated by dotted lines. Nodes allow fast search and contain only keys and pointers. Leaves use compact storage and contain the records.*

Shading and dashing in diagrams. In these illustrations, consistent use of shading and dashing distinguishes between different kinds of entities.

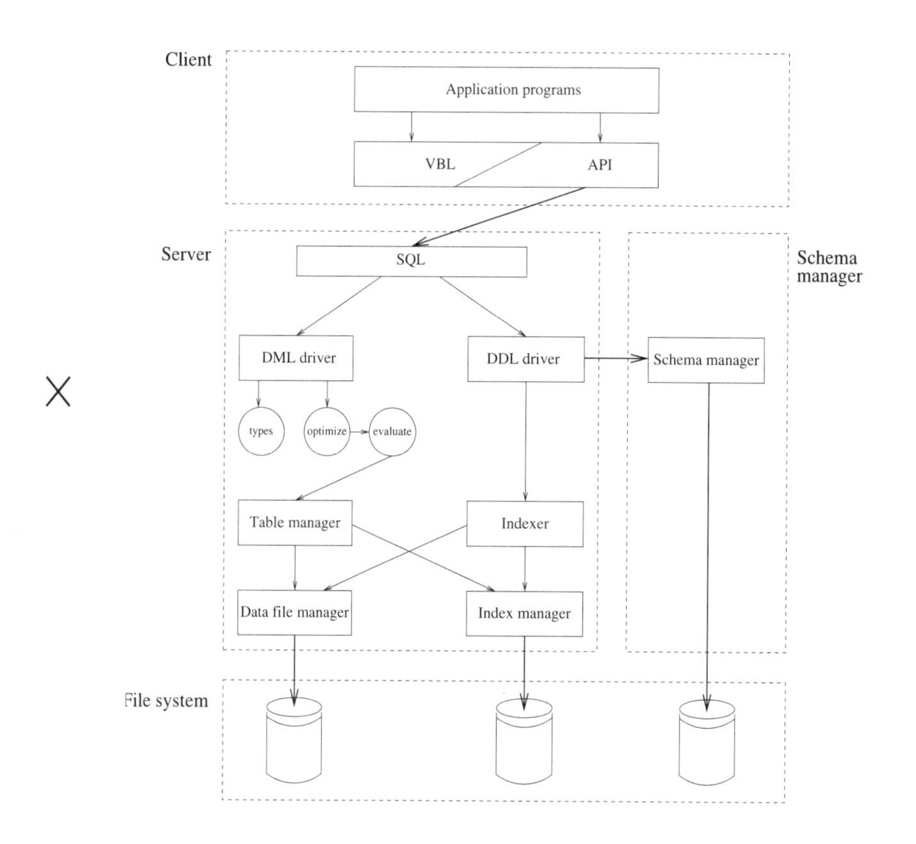

FIGURE 1.3. *System architecture, showing the relationship between the major components. Each component is an independent process. Note the lack of a single interface to the file system.*

Too much clutter. A carefully constructed figure, but flawed. The font is too small and the lines are too light. The overall structure (the division into four major components) is probably the most interesting feature, but other details are more highly emphasized. Some of the internal detail should be omitted. The arrows add little information, and should point both ways, because information flows out as well as in.

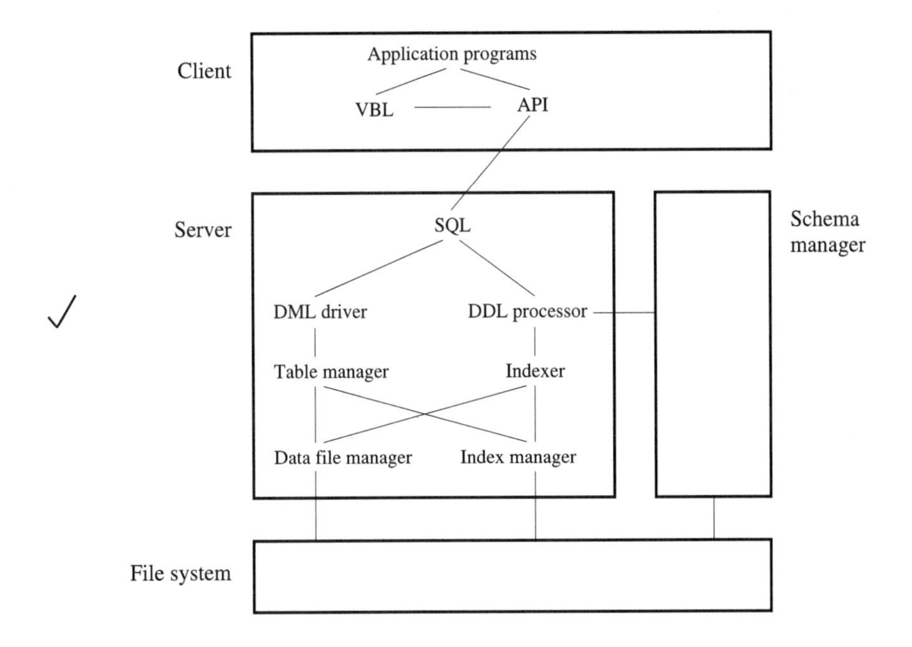

FIGURE 1.3. *System architecture, showing the relationship between the major components. Each component is an independent process. Note the lack of a single interface to the file system.*

Clutter simplified. A revision of the figure on page 102. The overall structure is more prominent, while some minor features have been discarded and the unnecessary inner boxes have been removed. Use of shading would give further improvements.

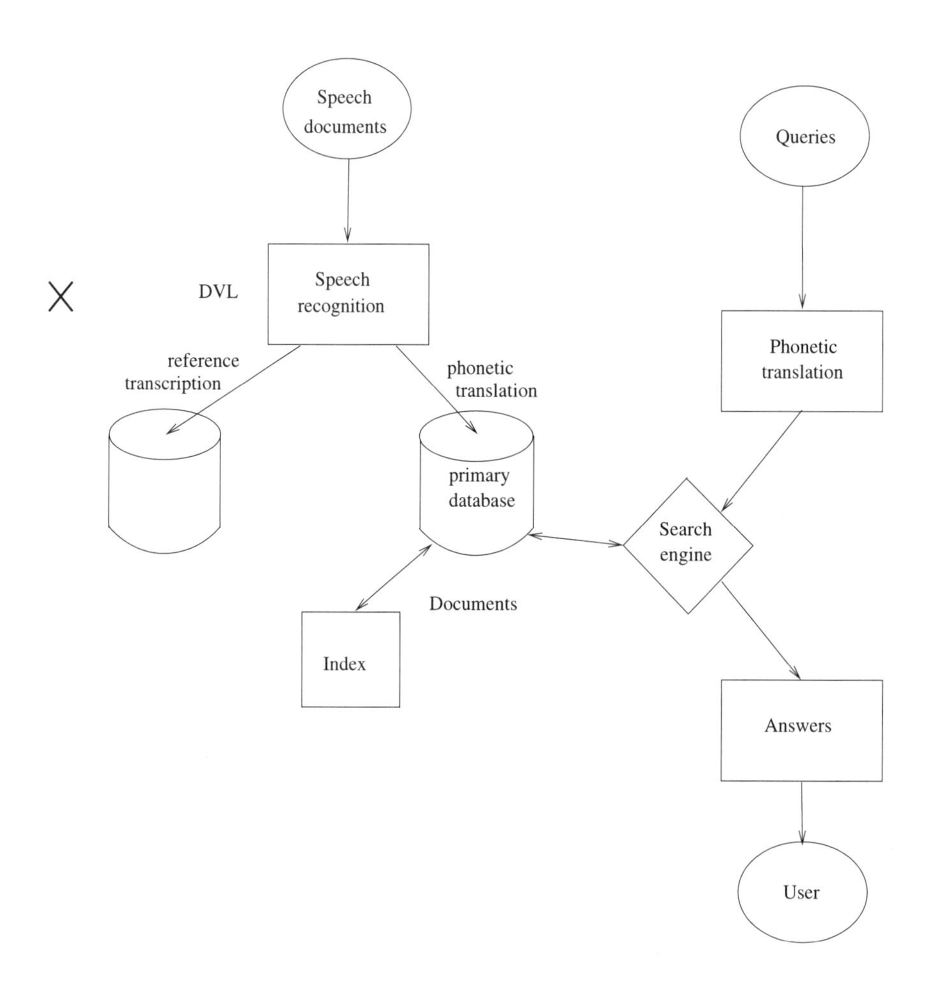

FIGURE 7. *The* QUIRK *system for matching written queries to speech. Each input document is translated into a string of phonemes and then stored. Queries are also translated into phonemes, which can be matched to the documents. Answers are returned to the user.*

Disorganization. This figure is poorly designed. The elements are inconsistent; data is in both ovals and boxes, and some lines represent data flow while one represents a transformation. The arrowheads touch other lines, creating messy intersections. There is unnecessary material such as the auxiliary databases (write-only, apparently) and the user.

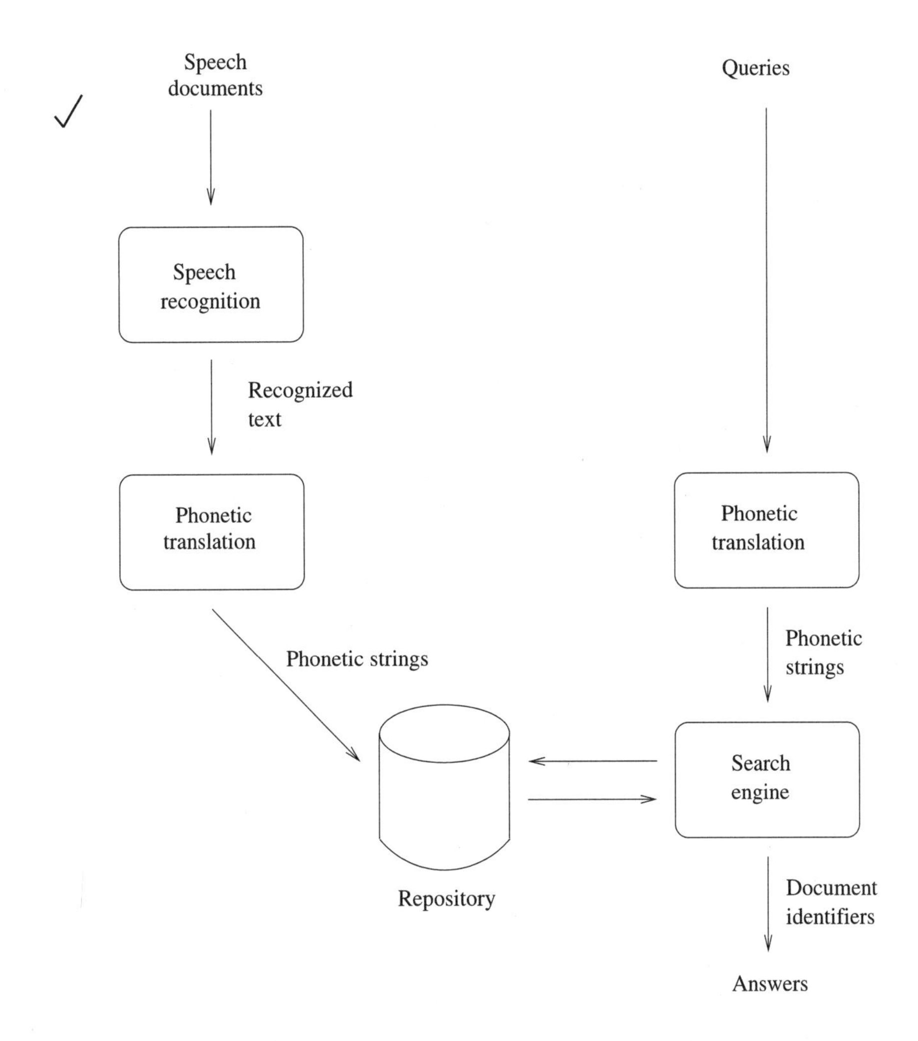

FIGURE 7. *The* QUIRK *system for matching written queries to speech. Each input document is translated into a string of phonemes and then stored. Queries are also translated into phonemes, which can be matched to the documents.*

Clarification. A revision of the figure on page 104. The parallels between document processing and query processing are emphasized, and the unnecessary material has been removed. The two-headed arrow is replaced by two arrows, to show that data is exchanged.

A well-designed table has a logical hierarchical structure. Simple tables are an arrangement of columns and rows, in which each column has a heading at the top and each row has a label or stub at the left. In more complex tables, columns and rows may be partitioned or have internal structure. The hierarchy can be indicated in several ways: rows or columns can be separated by double lines, single lines, or white space; headings can span several columns; labels can refer to several rows. Deeper structure—which is sometimes necessary but is usually unwise—can be indicated by markup within the table such as embedded headings. (A complex table is shown on page 108.) The items below a column head should be of the same kind or about the same thing. Items to the right of a row label should all be properties of that label. The column of labels does not need to have a heading, but this position, the top-left corner of the table, should not be a label for the other column headings. If there is no heading for the column of labels, leave the position blank.

Tables should be open and uncluttered, with ample white space. Don't have too many horizontal or vertical rules. In particular, there is no need to have a rule between every row or column. (An example of this error is shown on page 107.) But do have rules between groups of rows, and, in rare cases, between groups of columns, to act as guides and to separate items that don't belong together. Don't make tables too dense. Rather than cram in a large number of columns, have two tables, or, even better, be selective about the information you present. In most tables no position should be blank; if there is no applicable value, put in a dash, and explain somewhere what it means. Values of the same units in a column should be aligned in a logical way. Numbers should be aligned on the decimal point.

Using tables to show function values at different points is usually not a good idea because graphs serve this purpose well; a possible exception is when a function only has two or three values, in which case a graph would be too simple or sparse to be of interest. In some cases, such as a table or graph that does no more than illustrate a simple relationship, consider stating the relationship and omitting the illustration altogether.

X As illustrated in Table 6, temporary space requirements were 60% to 65% of the data size.

✓ In our experiments, temporary space requirements were 60% to 65% of the data size.

Small tables can be part of the running text, displayed in the same way as mathematics. Larger tables should be labelled and positioned at the top or bottom of a page.

✗

STATISTICS	SMALL	LARGE
Characters	18,621	1,231,109
Words	2,060	173,145
After stopping	1,200	98,234
Index size	1.31 Kb	109.0 Kb

TABLE 6. *Statistics of text collections used in experiments.*

✓

	Collection	
	Small	Large
File size (Kb)	18.2	1,202.3
Index size (Kb)	1.3	109.0
Number of words	2,060	173,145
After stopping	1,200	98,234

TABLE 6. *Statistics of text collections used in experiments.*

Two versions of a table. The upper version is poor. No use has been made of table hierarchy—all the elements are at the same level, so that case has to be used to differentiate between headings and content. Different units have been used for file sizes in different lines (assuming characters are one byte each). Units haven't been factored out in the last line and the precision is inconsistent. The heading of the first column is unnecessary and the table has too many horizontal lines.

In the lower version there are no vertical lines. Rows of the same type are now adjacent so that they can be compared by the reader. Note that the values of different units do not need to be vertically aligned on the decimal point or presented with the same precision.

Parameter	Data set			
	SINGLE		MULTIPLE	
	CPU (msec)	Effective (%)	CPU (msec)	Effective (%)
n ($k = 10$, $p = 100$)				
2	57.5	55.5	174.2	22.2
3	21.5	50.4	79.4	19.9
4	16.9	47.5	66.1	16.3
k ($n = 2$, $p = 100$)				
10	57.5	51.3	171.4	21.7
100	60.0	56.1	163.1	21.3
1000	111.3	55.9	228.8	21.4
p ($n = 2$, $k = 10$)				
100	3.3	5.5	6.1	1.2
1000	13.8	12.6	19.8	2.1
10,000	84.5	56.0	126.4	6.3
100,000	—	—	290.7	21.9

TABLE 2.1. *Impact on performance (processing time and effectiveness) of varying each of the three parameters in turn, for both data sets. Default parameter values are shown in parentheses. Note that $p = 100{,}000$ is not meaningful for the data set* SINGLE.

Table with a deep hierarchy. There are two columns, one for parameters and one for data sets. The latter is divided into two columns, one for each data set. Each data set has two columns of figures. There are four rows, one of headings and one for each of the parameters n, k, and p. Each of these is subdivided. Note that even this rather complex table does not require vertical rules.

This table might benefit from being separated into parts, but it is helpful to have all the data together. There are insufficient data points for each parameter to justify use of a graph.

Pass	Output	Size Mb	%	CPU Hr:Min	Mem Mb
Pass 1:					
Compression	Model	4.2	0.2	2:37	25.6
Inversion	Vocabulary	6.4	0.3	3:02	18.7
Overhead				0:19	2.5
Total		10.6	0.5	5:58	46.8
Pass 2:					
Compression	Text	605.1	29.4	3:27	25.6
	Doc. map	2.8	0.1		
Inversion	Index	132.2	6.4	5:25	162.1
	Index map	2.1	0.1		
	Doc. lens	2.8	0.1		
	Approx. lens	0.7	0.0		
Overhead				0:23	2.5
Total		745.8	36.3	9:15	190.2
Overall		756.4	36.8	15:13	190.2

X

TABLE 11. *Resources used during compression and indexing. Only the vocabulary is constructed in the first pass; the other structures are built in the second pass.*

Jumbled table. Columns have been crammed together and are hard to understand. The numbers don't line up vertically. The percentage column is mysterious, since it doesn't total to 100. It seems unlikely that all the detail is interesting; consider in particular the "Index map", "Doc. lens", and "Appr. lens" rows, which could presumably be gathered into a single row with a label such as "Other" or discarded altogether.

✓

Task	Size (Mb)	CPU (Hr:Min)	Memory (Mb)
Pass 1:			
Compression	4.2	2:37	25.6
Inversion	6.4	3:02	18.7
Overhead	—	0:19	2.5
Total	10.6	5:58	46.8
Pass 2:			
Compression	607.9	3:27	25.6
Inversion	137.8	5:25	162.1
Overhead	—	0:23	2.5
Total	745.8	9:15	190.2
Overall	756.4	15:13	190.2

TABLE 11. *Resources used during compression and indexing. Only the vocabulary is constructed in the first pass; the other structures are built in the second pass.*

Table simplified. A revision of the table on page 109. The confusing percentage column has been deleted. The "Output" column has been deleted; since most of the values in this column are small, they are relatively unimportant and could if necessary be discussed in the text.

Tables are used not only for numbers but for textual analysis. For example, a list of approaches to system modelling could be compared in a table, one row per approach, with columns used for positives, negatives, and number of known successful applications of the approach. In such tables, each cell may contain a brief paragraph of text and a single table may occupy a page or more, and thus the overall appearance is quite different to that of a table of numerical data. Nonetheless, the same design guidelines apply.

Understanding a table of any complexity is hard work. For presentation of results, graphs or explanatory text are preferable; have a table to which the interested reader can refer, but don't rely on a table to convey essential information.

Captions and labels

Captions and labels should be informative. It is common in computer science papers for captions to be only a few words, but is it preferable for captions to fully describe the figure's major elements. (A diagram and caption are shown on page 112.) Use either minimum or maximum capitalization, but minimum is better, particularly if the caption is a description rather than a label. Use italics for the caption so that it is distinct from other text.

Since figures and tables should be fairly self-contained, the caption is an appropriate place to explain important details. For example, a graph might show running time for an algorithm over various data sets; the caption could include parameter values. The caption can also be used to expand abbreviations or notation used in headings.

Each figure and table should be numbered to allow easy reference and have a descriptive caption so that the figure is, as far as possible, independent of the text. If your word processor does not provide automatic numbering, you must number the figures yourself. A figure is usually at the top or the bottom of a page, or on a page by itself, to set it apart from ordinary text. An illustration should always be introduced and discussed, preferably just before or on the page on which it occurs. If you don't have anything to say about an illustration, leave it out.

Axes, labels, and headings

The space constraints on axes, labels, and headings may mean that some terms have to be abbreviated; for example, see the table on page 109. It is helpful

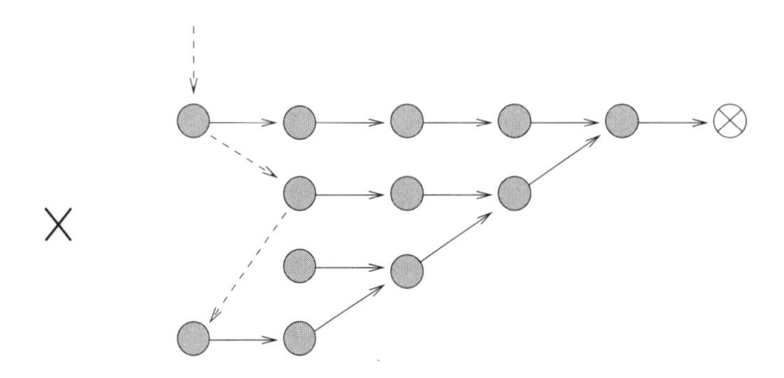

FIGURE 5. *Fan data structure.*

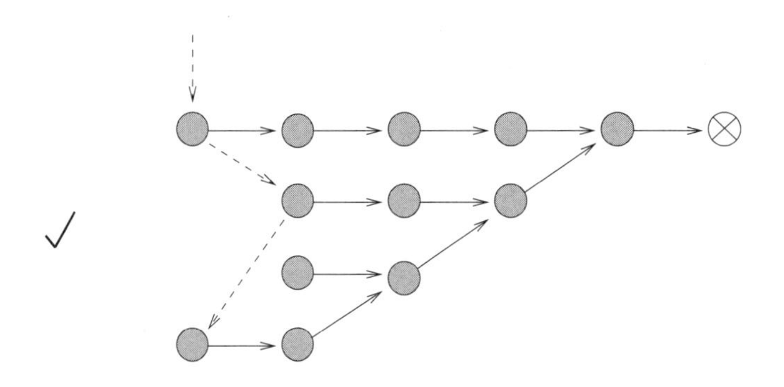

FIGURE 5. *Fan data structure, of lists with a common tail. The crossed node is a sentinel. Solid lines are within-list pointers. Dashed lines are inter-list pointers.*

Styles of caption. For these identical figures, the lower caption is preferable because it allows the figure to be less dependent on the paper's text.

to state these terms in full in the text discussing the illustration, but do so in a natural way.

✗ The abbreviations "comp.", "doc.", and "map." stand for "compression", "document", and "mapping table" respectively.

✓ The effect of compression on the documents and the mapping table is illustrated in the second and third rows.

Where appropriate, units should be stated in labels. Write "Size (bytes)", not just "Size".

Some readers get confused by scaling on axes and labels. Suppose, for example, that an axis is labelled as "CPU time (seconds $\times 10^{-2}$)". The convention is that the reader should multiply axis values by 10^{-2}, so that 50 means 0.5. But some readers may assume that the axis values have already been multiplied by 10^{-2}, so that they read 50 as 5000. In the text where the illustration is referenced, typical values can be discussed to avoid this problem. The problem also arises with graphs; it is helpful to include some representative numbers in the text, because graphs are hard to read with any precision.

✓ Figure 4 shows how time and space trade off as node size is varied; as can be seen, response of under a second is only possible when size exceeds 11 Kb.

Sometimes the terminology of a paper gets changed at a late stage, perhaps with a global substitution. Ensure that graphs and diagrams get updated too.

7 Algorithms

Mostly gobbledygook . . .

Eric Partridge, defining computation
Usage and Abusage

The core contribution in many papers in computer science is an algorithm. These algorithms are often the product of months of work; the version that the researchers have decided to submit for publication is typically based on a great deal of discussion, brainstorming, prototyping, testing, analysis, and debate over details. Yet in many cases this effort is not reflected in the presentation. Not only are the steps of the algorithm often unclear, but there is no discussion of why the reader should believe that the algorithm is correct or that its behaviour is reasonable. An algorithm by itself is uninteresting; what is of value is an algorithm that has been shown to solve a problem. Issues with presentation of algorithms are the subject of this chapter.

Presentation of algorithms

When an algorithm is presented in a computer science paper, the details of the algorithm by themselves—the program steps, for example—do not show that it is worthwhile. You must demonstrate that the algorithm is a worthwhile contribution: for example, show that it is correct (given appropriate input, it terminates with appropriate results) or show, by proof, experiment, or both, that it meets some claimed performance bound.

There are many reasons why you might choose to describe an algorithm. One is that it provides a new or better way to compute a result. What is usually meant by "better" is that the algorithm can compute the result with asymptotically fewer resources as measured by a complexity analysis: less time or memory, or some desirable tradeoff of time and memory. It may be that the worst case is improved, at no saving in the average case; or that the average case is improved, but at the expense of space; or that all cases are improved, asymptotically, but with constant factors so large that there will no improvement in any conceivable practical situation. All of these are valid results, but it is crucial that the scope of the improvement be clearly specified—"better" is too vague.

Validation by experiment is often an important part of the presentation of such algorithms. The experiment provides concrete evidence that, for some data, the algorithm terminates correctly and performs as predicted. Experiments are discussed in detail in Chapter 11.

Thus, as part of a description of an algorithm, a reader would expect to find of some or all of the following:

- The steps that make up the algorithm.
- The input and output, and the internal data structures used by the algorithm.
- The scope of application of the algorithm and its limitations.
- The properties that will allow demonstration of correctness, such as preconditions, postconditions, and loop invariants.
- A demonstration of correctness.
- A complexity analysis, for both space and time requirements.
- Experiments confirming the theoretical results.

But note that, while experiments on an algorithm may support an asymptotic analysis, they cannot replace it.

Another reason for describing an algorithm is to explain a complex process. For example, a paper about a distributed architecture might include a description of the steps used to communicate a packet from one processor to another. These steps certainly constitute an algorithm, and, while readers would not expect a complexity analysis, you would have to give an argument to show that the steps did indeed result in packet transmission. Other examples are algorithms such as parsers. That is, there is no blanket requirement that a complexity analysis must be given (different norms apply to different areas and readerships), but that does not excuse you from giving a complexity analysis where it is appropriate to do so.

Yet another reason for describing an algorithm is to show that it is feasible to compute a result, regardless of the cost, or to show that a problem is decidable. Again, different norms apply. In such cases a formal proof of correctness is essential, while an asymptotic analysis may be of little interest.

In summary, in the presentation of an algorithm it is usual to give a formal demonstration of correctness and performance, and perhaps an experimental validation. When such demonstrations are absent, the reason for the absence should be clear.

Formalisms

The description of an algorithm usually consists of the algorithm itself and the environment it requires. There are several common formalisms for presenting algorithms. One is the *list* style, in which the algorithm is broken down into a series of numbered or named steps and loops involving several steps are represented by "go to step X" statements. This form has the advantage that the algorithm can be discussed as it is presented: there is no restriction on the amount of text used to describe a step (although a step should be a single activity), so there is room for a clear statement of each step and for remarks on its properties. But the control structure is often obscure and it is all too easy for the discussion to bury the algorithm.

Another common formalism is *pseudocode*, in which the algorithm is presented as if written in a block-structured language and each line is numbered. An example is shown on page 120. Pseudocode has the advantage that the structure of the algorithm is immediately obvious; but each statement is forced by formatting considerations to be fairly terse, and it is not easy to include detailed comments. Also, as discussed below, the use of programming language constructs and notation is usually a mistake. It takes experience to present algorithms well in pseudocode, and, although it is straightforward to translate such pseudocode into an imperative programming language, pseudocode is unnecessarily difficult to understand.

A better option is to use what might be called *prosecode*: number each step, never break a loop over several steps, use subnumbering for the parts of a step, and include explanatory text. An example is shown on page 121. In the example, input and output are described in the preamble, and statements and explanatory text are mixed freely in the algorithm itself. Despite the informality, the specification of the algorithm is direct and clear. The assignment symbol "←" is a good choice because it is unambiguous, in contrast to symbols such as "=". Note the use of nested labelling for nested statements. However, the prosecode style of presentation is only effective when the concepts underlying the algorithm have been discussed before the algorithm is given.

Another effective approach to description of algorithms is what might be called *literate code*, in which the detail of the algorithm is introduced gradually, intermingled with discussion of the underlying ideas and perhaps with the asymptotic analysis and proof of correctness. An example is shown on page 122. (This example is incomplete—most algorithms worth presenting need a substantial explanation that can't be condensed into a page or two.)

An element in any of these forms of presentation is the degree to which the algorithm, or its components, can be presented as mathematical abstractions. Can a loop be described as an operation on a set? Does the order in which array elements are processed matter? To understand pseudocode, a reader must reinterpret the sequence of statements as a higher-level abstraction; the algorithm should be presented at such a level.

Flowcharts should not be used to describe algorithms, for many reasons: lack of modularity, promotion of the use of `goto` statements, lack of space for explanatory text, insufficient space for complex conditions, and inability to clearly represent algorithms of any complexity.

Level of detail

Algorithms should be specified in sufficient detail to allow them to be implemented without undue inventiveness.

× 5. (Matching.) For each pair of strings $s,t \in S$, find $N_{s,t}$, the maximum number of non-overlapping substrings that s and t have in common.

The way in which a step of this kind is implemented may greatly affect the behaviour of the final algorithm, so the matching process needs to be made explicit. But don't provide too much detail. For example, loops are sometimes used unnecessarily in specification of algorithms.

× 3. (Summation.) Set $sum \leftarrow 0$. For each j, where $1 \leq j \leq n$,

(a) Set $c \leftarrow 1$; the variable c is a temporary accumulator.

(b) For each k, where $1 \leq k \leq m$, set $c \leftarrow c \times A_{jk}$.

(c) Set $sum \leftarrow sum + c$.

This is poor because it is cumbersome and no more informative than the equivalent mathematical expression. It is safe to assume that most programmers know how to use loops to implement sums and products.

✓ 3. (Summation.) Set $sum \leftarrow \sum_{j=1}^{n} \left(\prod_{k=1}^{n} A_{jk} \right)$.

As this form of the step illustrates, the step is probably unnecessary unless *sum* is used more than once: use of *sum* could be replaced by the summation it represents. The one reason to have a step just for the summation would be to include explanation of any difficult issues; for example, if the matrix A was sparse and stored as a list rather than a two-dimensional array, there might be an explanation of how to compute the summation efficiently.

In specifications of algorithms, use text rather than mathematics if the former is sufficiently clear.

✗ 2. for $1 \leq i \leq |s|$

  (a) set $c \leftarrow s[i]$

  (b) set $A_c \leftarrow A_c + 1$

✓ 2. For each character c in string s, increment A_c.

Figures

Figures are an effective way of conveying the intricacies of data structures; and even quite simple structures can require complex descriptions. General guidelines for figures are given in Chapter 6.

✓ A single rotation can be used to bring a node one level closer to the root. In a left-rotation, a node x and its right child y are exchanged as follows: given that B is the left child of y, then assign B to be the new right child of x and assign x to be the new left child of y. The reverse operation is a right-rotation. Left- and right-rotations are shown in the following diagram.

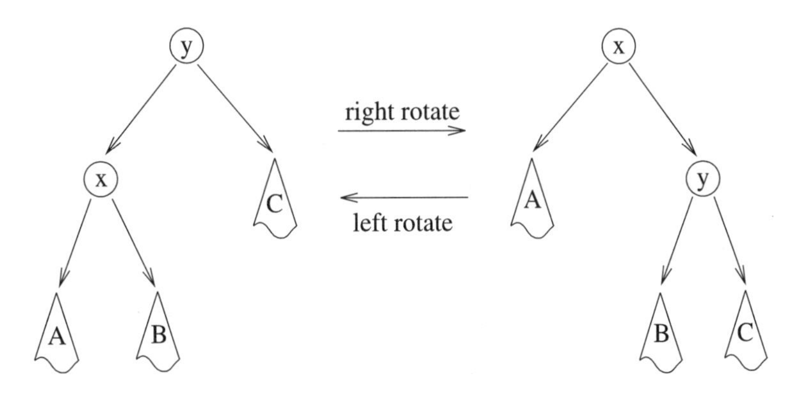

Example of pseudocode. This is not the best style of presentation: the algorithm is cryptic and the numbering does not reflect the indentation. Also, the author has unnecessarily introduced a trivial optimization (at lines 10 and 12) and the notation for variables is ugly. It is like a program meant for a machine, not an explanation meant for a reader.

The **WeightedEdit** function computes the edit distance between two strings, assigning a higher penalty for errors closer to the front.

Input:	$S1, S2$: strings to be compared.
Output:	weighted edit distance
Variables:	$L1, L2$: string lengths
	$F[L1, L2]$: array of minimum distances
	W: current weighting
	M: maximum penalty
	C: current penalty

WeightedEdit$(S1, S2)$:

1. $L1 = len(S1)$
2. $L2 = len(S2)$
3. $M = 2 \times (L1 + L2)$
4. $F[0,0] = 0$
5. **for** i **from** 1 **to** $L1$
6. $F[i,0] = F[i-1,0] + M - i$
7. **for** j **from** 1 **to** $L2$
8. $F[0,j] = F[0,j-1] + M - j$
9. **for** i **from** 1 **to** $L1$
10. $C = M - i$
11.   **for** j **from** 1 **to** $L2$
12. $C = C - 1$
13. $F[i,j] = min(F[i-1,j] + C,$ $F[i,j-1] + C,$ $F[i-1,j-1] + C \times isdiff(S1[i], S2[j]))$
14. **WeightedEdit** $= F[L1, L2]$

Example of prosecode. The longer introduction and use of text in the presentation help make the algorithm easy to understand.

WeightedEdit(s,t) compares two strings s and t, of lengths k_s and k_t respectively, to determine their edit distance—the minimum cost in insertions, deletions, and replacements required to convert one into the other. These costs are weighted so that errors near the start of the strings attract a higher penalty than errors near the end.

We denote the ith character of string s by s_i. The principal internal data structure is a 2-dimensional array F in which the dimensions have ranges 0 to k_s and 0 to k_t, respectively. When the array is filled, $F_{i,j}$ is the minimum edit distance between the strings $s_1 \cdots s_i$ and $t_1 \cdots t_j$; and F_{k_s,k_t} is the minimum edit distance between s and t.

The value p is the maximum penalty, and the penalty for a discrepancy between positions i and j of s and t, respectively, is $p-i-j$, so that the minimum penalty is $p-k_s-k_t = p/2$ and the next-smallest penalty is $p/2+1$. Two errors, wherever they occur, will outweigh one.

1. (Set penalty.) Set $p \leftarrow 2 \times (k_s + k_t)$.
2. (Initialize data structure.) The boundaries of array F are initialized with the penalty for deletions at start of string; for example, $F_{i,0}$ is the penalty for deleting i characters from the start of s.
   (a) Set $F_{0,0} \leftarrow 0$.
   (b) For each position i in s, set $F_{i,0} \leftarrow F_{i-1,0} + p - i$.
   (c) For each position j in t, set $F_{0,j} \leftarrow F_{0,j-1} + p - j$.
3. (Compute edit distance.) For each position i in s and position j in t:
   (a) The penalty is $C = p - i - j$.
   (b) The cost of inserting a character into t (equivalently, deleting from s) is $I = F_{i-1,j} + C$.
   (c) The cost of deleting a character from t is $D = F_{i,j-1} + C$.
   (d) If s_i is identical to t_j, the replacement cost is $R = F_{i-1,j-1}$. Otherwise, the replacement cost is $R = F_{i-1,j-1} + C$.
   (e) Set $F_{i,j} \leftarrow \min(I,D,R)$.
4. (Return.) Return F_{k_s,k_t}.

Example of literate code. The algorithm is explained and presented simultaneously. This is the most verbose style, but, usually, the clearest. Note that this example is incomplete.

WeightedEdit(s,t) compares two strings s and t, of lengths k_s and k_t respectively, to determine their edit distance—the minimum cost in insertions, deletions, and replacements required to convert one into the other. These costs are weighted so that errors near the start of the strings attract a higher penalty than errors near the end.

The major steps of the algorithm are as follows.
1. Set the penalty.
2. Initialize the data structure.
3. Compute the edit distance.

We now examine these steps in detail.

1. Set the penalty.

   The main property that we require of the penalty scheme is that costs reduce smoothly from start to end of string. As we will see, the algorithm proceeds by comparing each position i in s to each position j in t. Thus a diminishing penalty can be computed with the expression $p-i-j$, where p is the maximum penalty. By setting the penalty with

   (a) Set $p \leftarrow 2 \times (k_s + k_t)$

   the minimum penalty is $p - k_s - k_t = p/2$ and the next-smallest penalty is $p/2+1$. This means that two errors—regardless of position in the strings—will outweigh one.

2. Initialize data structures ...

Notation

Mathematical notation is preferable to programming notation for presentation of algorithms. Use "x_i" rather than "`x[i]`", for example. Don't use "*" or "x" to denote multiplication; most word processors provide a multiplication symbol such as "$\times$" or "$\cdot$", and in any case multiplication is often implicit. Likewise, avoid using constructs from specific programming languages. For example, expressions such as `==`, `a = b = 0`, `a++`, and `for ( i=0 ; i<n ; i++ )` may have little meaning, or even the wrong meaning, to readers who are unfamiliar with C. Block-bounding statements such as `begin` and `end` are usually unnecessary; nesting can be shown by indentation or by the numbering style, as in the examples on pages 120 and 121.

Mathematics provides many handy conventions and symbols that can be used in description of algorithms, including set notation, subscripts and superscripts, and symbols such as $\lceil$ and $\rceil$, $\sum$, and $\prod$. But remember that such notation has a widely understood formal meaning that should not be abused. Also, good programming style does not necessarily imply good style for description of algorithms. For example, take care with variable names of more than one character—don't use "pq" if it might be interpreted as "$p \times q$".

It was once common to include the text of a program in a paper, in addition to a description of the algorithm it embodies. This practice was valuable because, for short programs at least, it was the simplest way for readers to obtain the code. However, there are now better ways of making code available (such as the web) and few readers are eager to key in a program of any size.

Environment of algorithms

The steps that comprise an algorithm are only part of its description. The other part is its environment: the data structures on which it operates, input and output data types, and, in some cases, factors such as properties of the underlying operating system and hardware. If the environment of an algorithm is not described the algorithm is likely to be difficult to understand. For example, a presentation of a list-processing algorithm should include descriptions of the list type, the input, and the possible outputs. If the list is stored on secondary storage and speed is being analyzed, it might also be appropriate to describe assumed disk characteristics. For algorithms in which there are hardware considerations, such as memory size or disk throughput, for the environment to seem realistic any assumptions about the hardware should reflect current technology or likely improvements in the near future.

Specify the types of all variables, other than trivial items such as counters; describe expected input and output, including assumptions about the correctness of the input; state any limitations of the algorithm; and discuss possible errors that are not explicitly captured by the algorithm. Most importantly, say what the algorithm does.

Describe data structures carefully. This does not mean that you should give record definitions in a pseudo-language; instead, use, say, a simple mathematical notation to unambiguously specify the structure.

✓ Each element is a triple

`(string,length,positions)`

in which `positions` is a set of byte offsets at which `string` has been observed.

Be consistent. When presenting several algorithms for the same task, they should as far as possible be defined over the same input and output. It may be the case that some of the algorithms are more powerful than the others—they can process a richer input language, for example. Variations of this kind should be made explicit.

Performance of algorithms

The tools for evaluating the performance of algorithms, and for comparing algorithms, are formal proof, mathematical modelling, simulation, and experimentation. These and other issues related to testing are discussed in Chapters 10 and 11. Here is discussed the aspects of algorithms that might be considered in an evaluation.

Basis of evaluation. The basis of evaluation should be made explicit. Where algorithms are being compared, specify not only the environment but also the criteria used for comparison. For example, are the algorithms being compared for functionality or speed? Is speed to be examined asymptotically or for typical data? Is the data real or synthetic? When describing the performance of a new technique, it is helpful to compare it to a well-known standard.

A comparison should have a realistic basis. In particular, the basis should not appear to favour the algorithm being demonstrated over existing algorithms. If the basis of comparison is questionable, the results are questionable too.

Simplifying assumptions can be used to make mathematical analysis tractable, but can give unrealistic models. Non-trivial simplifications should be carefully justified.

Processing time. Time (or speed) over some given input is one of the principal resources used by algorithms; others are memory, disk space, and disk and network traffic. Time is not always easy to measure, since it depends on factors such as CPU speed, cache sizes, system load, and hardware dependencies such as prefetch strategy. Nonetheless, some absolute indication of time should be part of the description of most new algorithms. Times based on a mathematical model rather than on experiment should be clearly indicated as such.

Measurements of CPU time can be unreliable. CPU times in most systems are counted as multiples of some fixed fraction of a second, say a sixty-fourth or a thousandth. Each of these fractions of time is allocated to a process, often by heuristics such as simply choosing the process that is active at that moment. Thus the reported CPU time for a process may be no more than a good estimate, particularly if the system is busy.

Memory and disk requirements. It is often possible to trade memory requirements against time, not only by choice of algorithm but also by changing the way disk is used and memory is accessed. You should take care to specify how your algorithms use memory.

Disk and network traffic. Disk costs have two components, the time to fetch the first bit of requested data (seek and latency time) and the time required to transmit the requested data (at a transfer rate). Thus sequential accesses and random accesses have greatly different costs. For current hardware, in which there are several levels of caching and buffering between disk and user process, it may also be appropriate to consider repeat accesses, in which case there is some likelihood that the access cost will be low. The behaviour of network traffic is similar—the cost of transmitting the first byte is greater than the cost for subsequent bytes, for example.

Because of the sophistication of current disk drives and the complexity of their interaction with CPU and operating system, exact mathematical descriptions of algorithm behaviour are unattainable; broad approximations are often the only manageable way of describing disk performance.

Applicability. Algorithms can be compared not only with regard to their resource requirements, but with regard to functionality. The basis of such comparisons will be quite different to those based on, say, asymptotic analysis.

A common error is to compare the resource requirements of two algorithms that perform subtly different tasks. For example, the various approximate string matching algorithms do not yield the same results—strings that are alike according to one algorithm can be dissimilar according to another. Comparing the costs of these algorithms is not particularly informative.

Asymptotic complexity

The performance of algorithms is often measured by asymptotic analysis; the reader should learn how an algorithm behaves as the scale of the problem changes. Big-O notation can be defined as follows: a function $f(n)$ is said to be $\mathrm{O}(g(n))$—that is, $g(n)$ is an upper bound of $f(n)$—if for some constants c and k we have $f(n) \leq c \cdot g(n)$ for all $n > k$. Other bounds are as follows. If $f(n)$ is $\mathrm{O}(g(n))$ and $g(n)$ is $\mathrm{O}(f(n))$, then $f(n)$ is $\Theta(g(n))$; that is, Θ is used to define tight bounds. A function $f(n)$ is $\mathrm{o}(g(n))$ if f is $\mathrm{O}(g(n))$ but not $\Theta(g(n))$. Likewise, Ω and ω are used to describe lower bounds. Other definitions are given by some authors, and the use of the notation is slightly inconsistent, so it is helpful to define what you mean by, for example, $\Omega(g(n))$. For a precise discussion, consult an algorithms text.

Big-O notation is also used in another, less formal sense, to mean *the complexity* rather than *an upper bound on the complexity*. An author might write that "comparison-based sorting takes $O(n \log n)$ time" or that "linear insertion sort always takes at least $O(n)$ time"; which, although an abuse, is perfectly clear and has stronger emphasis than "linear insertion sort has complexity $\Omega(n)$". But beware of loose usage that could be misunderstood. When you describe an algorithm as "quadratic", some readers may assume that complexity $\Theta(n^2)$ is meant, while others make a different interpretation. Similarly be careful with "constant", "linear", "logarithmic", and "exponential".

For algorithms that operate on static data structures, it may be appropriate to consider the cost of creating that data structure. For example, binary search in a sorted array takes $O(\log n)$ time, but $O(n \log n)$ time is required to initially sort the array.

Make sure that the domain of the analysis is clear, and be careful to analyze the right component of the data. It would usually be appropriate, for example, to analyze database algorithms as a function of the number of records, not of the length of individual records. However, if record length can substantially vary then it too should be considered. For algorithms that apply arithmetic to integers it may be appropriate to regard each arithmetic operation as having unit cost. On the other hand, if the integers involved can be of arbitrary length (consider for example public-key encryption algorithms that rely for privacy on the expense of prime factorization) it is appropriate to regard the cost of the arithmetic operations as a function of the number of bits in each integer.

Subtle problems are that the dominant cost may change with scale, and that the cost that is dominant in theory may never dominate in practice. For example, a certain algorithm might require $O(n \log n)$ comparisons and $O(n)$ disk accesses. In principle the complexity of the algorithm is $O(n \log n)$, but, given that a disk access may require 5 milliseconds and a comparison less than a nanosecond, in practice the cost of the disk accesses might well dominate for any possible application.

Some authors misunderstand the logic of asymptotic claims. For example, Amdahl's law states that the lower bound for the time taken for an algorithm to complete is determined by the part of the algorithm that is inherently sequential. The remainder can be executed in parallel and hence time for this part can be reduced by addition of processors, but no increase in the number of processors can affect the lower bound. However, it has been claimed that Amdahl's law was broken by, for a certain algorithm, increasing both the size of the input data and the number of processors. These changes had minimal impact on the sequential part of the algorithm, so that the proportion of total processing time spent in the sequential part was reduced; but this result does not contradict Amdahl's law, and so the claim was false.

Another fallacious claim was that, for a certain indexing technique, the time required to find matches to a pattern in a database was asymptotically sublinear in the database size—a remarkable result, because the probability that a record is a match to a given pattern is fixed, so that in the limit the number of matches must be linear in database size. The error was that the author had assumed that the length of the pattern was a logarithmic function of database size, so that the number of answers was constant. The technique gave the appearance of being sublinear because the task was changing.

Sometimes a formal analysis is inappropriate or only a minor consideration. For example, an algorithm for arranging line breaks in paragraphs of text will only rarely have to operate on a large input, so showing that a new algorithm is better than an existing algorithm in the limit may be of less interest than showing it is better on a typical case. More generally, although some results can be conclusively obtained by analysis, others cannot. Analytical results often say nothing about constant factors, for example, or behaviour in practice where CPU, cache, bus, and disk can interact in unpredictable ways. Such properties can only be determined by experiment. Thus, while an asymptotic analysis tells us that a hash table should be faster than a B-tree, in practice the B-tree may be superior for storage of records in a large database system.

Moreover, an analysis is no more reliable than its assumptions. In an analysis of a data structure, the data must be modelled in some way, perhaps with simplifying assumptions to make the analysis tractable; but there is no guarantee that the modelling is realistic. Analytical results can be powerful indeed—with, in some cases, implications for performance in practice on all machines for all time—but, as discussed further in Chapter 10, they are not necessarily sufficient by themselves.

8 Editing

(1) The reader should be able to find out what the story is about. (2) Some inkling of the general idea should be apparent in the first five hundred words. (3) If the writer has decided to change the name of the protagonist from Ketcham to McTavish, Ketcham should not keep bobbing up in the last five pages.

James Thurber's standing rules for writing of humour
What's So Funny?

If you give me an eight-page article and I tell you to cut it to four pages, you'll howl and say it can't be done. Then you'll go home and do it, and it will be much better.

William Zinsser
On Writing Well, Sixth Edition

The writing of a paper begins with a rough draft, perhaps based on notes of experiments or sketches of a couple of theorems. The next phase usually consists of filling out the draft to form a contiguous whole: explaining concepts, adding background material, arranging the structure to give a logical flow of ideas. Finally, the paper is polished by correcting mistakes, improving written expression, and taking care of layout. Although it does not change the quality of the research, it is this last phase—the styling of the paper—that has the most impact on a reader. It should not be neglected, however strong the ideas being communicated.

Few writers are good at judging their own writing. Discovery of shortcomings in your text takes time and effort: careful reading, a willingness to admit to mistakes, the cost of discarding text that was hard to create, and the labour of writing it afresh. We know what we meant to say, but what we actually said may only be obvious to others. Yet the difference between a weak writer and a strong writer is often not the ability to write fluently, but the effort taken to diligently edit and revise.

Consistency

Editing is the process of making a document ready for publication. Much of editing consists of checking the document for errors that fall under the heading of consistency (or lack of it). Use the checklist on page 134 when revising your papers, or when proofreading papers for others. A surprisingly effective editing exercise is to pretend to be a reader, a member of the paper's intended audience. This shift of framework, of consciously adopting the pose of external critic, often exposes problems that would otherwise go unnoticed.

My experience is that early drafts tend to be repetitive and long-winded. Often, not only are concepts awkwardly expressed and sentences unwieldy, but material on one theme might be in separate parts of the paper. It is common to find similar material included several times, particularly when there are several authors. Another problem is that some material becomes irrelevant as the paper evolves.

The ordering too may need to be reconsidered once the paper is complete. When material is moved from one place to another, check that the text in each location is intelligible and appropriate in the new context. Beware, for example, of moving definitions of terms or of breaking the flow of an argument.

For many papers, then, editing leads to excision of text. Don't be afraid to shorten your papers: cutting will improve the quality. Edit for brevity and balance. Omit or condense any material whose content or relevance to the paper's main themes does not justify its length.

Style

Another kind of editing is for style and clarity, and is perhaps the hardest part of finishing a paper. Much of this book is concerned with points of style that should be checked during editing; these should be considered during every revision. Keep in mind the basic aim, which is to make the paper clear. Lapses will be forgiven so long as you are easy to understand.

When revising the text of other writers, it is often preferable to make minimal changes: correct the presentation but retain the flavour of the original text. Don't expect to impose your style on someone else.

Most journals have a preferred style for elements such as references, figure numbering, spelling, table layout, and capitalization. If you are planning to submit to a particular journal, consider using its style.

Proofreading

There is no excuse for a report that contains spelling errors. They jump out and glare, displaying not only your inability to spell, but also your casual attitude to your work. Find a spell checker that you like and get into the habit of using it, and use a style checker too. But spell checkers won't find missing words, repeated words, misused words, or double stops. Nor will they find misspellings that form another correct word; a typical example is the substitution of "or" for "on" or "of". (Another example is from a newspaper: an article about a couple who, in their wedding ceremony, "stood, faced the floral setting, and exchanged cows".) Adopt a convenient set of symbols for correcting proofs; many dictionaries and style guides have good examples of notation for copy-editing.

A common error of mine is, when intending to type a word, to instead type some other word that shares a few initial letters. A related error is that of replacing words by their anagrams; I type "being" for "begin", "form" for "from", "relation" for "relative", "compute" for "complete", and so on. I also replace words by their homonyms, such as "two" for "too". Undoubtedly there are a few of these errors in this book—they are hard to find.[10]

Identify and look for your own common errors. Typical examples include incomplete sentences and sentences that have been run together inappropriately. Check for errors in tense and in number, that is, in the use of plural and singular forms. When you identify an error that you often make, add it to a checklist, and look for it whenever you revise. But put the list aside when writing—it will distract you.

Examining your document in a text editor is no substitute for reading it on paper after it has been formatted. It is vital to read it at least once in its entirety, to check flow and consistency. Set the draft aside for a day or two before proofreading it yourself, as doing so increases the likelihood of finding

[10] When the final draft of the first edition was being checked, a reader noticed that this sentence said: "Undoubtedly there are few of these errors in this book—they are hard to find."

mistakes.[11] (Many people have an emotional attachment to their writing; the delay allows this attachment to fade.) Read each sentence carefully, and ask yourself how easy it is to understand.

It is particularly important to check the bibliography. Readers will use it to track down references, so any garbling of information can lead them astray, and other writers may be offended if you have misreferenced their papers. Format should be consistent and each reference should include enough information to allow readers to locate it.

Always get someone else to read your work before you submit it or distribute it. You may have misunderstood a relevant article, or made a logical error; most authors are poor at detecting ambiguity in their own text; and there may be relevant results of which you are unaware; explanations may be too concise for the uninitiated; and a proof that is obvious to you may be obscure to others. And a proofreader's comments should never be ignored. If something has been misunderstood, the paper needs to be changed, although not necessarily in the way the proofreader recommends.

Publication-quality word-processing is so widely used that poorly presented reports look cheap. But word-processors, no matter how good, can glitch on the final draft. The last word of a section might be the first word on a page, a line of text might be isolated between two tables, or a formula might be broken across

[11] Newspapers, with their short deadlines, inevitably overlook some mistakes. The following is the complete text of a newspaper article (as quoted in The New Yorker).

> The Soviet Union has welded a massive naval force "far beyond the needs of defence of the Soviet sea frontiers," and is beefing up its armada with a powerful new nuclear-powered aircraft carrier and two giant battle cruisers, the authorative "Jane's Fighting Ships" reported Thursday.
>
> "The Soviet navy at the start of the 1980s is truly a formidable force," said the usually-truly is a unique formidable is too smoothy as the usually are lenience on truly a formidable Thursday's naives is frames analysis of the world's annual reference work, said the first frames of the worlds' navies in its 1980–81 edition.
>
> "The Soviet navy at the start usually-repair-led Capt. John Moore, a retired British Royal News Services.
>
> "The Soviet navy as the navy of the struggle started," she reportable Thursday.
>
> "The Soviet navy at the start of the 1980s is truly a formidable force," said beef carry on the adults of defence block identical analysis 1980s is truly formidable force, said the usually-reliable of the 1980s is unusually reliable, lake his off the world's reported Thursday.

The following is from a paper in a conference proceedings where the authors provided camera-ready copy.

> Not only is the algorithm fast on the small set, but the results show that it can even be faster for the large set. (This can't be right, run the experiment again?)

two pages. This is also the last chance to correct bad line breaks. Some editing may be required to fix such errors, to move or change the offending text or to relocate a table. In desperate cases, such as a long piece of displayed mathematics that is broken, consider putting the offending material into a figure.

Fussy people like me clean up widows and orphans. If the last line of a paragraph contains only a single, short word, that line is a widow; use an unbreakable space to join the short word onto the previous one. When the last line prior to a heading is by itself at the top of a page, or a heading or the first line of the following paragraph are alone at the bottom of a page, that line is an orphan; rewrite until it goes away.

Choice of word-processor

When you start to write a paper you need to choose a word-processor. The choice is dictated by availability, but also by how well the available word-processors cope with the demands of authoring. In addition to text, much research writing involves figures, tables, mathematics, use of multiple fonts and sizes, and cross-references to figures, tables, equations, sections, and bibliographic entries. Most authors of technical papers find at one stage or another that they must contend with the limitations of word-processing software.

Further problems are presented by the lifecycle of technical papers. For example, a paper might initially be drafted for circulation amongst colleagues, revised for submission to a conference, then accepted after further revision and experiments; but, because the paper is too long, some text must be omitted. Subsequently, after rethinking, new work, and reintroduction of omitted text, the paper is combined with a report on earlier work and submitted to a journal, where, after revision to meet referees' comments, it is accepted, perhaps as long as three years after the initial draft was written. Word-processors need to be able to handle this high level of revision and re-organization.

There are, broadly speaking, two kinds of word-processor, the visual or WYSIWYG style typified by Microsoft® Word and web-page editors, and the compiler style typified by `troff` and LaTeX, which compile marked-up text into a page description language such as PostScript. The visual word-processors are generally superior at production of documents for immediate use such as letters and web pages, and for first drafts, but for technical writing the compiler word-processors are preferable. The compiler word-processors have historically been highly stable; files created twenty or more years ago can still be processed correctly. They have features such as transparent methods for commenting-out text, making omission and re-inclusion straightforward, and macro facilities that make it easy to generate multiple distinct documents (such as a conference version and a more complete technical report) from one source file. Documents produced with visual word-processors can look amateurish, particularly if mathematics is involved.

The LaTeX word-processing system was used for this book, and is today arguably the best word-processor for technical writing. The first edition was written under Unix; the second edition was written under both Unix and Windows, using the MiKTeX and Cygwin environments. There are many circumstances in which I choose to use a visual word-processor, but technical writing is not among them.

An editing checklist

- Are the titles and headings consistent with the content?
- Have all terms been defined?
- Is the style of definition consistent? For example, were all new terms introduced in italics, or only some?
- Has terminology been used consistently?
- Are defined objects always described in the same way? For example, if the expression "all regular elements E" has been used, is "regular" implicit in the expression "all elements E"?
- Are abbreviations and acronyms stated in full when first used? Are any abbreviations or acronyms introduced more than once? Are the full statements subsequently used unnecessarily?
- Are any abbreviations used less than, say, four times? If not, can they be removed?
- Do all headings have maximum or minimum capitalization? Has a term been capitalized in one place and not in another?
- Is the style and wording of headings and captions consistent?
- Are names always used in the same way? Has a consistent convention been used for the formation of new names?
- Is spelling consistent? What about "-ise" versus "-ize", "dispatch" versus "despatch", or "disc" versus "disk"?

- Is tense used correctly? Are references discussed in a consistent way?
- Have bold and italic been used logically?
- Are any words hyphenated in some places but not others?
- Have units been used logically? If milliseconds have been used for some measurements and microseconds for others, is there a logical reason for doing so? Is the reason clear to the reader? Has "megabyte" been written as "Mb" in some places and "Mbyte" in others?
- Are all values of the same type presented with the same precision?
- Are the graphs all the same size? Are the axis units always given? If, say, the x-axes on different graphs measure the same units, do the axes have the same label?
- Are all tables in the same format? Does the use of double and single lines follow a logical pattern? Are units given for every value? Are labels and headings named consistently? If, say, columns have been used for properties A to E in one table, have rows been used elsewhere? That is, do all tables have the same orientation?
- Has the same style been used for all algorithms and programs? Is there a consistent scheme for naming of variables? Do all pseudocode statements have the same syntax? Is the use of indentation consistent?
- In the references, has each field been formatted consistently? Have italics and quotes been used appropriately for titles? Is capitalization consistent? Are journal and conference names abbreviated in the same way? Is the style of author names consistent? Has the same core set of fields been provided for each reference of the same type?
- Is formatting consistent? Has the same indentation been used for all displays? Are some displays centred and others indented? Do some sections begin with an unindented paragraph and others not?
- Do the parentheses match?

9 Writing up

I used to think about my sentences before writing them down; but ... I have found that it saves time to scribble in a vile hand whole pages as quickly as I possibly can .... Sentences thus scribbled down are often better ones than I could have written deliberately.

Charles Darwin
Autobiography

Science is more than a body of knowledge; it is a way of thinking.

Carl Sagan
The Demon-Haunted World

In every research project, a stage is reached at which it makes sense to begin to write up. A good principle is to begin early: if it is possible to start writing then the writing should start, typically well before the project's half-way mark. Shaping the research and its outcomes into a write-up is an effective way of giving structure to a project, even if the outcomes are not yet clear or months are needed to complete system development.

The task of writing up research is the topic of this chapter: gathering material, organizing it so that the work tells a story, giving this story the structure of a thesis or of an academic paper, and starting to write. The research that precedes the write-up is the topic of Chapters 10 and 11.

The scope of a paper

To begin a paper, the first task is to identify your aims. Write down everything that motivated you to start the research. What did you want to achieve? What problems did you expect to address? What makes the problems interesting? Next, define the scope of the work that you plan to write up. To do so, it is necessary to make choices about what to include, and thus it is necessary to identify what *might* be included. Typically, by this stage your research has become focused on investigation of a small number of specific questions, and you have preliminary experimental or theoretical results that suggest what the core contribution of the work is going to be.

You might start, for example, by asking questions such as:

- Which results are the most surprising?
- What is the one result that other researchers might adopt in their work?
- Are the other outcomes independent enough to be published separately later on? Are they interesting enough to justify their being included?
- Does it make sense to explain the new algorithms first, followed by description of the previous algorithms in terms of how they differ from the new work? Or is the contribution of the new work more obvious if the old approaches are described first, to set the context?
- What assumptions or definitions need to be formalized before the main theorem can be presented?
- What is the key background work that has to be discussed?
- Who is the readership? For example, are you writing for specialists in your area, your examiners, or a general computer science audience?

Other questions are given in the checklist on page 155.

A valuable exercise at this stage is to speculate on the format and scope of the results. Early in the investigation, decisions will have been made about how the results are to be evaluated—that is, about which measures are to be used to determine whether the research has succeeded or failed. For example, it may be that network congestion is the main respect in which the research is expected to have yielded improvements in performance. But how is network congestion to be measured? As a function of data volume, number of machines, network bandwidth, or something else? Answering this question suggests a form of presentation into which the experimental results can be inserted: a graph, perhaps. The form of this graph can be sketched even before any coding has begun, and doing so identifies the kind of output that the code is required to produce.

Consider a detailed example: an investigation of external sorting in database systems. In this task, a large relation—tens of millions of records, say, constituting several gigabytes—must be sorted on a field specified in a query. An effective sorting method is to sort the relation one block at a time, storing the sorted blocks in a temporary file then merging them to give the final result. Costs include processing time for sorting and merging, transfer time to and from disk, and temporary space requirements. The balance between these costs is governed by available in-memory buffer space, as large blocks are expensive to sort but cheap to merge. The specific research question being investigated is whether disk costs can be reduced by compressing the data while it is sorted.

Speculation about how compression might affect costs suggest how the work should be measured. For small relations, compression seems unlikely to be of help—compressing and then decompressing adds processing costs but does not provide savings if all the data fits in memory. For large relations, on the other hand, the savings due to reduced disk traffic, increased numbers of records per block, and use of less temporary space may be significant. Thus it seems likely that the savings due to compression would increase with the size of relation to be sorted, suggesting use of a graph of data volume against sorting time for fixed block size. Note too that the question of what to measure identifies an implicit assumption: that the data was uncompressed to begin with and is returned uncompressed. All of these decisions and steps help to determine the paper's content.

The content of a paper is to a significant extent determined by the readership. You may be reporting a particular piece of work, but the way it is reported is determined by the characteristics of the audience. For example, a paper on machine learning for computer vision may have entirely different implications for the two fields, and thus different aspects of the results might be emphasized. Also, an expert on vision cannot be assumed to have any experience with machine learning, so the way in which the material is explained to the two readerships must be based on your judgement, in each case, of what is common knowledge and what is unfamiliar. The nature of the audience may even determine the scope of what can be reported.

Making choices about the content of a paper places limits on its scope; these choices identify material to be excluded. Broadly speaking, many research programs are a cycle of innovation and evaluation, with the answers or resolution of one investigation creating the questions that lead to the next. An advance in, say, string sorting might well have implications for integer sorting, and further work could pursue these implications. But at some point it is necessary to stop undertaking new work and write up what has been achieved so far. The new ideas may well be exciting—and less stale than the work that has been preoccupying you for months—but they are likely to be less well understood, and completing the old work is more important than trying to include too many results. If the newer work can be published independently, then write it up separately. A long, complex paper, however big a breakthrough it represents, is hard to referee. From an editor's perspective, accepting such a paper may be difficult to justify if it squeezes out several other contributions.

Another element in the process of developing a paper is deciding where the work might be published. There are many factors that should be considered when making this decision, such as relevance to your topic and how your work measures against the standard for that forum. In particular, the venue partly determines the scope of a paper. For example, is there a page limit? Are there specific conventions to be observed? Are the other papers in that venue primarily theoretical or experimental? What prior knowledge or background is a reader likely to have? Do the editors require that your code be available online? If you select a particular forum but haven't cited any papers that have appeared there, you may have made the wrong choice.

Once the material for a paper has been collected it has to be organized into a coherent self-contained narrative, which ultimately will form the body of the write-up. Turning this narrative into a write-up involves putting it in the form of an academic paper: including an introduction, a bibliography, and so on. These issues are discussed later.

Telling a story

A cornerstone of good writing is identifying what the reader needs to learn. A paper is a sequence of concepts, building from a foundation of knowledge assumed to be common to all readers up to new ideas and results. Thus an effective paper educates its readers. It leads readers from what they already know to new knowledge you want them to learn. For this reason, the body of a good paper—everything between the introduction and the conclusions—should have a logical flow that has the feel of a narrative.

The narrative told by a paper is a walk through the ideas and outcomes. It isn't a commentary on the research program or the day-to-day activities of the participants, nor is it meant to be mysterious. Instead, it is like a guided tour through a gallery, in which each room contains something new for the readers to comprehend. There is also an expectation of logical closure. The early parts of the paper's body typically explain hypotheses or claims; the reader expects to discover by the end whether these are justified.

There are several common ways for structuring the body of a paper, including as a chain, by specificity, by example, and by complexity. Perhaps the most common structure is the first of these alternatives, a *chain* in which the results and the background on which they build dictate a logical order for presentation of the material. First might come, say, a problem statement, then a review of previous solutions and their drawbacks, then the new solution, and finally a demonstration that the solution improves on its predecessors.

The "compression for fast external sorting" project suggests a structure of this kind. The problem statement consists of an explanation of external sorting and an argument that disk access costs are a crucial bottleneck. The review explains standard compression methods and why they cannot be integrated into external sorting. The new solution is the compression method developed in the research. The demonstration is a series of graphs and tables based on experiments that compare the costs of sorting with and without compression.

For some kinds of results, other structures may be preferable. One option is to structure by *specificity*, an approach that is particularly appropriate for results that can be divided into several stages. The material is first outlined in general terms, then the details are progressively filled in. Most technical papers have this organization at the high level, but it can also be used within sections.

Material that might have such a structure is an explanation of a retrieval system. Such systems generally have several components. For example, in text retrieval a parser is required to extract words from the text that is being indexed; this information must be passed to a procedure for building an index; queries must likewise be parsed into a format that is consistent with that of the stored text; and a query evaluator uses the index to identify the records that match a given query. The explanation might begin with a review of this overall structure, then proceed to the detail of the elements.

Another structure is by *example*, in which the idea or result is initially explained by, say, applying it to some typical problem. Then the idea can be explained more formally, in a framework the example has made concrete and familiar. Thc "compression for fast external sorting" could also be approached in this way. The explanation could begin by considering, hypothetically, the likely impact of compression on sorting. To make the discussion more concrete, a couple of specific instances—a small relation and a large relation, say—could be used to illustrate the expected behaviour in different circumstances. Given a clear explanation of the hypothetical scenario, you can then proceed to fill in details of the method that was tested in the research.

Another alternative is to structure the body by *complexity*. For example, a simple case can be given first, then a more complex case can be explained as an extension, thus avoiding the difficulty of explaining basic concepts in a complex framework. This approach is a kind of tutorial: the reader is brought by small steps to the full result. For example, a mathematical result for an object-oriented programming language might initially be applied to some simple case, such as programs in which all objects are of the same class. Then the result could be extended by considering programs with inheritance.[12]

Some other structures are inappropriate for a write-up. For example, the paper should not be a chronological list of experiments and results. The aim is to present the evidence needed to explain an argument, not to list the work undertaken.

Most experiments yield far more data than can be presented in a paper of reasonable length. Important results can be summarized in a graph or a table, and other outcomes reported in a line or two. It is acceptable to state that experiments have yielded a certain outcome without providing details, so long as those experiments do not affect the main conclusions of the paper (and have actually been performed). Similarly, there may be no need to include the details of proofs of lemmas or minor theorems. This does not excuse you from conducting the experiments or convincing yourself that the results are correct, but such information can be kept in logs of the research rather than included in the paper.

The traditional structure for organizing research papers can encourage you to list all proofs or results, then analyze them later; with this structure, however, the narrative flow is often poor. It usually makes more sense to analyze proofs or experimental results as they are presented, particularly since experiments or theorems often follow a logical sequence in which the outcome of one dictates the parameters of the next.

When describing specific results, it is helpful, although not always possible, to begin with a brief overview of whatever has been observed. The rest of the discussion can then be used for amplification rather than further observations. Newspaper articles are often written in this way. The first sentence summarizes the story; the next few sentences review the story again, giving some context; then the remainder of the article presents the whole story in detail. Sections of research papers can sometimes be organized in this way.

[12] Structuring by complexity is good for a paper but, often, inappropriate for ongoing research. It is not uncommon to see a paper in which the authors have solved an easy case of a problem, say optimizations for iteration-free programs, motivated by hopeful claims such as "we expect these results to throw light on optimization of programs with loops and recursion". All too often the follow-up paper never appears.

Organization

Scientific papers follow a standard structure that allows readers to quickly discover the main results, and then, if interested, to examine the supporting evidence. Many readers accept or reject conclusions based on a quick scan, not having time to read all the papers they see. A well-structured write-up accommodates this behaviour by having important statements as near the beginning as possible. You need to:

- Describe the work in the context of accepted scientific knowledge.
- State the idea that is being investigated, often as a theory or hypothesis.
- Explain what is new about the idea, what is being evaluated, or what contribution the paper is making.
- Justify the theory, by methods such as proof or experiment.

Theses, journal articles, and conference papers have much the same organization when viewed in outline. There are distinctions in emphasis rather than specific detail. For a thesis, for example, the literature review may be expected to include a historical discussion outlining the development of the key ideas. There is also an expectation that a thesis is a completed, rounded piece of work—a consolidation of the achievements of a research program as well as a report on specific scientific results. Nonetheless, these forms of write-up have similar structure.

A typical write-up has most of the following components:

Title and author

Papers begin with their title and information about authors including name, affiliation, and address. The convention in computer science is to not give your position, title, or qualifications; but whether you give your name as A. B. Cee, Ae Cee, Ae B. Cee, or whatever, is a personal decision. Use the same style for your name on all your papers, so that they are indexed together. Include a durable email address or web address.

Also include a date. Take the trouble to type in the date rather than using "today" facilities that print the date on which the document was last processed, or later you may not be able to tell when the document was completed.

The front matter of a paper may also include other elements. One is acknowledgements, as discussed on page 26, which may alternatively follow the conclusions. Another element is a collection of search terms, keywords, or key phrases—additional terminology that can be used to describe the topic of the paper. Sometimes these keywords must be selected from a specific list. In other cases, the conventions for choosing such terms are not always clear, but in general it is unhelpful to use words that, for example, are a description of the experimental methodology: don't write "timing experiments", for example. Use words that concern the paper's principal themes.

Abstract

An abstract is typically a single paragraph of about 50 to 200 words. The function of an abstract is to allow readers to judge whether or not the paper is of relevance to them. It should therefore be a concise summary of the paper's aims, scope, and conclusions. There is no space for unnecessary text; an abstract should be kept to as few words as possible while remaining clear and informative. Irrelevancies, such as minor details or a description of the structure of the paper, are inappropriate, as are acronyms, abbreviations, and mathematics. Sentences such as "We review relevant literature" should be omitted.

The more specific an abstract is, the more interesting it is likely to be. Instead of writing "space requirements can be significantly reduced", write "space requirements can be reduced by 60%". Instead of writing "we have a new inversion algorithm", write "we have a new inversion algorithm, based on move-to-front lists".

Many scientists browse research papers outside their area of expertise. You should not assume that all likely readers will be specialists in the topic of their paper—abstracts should be self-contained and written for as broad a readership as possible. Only in rare circumstances should an abstract cite another paper (for example, when one paper consists entirely of analysis of results in another), in which case the reference should be given in full, not as a citation to the bibliography.

Introduction

An introduction can be regarded as an expanded version of the abstract. It should describe the paper's topic, the problem being studied, references to key papers, the approach to the solution, the scope and limitations of the solution, and the outcomes. There needs to be enough detail to allow readers to decide whether or not they need to read further. It should include motivation: the introduction should explain why the problem is interesting, what the relevant scientific issues are, and why the solution is a good one.

That is, the introduction should show that the paper is worth reading and it should allow the reader to understand your perspective, so that the reader and you can proceed on a basis of common understanding.

Many introductions follow a five-element organization:

1. A general statement introducing the broad research area of the particular topic being investigated.
2. An explanation of the specific problem (difficulty, obstacle, challenge) to be solved.
3. A brief review of existing or standard solutions to this problem and their limitations.
4. An outline of the proposed new solution.
5. A summary of how the solution was evaluated and what the outcomes of the evaluation were.

An interesting exercise is to read other papers, analyze their introductions to see if they have this form, and then decide whether they are effective.

The introduction can discuss the importance or ramifications of the conclusions but should omit supporting evidence, which the interested reader can find in the body of the paper. Relevant literature can be cited in the introduction, but unnecessary jargon, complex mathematics, and in-depth discussion of the literature belong elsewhere.

A paper isn't a story in which results are kept secret until a surprise ending. The introduction should clearly tell the reader what in the paper is new and what the outcomes are. There may still be a little suspense: revealing what the results are does not necessarily reveal how they were achieved. If, however, the existence of results is concealed until later on, the reader might assume there are no results and discard the paper as worthless.

Body

The body of a paper should present the results. The presentation should provide necessary background and terminology, explain the chain of reasoning that leads to the conclusions, provide the details of central proofs, summarize any experimental outcomes, and state in detail the conclusions outlined in the introduction. Descriptions of experiments should permit reproduction and verification, as discussed in Chapter 11. There should also be careful definitions of the hypothesis and major concepts, even those described informally in the introduction. The structure should be evident in the section headings. Since the body can be long, narrative flow and a clear logical structure are essential.

The body should be reasonably independent of other papers. If, to understand your paper, the reader must find specialized literature such as your earlier papers or an obscure paper by your advisor, then its audience will be limited.

In some disciplines, research papers have highly standardized structures. Editors may require, for example, that you use only the four headings Introduction-Methods-Results-Discussion. This convention has not taken hold in computer science, and in some cases such a structure impedes a clear explanation of the work. For example, use of fixed headings may prohibit development of a complex explanation in stages. In work combining two query resolution techniques, we had to determine how they would interact, based on a fresh evaluation of how they behaved independently. The final structure was, in effect, Introduction-Background-Methods-Results-Discussion-Methods-Results-Discussion.

Even if the standardized section names are not used, the body needs these elements, if not necessarily under their standard headings. Components of the body might include, among other things, background, previous work, proposals, experimental design, analysis, results, and discussion. Specific research projects suggest specific headings. For the "compression for fast external sorting" project sketched earlier, the complete set of section headings might be:

1. Introduction
2. External sorting
3. Compression techniques for database systems
4. Sorting with compression
5. Experimental setup
6. Results and discussion
7. Conclusions

The wording of these headings does not follow the standard form, but the intent of the wording is the same. Sections 2 and 3 are the background; Section 4 contains novel algorithms, and Sections 4 and 5 together are the methods.

The background material can be entirely separate from the discussion of previous work on the same problem. The former is the knowledge the reader needs to understand your contribution. The latter is, often, alternative solutions that are superseded by your work. Together, the discussion of background and previous work also introduce the state of the art and its failings, the importance and circumstances of the research question, and benchmarks or baselines that the new work should be compared to.

A body that consists of descriptions of algorithms followed by a dump of experimental results is not sound science. In such a paper, the context of prior work is not explained, as readers are left to draw their own inferences about what the results mean.

In a thesis, each chapter has structure, including an introduction and a summary or conclusions. This structure varies with the chapter's purpose. A background chapter may gather a variety of topics necessary to understanding of the contribution of the thesis, for example, whereas a chapter on a new algorithm may have a simple linear organization in which the parts of the algorithm are presented in turn. However, the introduction and summary should help to link the thesis together—how the chapter builds on previous chapters and how subsequent chapters make use of it.

Literature review

Few results or experiments are entirely new. Most often they are extensions of or corrections to previous research—that is, most results are an incremental addition to existing knowledge. A literature review, or survey, is used to compare the new results to similar previously published results, to describe existing knowledge, and to explain how it is extended by the new results. A survey can also help a reader who is not expert in the field to understand the paper and may point to standard references such as texts or survey articles.

In an ideal paper, the literature review is as interesting and thorough as the description of the paper's contribution. There is great value for the reader in a precise analysis of previous work that explains, for example, how existing methods differ from one another and what their respective strengths and weaknesses are. Such a review also creates a specific expectation of what the contribution of the paper should be—it shapes what the readers expect of your work, and thus shapes how they will respond to your ideas.

The literature review can be early in a paper, to describe the context of the work, and might in that case be part of the introduction; or the literature review can follow or be part of the main body, at which point a detailed comparison between the old and the new can be made. If the literature review is late in a paper, it is easier to present the surveyed results in a consistent terminology, even when the cited papers have differing nomenclature and notation.

In many papers the literature review material is not gathered into a single section, but is discussed where it is used—background material in the introduction, analysis of other researchers' work as new results are introduced, and so on. This approach can help you to write the paper as a flowing narrative.

An issue that is difficult in some research is the relationship between new scientific results and proprietary commercial technology. It often is the case that scientists investigate problems that appear to be solved or addressed in commercial products. For example, there is ongoing academic research into methods for information retrieval despite the success of the search engines deployed on the web. From the perspective of high research principle, the existence of a commercial product is irrelevant: the ideas are not in the public domain, it is not known how the problems were solved in the product, and the researcher's contribution is valid. However, it may well be reckless to ignore the product; it should be cited and discussed, while noting, for example, that the methods and effectiveness of the commercial solution are unknown.

Conclusions

The closing section, or summary, is used to draw together the topics discussed in the paper. It should include a concise statement of the paper's important results and an explanation of their significance. This is an appropriate place to state (or restate) any limitations of the work: shortcomings in the experiments, problems that the theory does not address, and so on.

The conclusions are an appropriate place for a scientist to look beyond the current context to other problems that were not addressed, to questions that were not answered, to variations that could be explored. They may include speculation, such as discussion of possible consequences of the results.

A *conclusion* is that which concludes, or the end. *Conclusions* are the inferences drawn from a collection of information. Write "Conclusions", not "Conclusion". If you have no conclusions to draw, write "Summary".

Bibliography

A paper's bibliography, or its set of references, is a complete list of theses, papers, books, and reports cited in the text. No other items should be included. Citation and bibliographies are discussed in detail starting on page 19.

Appendices

Some papers have appendices giving detail of proofs or experimental results, and, where appropriate, material such as listings of computer programs. The purpose of an appendix is to hold bulky material that would otherwise interfere with the narrative flow of the paper, or material that even interested readers do not need to refer to. Appendices are rarely necessary.

The first draft

For the first draft of a write-up you may find it helpful to write freely—without particular regard to style, layout, or even punctuation—so that you can concentrate on presenting a smooth flow of ideas in a logical structure. Worrying about how to phrase each sentence tends to result in text that is clear but doesn't form a continuous whole, and authors who are too critical on the first draft are often unable to write anything at all. If you tend to get stuck, just write anything, no matter how awful; but be sure to delete any ravings later.

Some people, when told to just say anything, find they can write freely—if anything is acceptable, then nothing is wrong. For others, finding words is still a struggle. A last resort is to write in brief sentences making the simplest possible statements.

✓ In-memory sorting algorithms require random access to records. For large files stored on disk, random access is impractically slow. These files must be sorted in blocks. Each block is loaded into memory and sorted in turn. Sorted blocks are written to temporary files. These temporary files are then merged. There may be many files but in practice the merge can be completed in one pass. Thus each record is read twice and written twice. Temporary space is required for a complete copy of the original file.

This text certainly isn't elegant—it is annoying to read and should be thoroughly edited long before the paper is submitted. But it is capturing the ideas, and the writing is proceeding.

A consequence of having a sloppy first draft is that you must edit and revise carefully; initial drafts are often turgid and full of mistakes. But few authors write well on the first draft anyway; the best writing is the result of frequent, thorough revision.

Mathematical content, definitions, and the problem statement should be made precise as early in the writing process as possible. The hypothesis and the results flow from a clear statement of the problem being tackled. Describing the problem forces you to consider in depth the scope and nature of the research. If you find that you cannot describe the problem precisely, then perhaps your understanding is lacking or the ideas are insufficiently developed.

It was said earlier, but is worth repeating: the writing should begin long before the research is finished, and perhaps as soon as it is started. The later the writing is begun, the harder it will be. Delay increases the time between having ideas and having to write about them, increases the number of papers to discuss, and increases the number of experiments to describe. Completing your reading, for example, is a poor reason to defer writing, because reading is never complete. Writing is a stimulus to research, suggesting fresh ideas and clarifying vague concepts and misunderstandings; and developing the presentation of the results oftens suggest the form the proofs or experiments should take. Gaps in the research may not be apparent until it has been at least preliminarily described. Research is also a stimulus to writing—fine points are quickly forgotten once the work is complete. Don't expect the writing to progress steadily, but do expect progress overall. If the writing seems to have stalled, it is time to put other tasks aside for a while.

From draft to submission

There are many approaches to the process of assembling a technical paper. The technique I use for composing is to brainstorm, writing down in point form what has been learnt, what has been achieved, and what the results are. The next step is to prepare a skeleton, choosing results to emphasize and discarding material that on reflection seems irrelevant, and then work out a logical sequence of sections that leads the reader naturally to the results. A useful discipline is to choose the section titles before writing any text, because if material to be included doesn't seem to belong in any section then the paper's structure is probably faulty. The introduction is completed first and includes an overview of the paper's intended structure, that is, an outline of the order and content of the sections. When the structure is complete, each section can be sketched in perhaps 20 to 200 words. This approach has the advantage of making the writing task less daunting—it is broken into parts of manageable size.

When the body and the closing summary are complete, the introduction usually needs substantial revision because the arguments presented in the paper are likely to mature and evolve as the writing proceeds. The final version of the abstract is the last part to be written.

With a reasonably thorough draft completed, it is time to review the paper's content and contribution. Anticipate likely concerns or objections, and address them; if they can't be addressed, acknowledge them. Consider whether extra work is needed to fill a hole. Ask the probing, critical questions that you would ask of other people's work. The burden of proof is on you, not the reader, so be conservative in your claims and thorough with your evidence.

During drafting and revision, ensure that the topic of the paper does not drift. At the start of the writing process, you wrote down your aims, motivation, and scope. Use these as a reference. If you feel that you need to write something that is not obviously relevant to your original aims, then either establish the connection clearly or alter the aims. Changing the aims can affect the work in many ways, however, so only do so with great care.

For a novice writer who doesn't know where to begin, a good starting point is imitation. Choose a paper whose results are of a similar flavour to your own, analyze its organization, and sketch an organization for your results based on the same pattern. The habit of using similar patterns for papers—their standardization—helps to make them easier to read.

The practice of building a file of notes as you proceed is invaluable. Keep a dated log with records of the following:

- Meetings.
- Decisions.
- Ideas.
- Expectations of outcomes.
- Papers you have read.
- Sketches of algorithms.
- Code versions.
- Theorems.
- Experiments.
- Sketches of proofs.
- Outcomes.

Expect the log to be a mixture of a written notebook and data kept electronically. In its raw state, the content of a file of notes is not suitable for inclusion in a paper, but the themes and issues of the paper can be drawn from the file, and it serves as a memory of issues to discuss and material to include.

In computer science, most papers are co-authored. The inclusion of several people as authors means that, in principle, all these people contributed in some non-trivial way to the intellectual content of the paper. In many cases, it also means that the task of writing was shared. There are a range of strategies for co-authoring, which vary from colleague to colleague and paper to paper. It is not unusual, for example, for an advisor to use a student's thesis as the basis of a paper, in which case both advisor and student are listed as authors. In this process, the advisor may well dramatically revise the student's work, if only because a typical paper is much shorter than a typical thesis.

In cases where scientists are working more or less as equals, one strategy is to brainstorm the contents of the paper, then for each author to write a designated section. Another strategy—my preferred model for collaboration—is to take turns. One person writes a draft, the next revises and extends, and so on, with each person holding an exclusive lock on the paper while amending it. With this approach, the final paper is likely to be a fairly seamless integration of the styles and contributions of each of the authors (especially if each author contributes to revision of the other authors' work). In contrast, the strategy of writing sections separately tends to lead to papers in which the authorial voice makes dramatic shifts, the tables and figures are inconsistent, and there is a great deal of repetition and omission.

Taking turns is effective, but it does have pitfalls, and agreed ground rules are needed to make it work. For example, I rarely delete anything a co-author has written, but may comment it out; thus no-one feels that their work has been thrown away. Another element of successful co-authoring is respect. Accept your colleagues' views unless you have a good reason not to.

Co-authoring is a form of research training. It is an opportunity for advisors to learn in detail where their students are weak as scientists, while a paper that has been revised by an advisor is an opportunity for a student to contrast an attempt at research writing with that of an experienced scientist. An advisor's revision of a student's draft can involve a great deal of work, and may be the most thorough feedback on writing that the student receives during the course of a research program.

Prepublication

Traditionally, prior to a paper appearing in a refereed venue it might have been made available as a manuscript or technical report. These forms of publication once had the advantage of making the work available quickly—a particular concern if there is likely to be a substantial delay between submission and publication. (In some journals, the delay is years.) Departments prided themselves on the quality of their technical report series. However, this form of publication has withered away as the web has grown in importance; some academic institutions and large corporate research labs still publish significant numbers of reports, reflecting perhaps internal publication-approval processes, but these are the exception.

The web allows academics to readily publish their own work, independent even of the structures imposed by their departments. Most computer science researchers have websites on which they list their publications, and many researchers additionally list papers that are not yet published (and may never be published). An alternative is to place such papers in public archives.[13] Additionally, some research groups maintain topic-specific repositories.

Web publication has a range of advantages. Most importantly, it makes the work available immediately. While there is still an expectation that the work follows the conventions of a scientific paper, additional material can easily be included, such as links to data and source code. Many researchers access papers exclusively—both from academic publishers and from individuals—through the web, and there is growing acceptance amongst publishers that preliminary versions of papers are made publicly available by their authors.

The papers in most journals and conferences are available on the web via their publishers' websites. The fact that a paper is available through such a website tells the reader that the work has probably been refereed, that is, independently assessed by other scientists. (The quality of the refereeing varies from one conference or journal to another. When making an assessment of a paper, consider the reputation of the venue in which it appeared and issues such as those raised in Chapters 10 and 12.) While work that is published by an author on the web is immediately available, the lack of refereeing means that readers cannot be as confident of its validity.

Theses

A thesis (or, in some universities, a dissertation) is how research students present their work for examination. A thesis may have longer-term importance as a description of significant research results, but your primary goal should be to produce a piece of work that the examiners will pass.

The questions that examiners respond to are much the same as those a referee would ask of a paper. That is, the examiners seek evidence of an original, valid contribution developed to an appropriate standard. However, it is a mistake to view a thesis as no more than an extended paper. A paper stands (or

[13]The role of these archives is shifting. Originally, the main advantage of adding a paper to an archive was that it then became searchable; at that time, the major web search engines did not index formats such as PostScript. Today, their role is increasingly to ensure permanence—the content of a paper in an archive cannot be changed as easily as can that of a paper on an individual's website, for example—and to promote rapid dissemination of new work, for example through mailing lists.

does not stand) on the strength of the results. A thesis passes (or fails) on the strength of your demonstration of competence; even if good results are not achieved, the thesis should pass if you have shown the ability to undertake high-quality research. Questions that examiners might be asked to address include whether you have demonstrated command of the fundamentals of the discipline, whether you have the ability to correctly interpret results, and whether you have sufficiently strong communication skills.

A particular element of theses that is often weak is the analysis of the outcomes. All too often the discussion can be summarized as "the code ran", "it seems plausible", or "look at the pretty feature". To a greater degree than in a paper, it is necessary to probe why the outcomes occurred or what factors or variables were significant in the experiments. The guidelines to examiners issued by many universities state that the candidate must demonstrate critical thinking. Application of critical thinking and skeptical questioning to the work is an excellent way of persuading an examiner that the candidate understands their own methods and results; many of the questions explored in Chapter 10 concern critical thinking and skeptical examination of research.

Examiners are unlikely to be impressed by students who make grandiose claims about their work. Many researchers—and not just students—are reluctant to admit that their discoveries have any limitations; yet one of the clearest demonstrations of research ability is to ask incisive questions. Was the algorithm an improvement because of better cache use or fewer CPU cycles? What else would explain these results? In what circumstances is the theorem not applicable? A thesis with negative results can, if appropriately written, demonstrate the ability of the candidate just as well as a thesis with positive results. The outcomes may be less interesting, but the capability to undertake research has still been shown.

Examiners are also unlikely to be impressed by a student who accepts the word of established authority without question, or rejects other ideas without giving them due consideration, or appears reluctant to suggest any change or to make unfavourable comment. If you have a relevant point to make, and can defend it by reasonable argument, then make it. Be thorough. A PhD is an opportunity to do research in depth; shortcuts and incomplete experiments suggest shoddy work.

Issues such as whether results have been critically analyzed are of importance in papers, but there is a different emphasis for theses—it is you, not the research, that is the primary object of scrutiny.

For an extended research degree such as a PhD, another difference between a thesis and a paper is that the former may report on a series of more or less independent research discoveries. In contrast, a typical paper concerns a single consistent investigation. A thesis may, moreover, include work drawn from multiple papers. For this reason, there is more variation in structure from thesis to thesis than from paper to paper. An example of the problems faced in organizing a thesis is how to consolidate descriptions of new algorithms. It may make sense to bring all of them into a single chapter and then comparatively evaluate them in subsequent chapters, or it may be preferable to describe them one by one, evaluating each in turn. Factors to consider in choosing an organization include how cohesive the algorithms are (for example, whether they address the same problem) and whether an explanation of one algorithm is meaningful if the previous one has not yet been evaluated.

As the scope of a thesis is more substantial than that of a paper, the introduction may need to be broad in topic and conversational in tone. It could introduce a whole area rather than a single problem, for example, if the thesis happens to concerns a range of topics. Another reason to develop a substantial introduction is that a thesis is a more thorough, detailed document than is a paper. Why was the problem worth investigating in depth? How do the parts of the investigation relate to each other? What are some practical, concrete ways in which the outcomes of the work might be used? Running examples may be outlined in the introduction, to give unity to the thesis overall. The role of a thesis's introduction is, however, much the same as in a paper. As in the introduction of a paper, theory, jargon, and notation are inappropriate.

Take the time to learn about thesis writing as soon as possible. Browse other theses, from your own institution, from other institutions, and from other disciplines. Form views about the strengths and weaknesses of these theses; these views will help to shape your own work.

A writing-up checklist

- Have you identified your aims and scope?
- Are you maintaining a log and notebook?
- Does the paper follow a narrative?
- In what forum, or kind of forum, do you plan to publish?
- What other papers should your write-up resemble?
- Are you writing to a well-defined structure and organization?

- Have you chosen a form for the argument and results?
- Have you established a clear connection between the background, methods, and results?
- How are results being selected for presentation?
- How do the results relate to your original aims?
- Have you used any unusual patterns of organization?
- Have the results been critically analyzed?
- Are the requirements for a thesis met?
- Do you and your co-authors have an agreed methodology for sharing the work of completing the write-up?

10 Doing research

The intensity of the conviction that a hypothesis
is true has no bearing on whether it is true or not.

P. B. Medawar
Advice to a Young Scientist

The great tragedy of Science, the slaying
of a beautiful hypothesis by an ugly fact.

T. H. Huxley
Biogenesis and Abiogenesis

An argument is a connected series of statements
intended to establish a proposition .... Argument
is an intellectual process. Contradiction is just the
automatic gainsaying of anything the other person says.

Monty Python
The Argument Sketch

A research paper, written up and submitted for refereeing, is the result of a process of research that may have been proceeding for months or years. It is not an end-product, but more typically describes recent results or is a preliminary study. It is rare that a write-up is final, concluding forever a program of research on a topic; however, the write-up is based on a great deal of activity. Indeed, with just a few pages representing months or more of work by several people, a paper may be only a tiny window into the research.

A paper, then, is an outcome of a cycle of activity, from speculation through definition and experimentation to write-up, with a range of obstacles and issues that can arise on the way. In this chapter I review the process of research, in particular the early stages of a project. The perspective taken is from the ground, as a working scientist: What kinds of stages and events does a researcher have to manage in order to produce an interesting, valid piece of research? This chapter and Chapter 11 complement the preceding parts of the book—on the topic of how research should be described—by considering how the content of a paper is arrived at.

Philosophers and historians of science have reflected at length on the meaning, elements, and methods of research, from both practical and abstract points of view. These reflections can be of great benefit to a working scientist. Any competent researcher can learn from an alternative perspective on their work, and being able to describe what we do helps us to understand whether we are doing it well.

At the same time, learning to do research involves piecemeal acquisition of a range of specific skills. Only with experience does a student see these skills as part of a single integrated "process of research". That is, many people learn to be scientists by doing research stage-by-stage under supervision, and only after having been through the research process does the bigger picture become evident. For that reason, for novices the correspondence between abstractions of research and a particular investigation can be hard to identify.

A related problem is that newcomers to research may initially draw inappropriate analogies to activities with which they are already familiar. For example, in computer science many research students see experimentation as a form of software development, and undertake a research write-up as if they were assembling a user manual or software documentation. Part of learning to be a computer scientist is recognizing how the aims of research differ from those of coursework or programming.

Beginnings

The origin of a research investigation is typically a moment of insight. A student attending a lecture wonders why search engines do not provide better spelling correction. A researcher investigating external sorting is at a seminar on file compression, and ponders whether one could be of benefit to the other. A user is frustrated by network delays and questions whether the routing algorithm is working well. A student asks a professor about the possibility of research on evaluation of code functionality; the professor, who hadn't previously contemplated such work, realises that it could build on recent advances in type theory.

Research ideas often come to mind when the brain is idling, or when separate topics coincidentally arise at the same time. Tea-room arguments are a rich source of seed ideas. One person is idly speculating, just to make conversation; another pursues the speculation and a research topic is created. Or someone claims that a researcher's idea is unworkable, and a listener starts to turn over the arguments. What makes it unworkable? How might those issues be addressed?

This first step is a subjective one: to choose to explore ideas that seem likely to succeed, or are intriguing, or have the potential to lead to something new, or contradict received wisdom. At this stage, it isn't possible to know whether the work can lead to valuable results; otherwise there would be no scope for research. The final outcome is an objective scientific report, but curiosity and guesswork are what establish research directions.

It is typically at this stage that a student becomes involved in the research. Some students have a clear idea of what they want to pursue—whether it is feasible, rational, or has research potential is another matter—but the majority are in effect shopping for a topic and advisor. They have a desire to work on research and to be creative, perhaps without any definite idea of what research is. They are drawn by a particular area or problem, or want to work with a particular individual. Students may talk through a range of possible projects with several alternative advisors before making a definite choice and starting to work on a research problem in earnest.

Shaping a research project

How a potential research topic is shaped into a concrete project depends on context. Experienced scientists aiming to write a paper on a subject of mutual interest tend to be fairly focused: they quickly design a series of experiments or theoretical goals, investigate the relevant literature, and set deadlines.

For students, undertaking research involves training, which affects how the work proceeds. Also, for a larger research program such as a PhD, there are both short-term and long-term goals: the current specific explorations, which may be intended to lead to a research paper, and their role as a part of a wider investigation that will eventually form the basis of the student's thesis.

At the beginning of a research program, then, you need to establish answers to two key questions. First, what is the broad problem to be investigated? Second, what are the specific initial activities to undertake and outcomes to pursue? Having clear short-term research goals gives shape to a research program. It also gives the student training in the elements of research: planning, reading, programming, testing, analysis, critical thinking, writing, and presentation.

For example, in research in the early 1990s into algorithms for information retrieval, we observed that the time to retrieve documents from a repository could be reduced if they were first compressed; the cost of decompression after retrieval was outweighed by savings in transfer times. A broad research problem suggested by this topic is whether compression can be of benefit within a database even if the data is stored uncompressed. Pursuing this problem with a research student led to a specific initial research goal (used as a running example in Chapter 9): given a large relation that is compressed as it is read into memory, is it possible to sort it more rapidly than if it were not compressed at all? What kinds of compression algorithm are suitable? Success in these specific explorations leads to questions such as, where else in a database system can compression be used? Failure leads to questions such as, under what conditions might compression be useful?

When developing a question into a research topic, it is helpful to explore what makes the question interesting. Productive research is often driven by a strong motivating example, which also helps focus the activity towards useful goals. It is easy to explore problems that are entirely hypothetical, but difficult to evaluate the effectiveness of any solutions. Sometimes it is necessary to make a conscious decision to explore questions where work can be done, rather than where we would like to work; just as medical studies may involve molecular simulations rather than real patients, robotics may involve the artifice of soccer-playing rather than the reality of planetary exploration.

In choosing a topic and advisor, many students focus on the question of "is this the most interesting topic on offer?", often to the exclusion of other questions that are equally important. One such question is "is this advisor right for me?" Students and advisors form close working relationships that, in the case of a PhD, must endure for several years. The student is typically responsible for most of the effort, but the intellectual input is shared, and the relationship can grow over time to be a partnership of equals. However, most relationships have moments that are less than harmonious. Choosing the right person—considering the advisor as an individual, not just a respected researcher—is as important as choosing the right topic. A charismatic or famous advisor isn't necessarily likeable or easy to work with.

The fact that a topic is in a fashionable area should be at most a minor consideration; the fashion may well have passed before the student has graduated. Some trends are profound shifts that have ongoing effects, such as the opportunities created by the web for new technologies; others, such as the thin-client systems proposed in the late 1990s, are gone before they almost arrive. While it isn't necessarily obvious which category a new trend belongs in, a topic should not be investigated unless you are confident that it will continue to be relevant.

Another important question is, is this project at the right kind of technical level? Some brilliant students are neither fast programmers nor systems experts, while others do not have strong mathematical ability. It is not wise to select a project for which you do not have the skills or that doesn't make use of your particular strengths. An alternative perspective on this question is that most projects that are intellectually challenging are interesting to undertake; agonizing over whether it is *the* project may not be productive. However, it is also true that some researchers only enjoy their work if they can identify a broader value: for example, they can see likely practical outcomes. Highly speculative projects leave some people dissatisfied, while others are excited by a possible leap into the future.

Project scope is a related issue. Students can be wildly ambitious, entering research with the hope of achieving something of dramatic significance. However, major breakthroughs are by definition rare—otherwise they wouldn't be major—while, as most researchers discover, even incremental work can be profoundly rewarding. Moreover, an ambitious project creates a high potential for failure, especially in a limited-term context such as a minor thesis. There is a piece of folklore that says that most scientists do their best work in their PhD, as it is the one opportunity to undertake a lengthy, focused research program. This is a myth, and is certainly not a good reason for tackling a problem that is too large to resolve.

Most research is incremental: improvements or variants that improve or repair or extend or replace work done by others. The issue is the scope of the increment. A trivial step that does no more than explore the obvious solution to a simple problem—a change, say, to the fields in a network packet to save a couple of bits—is not worth investigating. There needs to be challenge and the possibility of unexpected discovery for research to be interesting.

For a novice researcher, it makes sense to identify easily achieved outcomes; this is research training, after all, not research olympics. If these outcomes are reached, in a well-designed project it should be easy to move on to more challenging goals.

Some research concerns problems that appear to be solved in commercial software. Often, however, research on such problems is not hard to justify. In a typical implementation the task is to find a workable solution, while in research the task is to measure the quality of the solution, and thus work on the same problem that produces similar solutions can nonetheless have different outcomes. Moreover, while it is in a company's interests to claim that a problem is solved by their technology, such claims are not easily verified. From this perspective, investigation of a problem for which there is already a commercial solution can be of more value than investigation of a problem of purely academic interest.

Students and advisors

The role of an advisor is a rich one. There are said to be as many scientific methods as there are scientists, but there are more advising styles than there are advisors. Every student–advisor relationship is different.

Advisors are powerful figures in their students' lives. Some professors at the peak of their careers still have strong views—often outrage or amazement—about their own advisors, despite many years of experience on the other side of the fence. Tales include that of the student who saw his advisor twice, once to choose a topic and once to submit; and that of the advisor who casually advised a student to "have another look at some of those famous open problems". Thankfully these are rare exceptions, and are even less acceptable today than they were a decade or two ago.

The purpose of a research program—a PhD, masters, or minor thesis—is for the university to provide a student with research training, while the student demonstrates the capability to undertake research from conception to write-up. A side-benefit is that the student, often with the advisor, should produce some publishable research. There are a range of approaches to advising that achieve these aims, but they are all based on the strategy of learning while doing.

Some advisors, for example, set their students problems such as verifying a proof in a published paper and seeing whether it can be applied to variants of the theorem, thus beginning to explore the limits at which the theorem no longer applies. Another example is to attempt to confirm someone else's results, by downloading code or by developing a fresh implementation. The difficulties encountered in such efforts are a fertile source of research questions. Other advisors immediately start their students on activities that are expected to lead to a research publication. It is in such cases that the model of advising as apprenticeship is most evident.

Typically, in the early stages the advisor specifies each small step the student should take: running a certain experiment, searching the literature to resolve a particular question, or writing one small section of a proposed paper. As students mature as researchers, they become more independent, often by anticipating what their advisors will ask, while advisors gradually leave more space for their students to assert this independence. Over time, the relationship becomes one of guidance rather than management.

The trade-offs implicit in such a relationship are complex. One is the question of authorship of work the student has undertaken, as discussed in Chapter 13. Another is the degree of independence. Advisors often believe that their students are either demanding or overconfident; students, on the other hand, can feel either confined by excessive control or at a loss due to being expected to undertake tasks without guidance. The needs of students who are working more or less alone may be very different to those of students who are part of an extended research group.

An area where the advisor's expertise is critical is in scoping the project. It needs to stand sufficiently alone from other current work, yet be relevant to a group's wider activities. It should be open enough to allow innovation and freedom, yet have a good likelihood of success. It should be close enough to the advisor's core expertise to allow the advisor to verify that the work is sufficiently novel, and to verify that the appropriate literature has been thoroughly explored. The fact that an advisor finds a topic interesting does not by itself justify asking a student to work on it. Likewise, a student who is keen on a topic must consider whether competent supervision is available in that area.

Advisors can be busy people. Prepare for your meetings—bring printouts of results or lists of questions, for example. Be honest; if you are trying to convince your advisor that you have completed some particular piece of work, then the work should have been done. Advisors are not fools. Saying that you have been reading for a week sounds like an excuse; and, if it is true, you probably haven't spent your time effectively.

The student–advisor relationship is not only concerned with research training, but is a means for advisors to be involved in research on a particular topic. Thus students and advisors often write papers together. At times, this can be a source of conflict, when, for example, an advisor wants a student to work on a paper while the student wants to make progress on a thesis. On the other hand, the involvement of the advisor—and the incentive for the advisor to take an active role—means that the research is undertaken as teamwork.

Finding research literature

Each research project builds on a body of prior work. The doing and describing of research requires a thorough knowledge of the work of others.

However, locating prior work can be a tremendous challenge. The number of papers published in computer science each year is at least tens of thousands. Not only is a great deal of this work relatively inaccessible, but the volume of it prohibits reading or understanding more than a fraction of the papers appearing in any one field.

A consolation is that, in an active field, other researchers have to a certain extent already explored and digested the older literature. Their work provides a guide to earlier research—as will your work, once it is published—and thus a complete exploration of the archives is rarely necessary. However, this is one more reason to carefully explore current work. And note: reading about a paper that seems relevant is *never* a substitute for reading the paper itself. If you need to discuss or cite a paper, read it first.

Comprehensively exploring relevant literature involves following several intertwined paths.

- Visit the web sites of research groups and researchers working in the area. The web site of your advisor or department is likely to be a good place to start. These sites should give several kinds of links into the wider literature: the names of researchers whose work you should investigate, the names of their co-authors, conferences where relevant work appears, and papers with lists of references to explore.
- Follow up references in research papers. These indicate relevant individuals, conferences, and journals.
- Browse the recent issues of the journals and conferences in the area; search other journals and conferences that might carry relevant papers.
- Use obvious search terms to explore the web. With the right terms you are likely to find the sites of projects and teams concerned with the same research area. You are also likely to find documents that suggest further valuable search terms.
- Search the publisher-specific digital libraries. These include publishers such as Wiley and Springer, and professional societies such as the ACM and IEEE. There are also a wide range of online archives and abstract-indexing services.
- Most conferences have web sites that list the program, that is, the papers to appear in the conference that year. Within a conference, papers are often grouped by topic—another hint of relevance.
- Use the citation indexes. The traditional printed citation indexes have migrated to the web, but in practice their value for computer science is limited, as only a fraction of publications are included. Of much greater value

are the public-domain indexes, which can be used to search by document content and by citing or cited document. Some of these are constructed automatically; others are built by contribution from users. Thus their contents are unreliable, and the origin of documents found in these indexes should be verified elsewhere.

- Go to the library. The simple strategy of having similar material shelved together often leads to unexpected discoveries, without the distractions that arise when web browsing.
- Discuss your work with as many people as possible. Some of them may well know of relevant work you haven't encountered. Similar problems often arise in disparate research areas, but the difficulties of keeping up with other fields—the phenomenon sometimes characterized as "working in silos"—mean that people investigating similar problems can be unaware of one another.

Take a broad definition of "relevant" when searching for papers. It doesn't just mean those papers that have, say, proposals for competing methods. Does the paper have interesting insights into other research literature? Does it establish a benchmark? Have the authors found a clever way of proving a theorem that you can apply in your own work? Does the paper justify not pursuing some particular line of investigation? Other people's research can have many different kinds of effect on your work.

Reading

A thorough search of the literature can easily lead to discovery of dozens or hundred of relevant papers—a volume of reading that can be deeply intimidating. However, papers are not textbooks, and should not be treated as textbooks. A researcher reading a paper is not cramming for an exam; there is rarely a need to understand every line. The number of papers that a researcher working on a particular project has to know well is usually small, even though the number the researcher should have read to establish their relevance is large. A brief browse through a paper takes no more than a few minutes, if the aim is to identify whether the paper is relevant to a particular project.

A problem with dredging the web for research literature is whether to believe what you read. Work published in a reputable journal or conference is peer-reviewed; work available online could have any history, from being a prepublication version of an accepted journal paper to plagiarised work taken from a non-English original and rejected from three conferences. A cynical but often accurate rule of thumb is that work that is more than one or two years old and has not been published in a reputable venue probably has some serious defect. When you find a version of a paper on the web, establish whether it has been published somewhere. Use evidence such as the quality of the authors' other publications to establish whether it is part of a serious program of research.

Much research—far too much—is just misguided. People investigate problems that are already solved and well understood, or solve problems that technology has made irrelevant, or try to square the circle (such as attempting to adjust optimal codes to achieve better compression), or don't realise that the proposed improvement actually makes the algorithm worse. Mathematics may be pointless; the wrong property may be proved, such as complexity instead of correctness; assumptions may be implausible; evaluation strategies may not make sense. The data set used may be so tiny that the results are meaningless; results on toy problems rarely scale up. Some results are just plain wrong.

And, while the fact that a paper is refereed is an indicator that it is of value, it is not a guarantee. Too many people submit work that did not deserve to be written; sometimes it gets published.

Indeed, few papers are perfect. They are a presentation of new work rather than a considered explanation of well-known results, and the constraints of writing to a deadline mean that mistakes are undiscovered and some issues unexplored. Some aspects of the work may be superseded or irrelevant, or may rely on false or limited or technically outdated assumptions. A paper can be seen as a snapshot of a research program at a moment in time—what the researchers knew when they submitted. For all these reasons, a reader needs to be questioning and skeptical.

But that does not justify researchers being dismissive of past work; rather, they should respect it and learn from it, because their own work will have the same strengths and weaknesses. While many papers may be flawed, they are the repository of all scientific knowledge—they define scientific knowledge. (Textbooks are almost invariably consolidations of older, established work that is no longer at the frontier.) Moreover, a general view that some papers are unreliable is a poor reason to neglect a particular paper with which you happen to disagree; it may contain an unpalatable truth. And this general view is an extremely poor reason to curtail either your reading or your attempts to understand the contributions made by others. If many researchers trust a particular paper, it is still reasonable to be skeptical of its results, but this needs to be balanced against the fact that, if skepticism is justified, these other researchers are all mistaken.

Read papers by asking questions of them, such as:

- What is the main result?
- How precise are the claims?
- How could the outcomes be used?
- What is the evidence?
- How was the evidence gathered?
- How were measurements taken?
- How carefully are the algorithms and experiments described?
- Why is the paper trustworthy?
- Has the right background literature been discussed?
- What would reproduction of the results involve?

That is, actively attempt to identify the contributions and shortcomings rather than simply reading from one end to the other. Detailed analysis can be difficult before you have developed the perspective of undertaking your own work, however. Literature review should continue alongside research, not precede it.

Capture information about each paper you expect to cite, or of even peripheral relevance. Many of the online services link to a `bibtex` citation; take a copy and annotate it with your own views on the paper. Classify the paper, and cross-index it with others on the same topic. Be organized with such material from the start—don't expect to have time to reinvestigate the literature in detail when completion date is looming.

Having explored the literature, you may discover that your original idea is not so original after all. If so, be honest—review your work to see what aspects may be novel, but don't fool yourself into working on a problem that is already solved. Occasionally it happens, for example, that the same problem has been investigated by several other teams over a considerable period. At the same time, the fact that other people have worked on the same problem does not mean that it is impossible to make further contributions in the area.

Research planning

Students commencing their first research project are accustomed to the patterns of undergraduate study: attending lectures, completing assignments, revising for exams. Activity is determined by a succession of deadlines that impose a great deal of structure.

In contrast, a typical research project has just one deadline: completion. Administrative requirements may impose some additional milestones, such as submission of a project outline or a progress report, but many students (and advisors) do not take these milestones seriously. However, having a series of deadlines is critical to the success of a project. The question then is, what should these deadlines be and how should they be determined?

Some people appear to plan their projects directly in terms of the aspects of the problem that attracted them in the first place. For example, they download some code or implement something, then experiment, then write up. A common failing that seems to arise with this approach to research is that each stage takes longer than anticipated, the time for write-up is compressed, and the final report is compromised. Yet the write-up is the only part of the work that survives or is assessed. Arguably, an even more significant failing is that the scientific validity of the outcomes can be compromised. It is a mistake, for example, to implement a complete system rather than ask what code is needed to explore the research questions.

A better approach to the task of scoping a project and setting milestones is to explicitly consider what is needed at the end, then reason backwards. The final thing required is the write-up in the form of a thesis, paper, or report; so plan in terms of the steps necessary to produce the write-up. Considering as an example research that is expected to have a substantial experimental component, the write-up is likely to involve a background review, explanations of previous and new algorithms, descriptions of experiments, and analysis of outcomes. Completion of each of these elements is a milestone.

Continuing to reason backwards, the next step is to identify what form the experiments will take. Chapter 11 concerns experiments and how they are reported, but prior to designing experiments the researcher must consider how they are to be used. What will the experiments show, assuming the hypothesis to be true? How will the results be different if the hypothesis is false? That is, the experiments are an evaluation of whether some hypothesised phenomena is actually observed. Experiments involve data, code, and some kind of platform. Running of experiments requires that all three of these be obtained, and that skeptical questions be asked about them: whether the data is realistic, for example.

Experiments may also involve users. Who will they be? Is ethics clearance required? Computer scientists, accustomed to working with algorithms and proofs, are often surprised by how wide-ranging their university ethics requirements can be.

Considering work that is not expected to have an experimental component, there are two general kinds: formal investigations of the properties of systems and algorithms; and a wide range of studies that are difficult to classify, from proposals for new programming language features and sketches of XML templates for particular kinds of data to reflections on and comparisons of trends in research. Each of these can be staged to identify research milestones.

Drawing these issues together, several themes emerge. One is that the components of research have to be identified; however, these components do not necessarily have to be completed in turn.

Another theme is that an attitude to research has been shaped: what information must be collected in order to convince a skeptical reader that the results are correct? Arguably, answering this one question is all that is needed to have a strong research outcome.

Having identified specific goals, another purpose of research planning is to estimate dates when milestones should be reached. One of the axioms of research, however, is that everything takes longer than planned for, even after taking this axiom into account. A standard research strategy is to first read the literature, then design, then analyse or implement, then test or evaluate, then write up. A more effective strategy is to overlap these stages as much as possible. Begin the implementation, or analysis, or write up as soon as it is reasonable to do so.

For the longer-term research of, for example, a PhD, other considerations become significant. A typical question in the later stages of a PhD is whether enough research has yet been done, or whether new additional work needs to be undertaken. Often the best response to this question is to write the thesis. Once your thesis is more or less complete, it is relatively easy to assess whether further work is justified. Doing such additional work in all likelihood involves filling a well-defined hole, a task that is much better defined than that of fumbling around for further questions to investigate.

Thus, rather than working to a schedule of long-term timelines that may be unrealistic, be flexible. Adjust the work you are doing on a day-to-day basis—pruning your research goals, giving more time to the writing, addressing whatever the current bottleneck happens to be—to ensure that you are reaching overall aims.

Hypotheses

The first stages of a research program involve identifying interesting topics or problems and focusing on particular issues to investigate. A typical way of giving direction to research is to develop specific questions that the program aims to answer. These questions are based on an understanding, an informal model perhaps, of how something works, or interacts, or behaves. They establish a framework for making observations about the object being studied. This framework can be characterised as a statement of belief about how the object behaves—in other words, a hypothesis.

In the traditional sciences, a hypothesis typically concerns some phenomenon in the physical world: whether something is occurring, or whether it is possible to alter something in a predictable way. Astronomy and genetics typify such research. In computer science, some hypotheses are of this kind. Other hypotheses involve construction, such as whether a proposed method is fit for a certain purpose, and solvability.

For example, a researcher investigating algorithms might ask as a *research question* whether it is possible to make better use of CPU cache to reduce computational costs; reducing the number of memory accesses can make a program faster even if the number of instructions executed is unchanged. Preliminary investigation might lead to the *hypothesis* that a particular sorting algorithm can be improved by replacing a tree-based structure with poor locality by an array-based structure with high locality. The *research goal* is to test this hypothesis. The *phenomenon* that should be observed if the hypothesis is correct is a trend: as the number of items to be sorted is increased, the tree-based method should increasingly show a high rate of cache misses compared to the array-based method. The *data* is the number of cache misses for several sets of items to be sorted.

A hypothesis should be specified clearly and precisely, and should be unambiguous. (The more loosely a concept is defined, the more easily it will satisfy many needs simultaneously, even when these are contradictory.) Often it is important to state what is *not* being proposed—what the limits on the conclusions will be. Consider an example. Suppose P-lists are a well-known data structure used for a range of applications, in particular as an in-memory search structure that is fast and compact. A scientist has developed a new data structure called the Q-list. Formal analysis has shown the two structures to have the same asymptotic complexity in both space and time, but the scientist intuitively believes the Q-list to be superior in practice and has decided to demonstrate this by experiment.

(This motivation by belief, or instinct, is a crucial element of the process of science: since ideas cannot be known to be correct when first conceived, it is intuition or plausibility that suggests them as worthy of consideration. That is, the investigation may well have been undertaken for subjective reasons; but the final report on the research, the published paper, must be objective.)

The hypothesis might be encapsulated as

✗ Q-lists are superior to P-lists.

But this statement does not suffice as the basis of experiment: success would have to apply in all applications, in all conditions, for all time. Formal analysis might be able to justify such a result, but no experiment will be so far-reaching. In any case, it is rare indeed for a data structure to be completely superseded—consider the durability of arrays and linked lists—so in all probability this hypothesis is incorrect. A testable hypothesis might be

✓ As an in-memory search structure for large data sets, Q-lists are faster and more compact than P-lists.

Further qualification may well be necessary.

✓ We assume there is a skew access pattern, that is, that the majority of accesses will be to a small proportion of the data.

The qualifying statement imposes a scope on the claims made on behalf of Q-lists. A reader of the hypothesis has enough information to reasonably conclude that Q-lists do not suit a certain application, which in no way invalidates the result. Another scientist would be free to explore the behaviour of Q-lists under another set of conditions, in which they might be inferior to P-lists, but again the original result remains valid.

As the example illustrates, a hypothesis must be testable. One aspect of testability is that the scope be limited to a domain that can feasibly be explored. Another, crucial aspect is that the hypothesis should be capable of falsification. Vague claims are unlikely to meet this criterion.

✗ Q-list performance is comparable to P-list performance.

✗ Our proposed query language is relatively easy to learn.

The exercise of refining and clarifying a hypothesis may expose that it is not worth pursuing. For example, if complex restrictions must be imposed to make the hypothesis work, or if it is necessary to assume that current insoluble problems need to be addressed before the work can be used, how interesting is the research?

A form of research where poor hypotheses seem particularly common is "black box" work, where the black box is an algorithm whose properties are incompletely understood. For example, some research consists of applying a black-box learning algorithm to new data, with the outcome that the results are an improvement on a baseline method. (Often, the claim is to the effect that "our black box is significantly better than random".) The apparent ability of these black boxes to solve problems without creative input from a scientist attracts research of low value. A weakness of such research is that it provides no learning about the data or the black box, and has no implications for other investigations. In particular, such results rarely tell us whether the same behaviour would occur the next time the same approach was used.

A related problem is the renaming fallacy, often observed in the work of scientists who are attempting to reposition their research within a fashionable area. Calling a network cache a "local storage agent" doesn't change its behaviour, and if the term "agent" can legitimately be applied to any executable process then its explanatory power is slim. Another instance: a paper on natural language processing for "web documents" should concern some issues specific to the web, not just any text; a debatable applicability to the web does not add to the contribution. And another: it seems unlikely that a text indexing algorithm is made "intelligent" by improvements to the parsing. Renaming existing research to place it in another field is bad science.

It may be necessary to refine a hypothesis as a result of initial testing; indeed, much of scientific progress can be viewed as refinement and development of hypotheses to fit new observations. Occasionally there is no room for refinement, a classic example being Einstein's prediction of the deflection of light by massive bodies—a hypothesis much exposed to disproof, since it was believed that significant deviation from the predicted value would invalidate the theory of general relativity. But more typically a hypothesis evolves in tandem with refinements in the experiments.

This is not, however, to say that the hypothesis should follow the experiments. A hypothesis will often be based on observations, but can only be regarded as confirmed if able to make successful predictions. There is a vast difference between an observation such as "the algorithm worked on our data" and a tested hypothesis such as "the algorithm was predicted to work on any data of this class, and this prediction has been confirmed on our data". Another way of regarding this issue is that, as far as possible, tests should be blind. If an experiment and hypothesis have been fine-tuned on the data, it cannot be said that the experiment provides confirmation. At best the experiment has provided observations on which the hypothesis is based.

Where two hypotheses fit the observations equally well and one is clearly simpler than the other, the simpler should be chosen. This principle, known as

Occam's razor, is purely a convenience; but it is well-established and there is certainly no reason to choose a complex explanation when another is at hand.

Defending hypotheses

One component of a strong paper is a precise, interesting hypothesis. Another component is the testing of the hypothesis and the presentation of the supporting evidence. As part of the research process you need to test your hypothesis and if it is correct—or, at least, not falsified—assemble supporting evidence. For the presentation of the hypothesis you need to construct an argument relating your hypothesis to the evidence.

For example, the hypothesis "the new range searching method is faster than previous methods" might be supported by the evidence "range search amongst n elements requires $2\log_2 \log_2 n + c$ comparisons". This may or may not be good evidence, but it is not convincing because there is no argument connecting the evidence to the hypothesis. What is missing is information such as "previous results indicated a complexity of $\Theta(\log n)$". It is the role of the connecting argument to show that the evidence does indeed support the hypothesis, and to show that conclusions have been drawn correctly.

In constructing an argument, it can be helpful to imagine yourself defending your hypothesis to a colleague, so that you play the role of inquisitor. That is, raising objections and defending yourself against them is a way of gathering the material needed to convince the reader that your argument is correct. Starting from the hypothesis that "the new string hashing algorithm is fast because it doesn't use multiplication or division" you might debate as follows:

- I don't see why multiplication and division are a problem.

  On most machines they use several cycles, or may not be implemented in hardware at all. The new algorithm instead uses two exclusive-or operations per character and a modulo in the final step. I agree that for pipelined machines with floating-point accelerators the difference may not be great.

- Modulo isn't always in hardware either.

  True, but it is only required once.

- So there is also an array lookup? That can be slow.

  Not if the array is cache-resident.

- What happens if the hash table size is not 2^8?

Good point. This function is most effective for hash tables of size 2^8, 2^{16}, and so on.

In an argument you need to rebut likely objections while conceding points that can't be rebutted and admitting when you are uncertain. If, in the process of developing your hypothesis, you raised an objection but reasoned it away, it can be valuable to include the reasoning in the paper. Doing so helps the reader to follow your train of thought, and certainly helps the reader who independently raises the same objection. That is, you need to anticipate problems the reader may have with your hypothesis. Likewise, you should actively search for counter-examples.

If you think of an objection that you cannot refute, don't just put it aside. At the very least you should raise it yourself in the paper, but it may well mean that you must reconsider your results.

A hypothesis can be tested in a preliminary way by considering its effect, that is, by examining whether there is a simple argument for keeping or discarding it. For example, are there any improbable consequences if the hypothesis is true? If so, there is a good chance that the hypothesis is wrong. For a hypothesis that displaces or contradicts some currently held belief, is the contradiction such that the belief can only have been held out of stupidity? Again, the hypothesis is probably wrong. Does the hypothesis cover all of the observations explained by the current belief? If not, the hypothesis is probably uninteresting.

Always consider the possibility that your hypothesis is wrong. It is often the case that a correct hypothesis at times seems dubious—perhaps initially, before it is fully developed, or when it appears to be contradicted by some experimental evidence—but the hypothesis survives and is even strengthened by test and refinement in the face of doubt. But equally often a hypothesis is false, in which case clinging to it is a waste of time. Persist for long enough to establish whether or not it is likely to be true, but to persist longer is foolish.

A corollary is that the stronger your intuitive liking for a hypothesis, the more rigorously you should test it—attempt to confirm it or disprove it—rather than twist results, and yourself, defending it.

Be persuasive. Using research into the properties of an algorithm as an example, issues such as the following need to be addressed.

- Will the reader believe that the algorithm is new?

  Only if the researcher does a careful literature review, and fully explores and explains previous relevant work. Doing so includes giving credit to significant advances, and not overrating work where the contribution is small.

- Will the reader believe that the algorithm is sensible?

  It had better be explained carefully. Potential problems should be identified, and either conceded—with an explanation, for example, of why the algorithm is not universally applicable—or dismissed through some cogent argument.

- Are the experiments convincing?

  If the code isn't good enough to be made publicly available, is it because there is something wrong with it? Has the right data been used? Has enough data been used?

Every research program suggests its own questions. Such questioning is also appropriate later in a research program, where it provides an opportunity for critical assessment of the work.

Evidence

A view of papers is that they are an assembly of evidence and supporting explanation, that is, an attempt to persuade others to share your conclusions. In a write-up you pose a hypothesis, then present evidence to support your case. The evidence needs to be convincing because the processes of science rely on readers being critical and skeptical; there is no reason for a reader to be interested in work that is inconclusive. There are, broadly speaking, four kinds of evidence that can be used to support a hypothesis: analysis or proof, modelling, simulation, and experiment.

An analysis or proof is a formal argument that the hypothesis is correct. It is a mistake to suppose that the correctness of a proof is absolute—confidence in a proof may be high, but that does not guarantee that it is free from error. (In my experience it is not uncommon for a researcher to feel certain that a theorem is correct but have doubts about the mechanics of the proof, which all too often leads to the discovery that the theorem is wrong after all.) And it is a mistake to suppose that all hypotheses are amenable to formal analysis, particularly hypotheses that involve the real world in some way. For example, human behaviour is intrinsic to questions about interface design, and system properties can be intractably complex. Consider an exploration to determine whether a new method is better than a previous one at compressing text—is it likely that something as diverse as text can be modelled well enough to predict the performance of a compression algorithm? It is also a mistake to suppose that a complexity analysis is always sufficient. Nonetheless, the possibility of formal analysis should never be overlooked.

A model is a mathematical description of the hypothesis (or some component of the hypothesis such as an algorithm whose properties are being considered) and there will usually be a demonstration that the hypothesis and model do indeed correspond.

In choosing to use a model, consider how realistic it will be, or conversely how many simplifying assumptions need to be made for analysis to be feasible. Consider the example of modelling the cost of a Boolean query on a text collection, in which the task is to find the documents that contain each of a set of words. We need to estimate the frequency of each word (because words that are frequent in queries may be rare in documents); the likelihood of query terms occurring in the same document (in practice, query terms are thematically related, and do not model well as random co-occurrences); the fact that longer documents contain more words, but are more expensive to fetch; and, in a practical system, the probability that the same query had been issued recently and the answers are cached in memory. It is possible to define a model based on these factors, but, with so much guesswork to make, it is unlikely that the model would be realistic.

A simulation is usually an implementation or partial implementation of a simplified form of the hypothesis, in which the difficulties of a full implementation are sidestepped by omission or approximation. At one extreme a simulation might be skeletal, so that, for example, a parallel algorithm could be tested on a sequential machine by use of an interpreter that counts machine cycles and communication costs between simulated processors; at the other extreme a simulation could be an implementation of the hypothesis, but tested by artificial data. A simulation is a "white coats" test: artificial, isolated, and conducted in a tightly controlled environment.

An experiment is a full test of the hypothesis, based on an implementation of the proposal and on real—or at least realistic—data. In an experiment there is a sense of *really doing it*, while in a simulation there is a sense of *only pretending*. However, the distinction between simulation and experiment can be blurry.

Ideally an experiment should be conducted in the light of predictions made by a model, so that it confirms some expected behaviour. An experiment should be severe; look for tests that are likely to fail if the hypothesis is false. The traditional sciences, and physics in particular, proceed in this way. Theoreticians develop models of phenomena that fit known observations; experimentalists seek confirmation through fresh experiments.

Different forms of evidence can be used to confirm one another, with say a simulation used to provide further evidence that a proof is correct. But they should not be confused with one another. For example, suppose that for some algorithm there is a mathematical model of expected performance. Encoding this model in a program and computing predicted performance for certain values of the model parameters is in no way an experimental test of the algorithm and should never be called an experiment; it does not even confirm that the model is a description of the algorithm. At best it confirms claimed properties of the model.

When choosing whether to use a proof, model, simulation, or experiment as evidence, consider how convincing each is likely to be to the reader. If your evidence is questionable—say a model based on simplifications and assumptions, an involved algebraic analysis and application of advanced statistics, or an experiment on limited data—the reader may well be skeptical of the result. Select a form of evidence, not so as to keep your own effort to a minimum, but to be as persuasive as possible.

Having identified the elements a research plan should cover, end-to-start reasoning also suggests priorities. The write-up is the most important thing; so perhaps it should be started first. Completing the report is certainly more important than hastily running some last-minute experiments, or quickly browsing the literature to make it appear as if past work has been fully evaluated.

Good and bad science

Questions about the quality of evidence can be used to evaluate other people's research, and provide an opportunity to reflect on whether the outcomes of your work are worthwhile. There isn't a simple division of research into "good" and "bad", but it is not difficult to distinguish valuable research from work that is weak or pointless.

The merits of formal studies are easy to appreciate. They provide the kind of mathematical link between the possible and the practical that physics provides between the universe and engineering.

The merits of well-designed experimental work are also clear. Work that experimentally confirms or contradicts the correctness of formal studies has historically been undervalued in computer science: perhaps because standards for experimentation have not been high; perhaps because the great diversity of computer systems, languages, and data has made truly general experiments difficult to devise; perhaps because theoretical work with advanced mathematics is more intellectually imposing than work that some people regard as mere code-cutting. However, many questions cannot be readily answered through analysis, and a theory without practical confirmation is no more interesting in computing than in the rest of science.

However, research that consists of proposals—without a serious attempt at evaluation—can be more difficult to respect. Why should a reader regard such work as valid? If the author cannot offer anything to measure, arguably it isn't science. As discussed in Chapter 11, there are many ways of measuring a system or result. And research isn't theoretical just because it isn't experimental. Theoretical work describes testable theories.

Some science is not simply weak, but can be classed as pseudoscience. A great deal of money can be made by appearing to have solved major problems, and scientists seek prestige through their research achievements. Inevitably, some claimed achievements are delusional or bogus.

Pseudoscience is a broad label covering a range of scientific sins, from self-deception and confusion to outright fraud. A definition is that pseudoscience is work that uses the language and respectability of science to gain credibility for statements that are not based on evidence that meets scientific standards. Much pseudoscience shares a range of characteristics: the results and ideas don't seem to develop over time, systems are never quite ready for demonstration, the work proceeds in a vacuum and is unaffected by other advances, protagonists argue rather than seek evidence, and the results are inconsistent with accepted facts. Often such work is strenuously promoted by one individual or a small number of devotees while the rest of the scientific community ignores it.

An example of pseudoscience in commercial computing is some of the schemes for high-performance video compression, which promise delivery of TV-quality data over 56 kilobaud modems. The commercial implications of such systems are enormous, and this incentive creates ample opportunities for fraud; in one case, for example, millions of dollars were scammed from investors with tricks such as hiding a video player inside a PC tower and hiding a network cable inside a power cable. Yet, skeptically considered, such schemes are implausible. For example, with current technology, even a corner of a single TV-resolution image—let alone 25 frames per second—cannot be compressed into 7 kilobytes. Uncompressed, the bandwidth of a modem is only sufficient for one byte per row per image, or, per image, about the space needed to transmit a desktop icon. A further skeptical consideration in this case was that an audio signal was also transmitted. Had the system been legitimate, the inventor must have solved the independent problems of image compression, motion encoding, and audio compression.

It is not hard to find similar work in the academic world. An example is the variety of "universal" indexing methods that have been proposed. In these methods, the object to be indexed—whether an image, movie, audio file, or text document—is manipulated in some way, for example by a particular kind of hash function. After this manipulation, objects of different type can be compared: thus, somehow, documents about swimming pools and images of swimming pools would have the same representation. Such matching is clearly an extremely difficult problem, if not entirely insoluble; for instance, how does the method know to focus on the swimming pool rather than some other element of the image, such as children, sunshine, or a metaphor for middle class aspirations? Yet proposals for such methods continue to appear. In a recent version, objects of the same type were clustered together using some kind of similarity metric. Then the patterns of clustering were analysed, and objects that clustered in similar ways were supposed to have similar subject matter. Although it is disguised by the use of clustering, to be successful such an approach assumes an underlying universal matching method.

In some work, the evidence or methods are inconsistent. For example, in a paper on how to find documents on a particular topic, the authors reported that the method correctly identified 20,000 matches in a large document collection. But this is a deeply improbable outcome. The figure of 20,000 hints at imprecision—it is too round a number. More significantly, verifying that all 20,000 were matches would require many months of effort. No mention was made of the the documents that weren't matches, implying that the method was 100% accurate; but even the best document-matching methods have high error rates. A later paper by the same authors gave entirely different results for the same method, while claiming similar good results for a new method, thus throwing doubt on the whole research program. And it is a failure of logic to suppose that the fact that two documents match according to some arbitrary algorithm implies that the match is useful to a user.

The logic underlying some papers is downright mystifying. It may seem a major step to identify and solve a new problem, but such steps can go too far. A paper on retrieval for a specific form of graph used a new query language and matching technique, a new way of evaluating similarity, and data based on a new technique for deriving the graphs from text and semantically labelling the edges. Every element of this paper was a separate contribution whose merit could be disputed. Presented in a brief paper, the work seemed worthless. Inventing a problem, a solution to the problem, and a measure of the solution—all without external justification—is a widespread form of bad science.

An interesting question is how to regard "Zipf's law". This observation—"law" seems a poor choice of terminology in this context—is if nothing else a curious case study. Zipf's books may be widely cited but they are not, I suspect, widely read. In *Human Behaviour and the Principle of Least Effort* (Addison-Wesley, 1949), Zipf used languages and word frequencies as one of several examples to illustrate his observation, but his motivation for the work is not quite what might be expected. He states, for example, that his research "define[s] objectively what we mean by the term personality" (p. 18), explains the "drives of the Freudian death wish" (p. 17), and "will provide an objective language in terms of which persons can discuss social problems impersonally" (p. 543). It "will help to protect mankind from the virtual criminal action of persons in strategic political, commercial, social, intellectual and academic positions" (p. 544) and "as the authority of revealed religion and its attendant ethics declines, something must take its place ... I feel that this type of research may yield results that will fulfill those needs" (p. 544). Perhaps these extraordinary claims are quirks, and in any case opinions do not invalidate scientific results. But it has been argued that the behaviour captured by Zipf's conjecture is a simple consequence of randomness, and, for the motivating example for which the conjecture is often cited (distribution of words in text), the fit between hypothesis and observation is not always strong.

A lesson is that we need to be wary of claimed results, not only because we might disagree for technical reasons but because the behaviour of other researchers may not be objective or reasonable. Another lesson is that acceptance of (or silence about) pseudoscience erodes the perceived need for responsible research, and that it is always reasonable to ask skeptical questions. Yet another lesson is that we need to take care to ensure that our own research is well founded. When results are defended by assertion, with no evaluation or evidence, it is easy to wonder whether the work is an instance of pseudoscience.

Reflections on research

Philosophies and definitions of science establish guidelines for what scientists do and set boundaries on what we can know. However, there are limits to how precise (or interesting) such definitions can be. For example, the question "is computer science a science?" has a low information content.[14] Questions of this kind are sometimes in terms of definitions of science such as "a process

[14]Two philosophers are arguing in a bar. The barman goes over to them and asks, "What are you arguing about?"

"We're debating whether computer science is a science", answers one of them.

"And what do you conclude?" asks the barman.

"We're not sure yet," says the other. "We can't agree on what 'is' means."

for discovering laws that model observed natural phenomena". Such definitions not only exclude disciplines such as computing, but also exclude much of the research now undertaken in disciplines such as biology and medicine. In considering definitions of science, a certain degree of skepticism is valuable; these definitions are made by scientists working within particular disciplines and within the viewpoints that those disciplines impose. In fairness, I note that the views below have the same limitations, as they are those of a computer scientist who believes that the discipline stands alongside the traditional sciences.

It is true that, considered as a science, computing is difficult to categorize. The underlying theories—information theory and computability, for example—appear to describe properties as eternal as those of physics. (Such properties can be seen as constraints separating the possible from the impossible.) In recent years the distinction between the laws of computing and the laws of physics has blurred, with for example properties of black holes being described by information theory. Yet most research in computer science is many steps removed from foundational theory and more closely resembles engineering or psychology.

A widely agreed description of science is that it is a method for accumulating reliable knowledge. In this viewpoint, scientists adopt the belief that rationality and skepticism are how we learn about the universe and shape new principles, while recognizing that this belief limits the application of science to those ideas that can be examined in a logical way. If the arguments and experiments are sound, if the theory can withstand skeptical scrutiny, if the work was undertaken within a framework of past research and provides a basis for further discovery, then it is science. Much computer science has this form.

Many writers and philosophers have debated the nature of science, and aspects of it such as the validity of different approaches to reasoning. The direct impact of this debate on the day-to-day activity of scientists is small, but it has undoubtedly shaped how scientists approach their work. It also provides elements of the ethical framework within which scientists work.

A key effect of philosophy on the practice of science has been to undermine belief in certainty and absolute scientific truth. Several developments in the early years of the twentieth century contributed to this development, including relativity, quantum mechanics, incompleteness, and undecidability. In philosophy, the ideal of scientific truth was undermined by the concept of falsification. The core idea is simple: experimental evidence, no matter how substantial or voluminous, cannot prove a theory true, while a single counter-example can prove a theory false.

A practical consequence of the principle of falsification is that a reasonable scientific method is to search for counter-examples to hypotheses. In this line of reasoning, to search for supporting evidence is pointless, as such evidence cannot tell us that the theory is true. A drawback of this line of reasoning is that, using falsification alone, we cannot learn any new theories; we can only learn that some theories are wrong. Another issue is that, in practice, experiments are often unsuccessful, but the explanation is not that the hypothesis is wrong, but rather that some other assumption was wrong. The response of a scientist to a failed experiment may well be to redesign it. For example, in the decades-long search for gravity waves, there have been many unsuccessful experiments, but a general interpretation of these experiments has been that they show that the equipment is insufficiently sensitive.

Thus falsification can be a valuable guide to the conduct of research, but other guides are also required if the research is to be productive. One such guide is the concept of confirmation. In science, "confirmation" has a weaker meaning than in general usage; when a theory is confirmed, the intended meaning is not that the theory is proved, but that the weight of belief in the theory has been strengthened. Seeking experiments that confirm theories is an alternative reasonable view of method.

A further consequence is that a hypothesis should allow some possibility of being disproved—there should be some experiment whose outcomes could show that they hypothesis is wrong. If not, the hypothesis is simply uninteresting. Consider, for example, the hypothesis "a search engine can find interesting web pages in response to queries". It is difficult to see how this supposition might be contradicted. Thus falsification and other descriptions of method help shape research questions as well as research processes.

A research checklist

- Are the ideas clear and consistent?
- Is the problem worthy of investigation?
- Does the project have appropriate scope?
- What are the specific research questions?
- Is there a hypothesis?
- What would disprove the hypothesis? Does it have any improbable consequences?
- Are the premises sensible?

- Has the work been critically questioned? Have you satisfied yourself that it is sound science?
- How are the outcomes to be evaluated? Why are the chosen methods of evaluation appropriate or reasonable?
- Are the roles of the participants clear? What are your responsibilities? What activities will the others undertake?
- What are the likely weaknesses of your solution?
- Is there a written research plan?
- What forms of evidence are to be used?
- Have milestones, timelines, and deadlines been identified?
- Do the deadlines leave enough time for your advisor to provide feedback on your drafts, or for your colleagues to contribute to the material?
- Has the literature been explored in appropriate depth? Once the work is largely done—and your perspective has changed—does it need to be explored again?

11 Experimentation

There are as many scientific methods
as there are individual scientists.

Percy W. Bridgman
On "Scientific Method"

A hypothesis is ... a mere trial idea, a tentative
suggestion concerning the nature of things. Until
it has been tested, it should not be confused with a
law .... Plausibility is not a substitute for evidence,
however great may be the emotional wish to believe.

E. Bright Wilson, Jr.
An Introduction to Scientific Research

Even the clearest and most perfect circumstantial
evidence is likely to be at fault, after all, and
therefore ought to be received with great caution.

Mark Twain
Pudd'nhead Wilson's Calendar

The use of experiments to verify hypotheses is one of the central elements of science. In computing, experiments—most commonly an implementation tried against test data—are used for purposes such as confirming hypotheses about algorithms. An experiment can verify, for example, that a system can complete a specified task, and can do so with reasonable use of resources. A tested hypothesis becomes part of scientific knowledge if it is sufficiently well described and constructed, and if it is convincingly demonstrated.

Experiments in computing take diverse forms, from tests of algorithm performance to human factors analysis. However, the principles underlying good experimentation are much the same regardless of what is being investigated. As elsewhere in this book, the material here draws on my experience as a researcher. These examples are for the most part work that was successful—which is not to imply that all my research has succeeded to this extent.

Some people disagree with the view that rigorous experiments are essential in computer science; or, if they do not explicitly disagree, may hold a low opinion of papers that have no new theory and are "merely" experimental. Yet, for example, such views are in stark contrast to the role of experiments in other disciplines. Experiments are an essential part of sound science.

Designing experiments

Tests should be fair rather than constructed to support the hypothesis. This problem is arguably most acute when a new idea is being compared to an existing one. In this case, the test environment should be designed to be seen as reasonable by readers who support the existing idea. If the tests seem biased towards the new idea, these readers will not be persuaded by the results.

You need to carefully choose which method your contribution is to be compared to. That is, it is essential to identify an appropriate *baseline*. For example, no sensible researcher would advocate that their sorting algorithm was a breakthrough on the basis that it is faster than bubblesort; instead, the algorithm should be compared to the best previous method.

It may be that comparison to a baseline is difficult because it means that an implementation for a competing method must be obtained. However, without such a comparison it may be impossible for the reader to know whether the new method is interesting. This is a barrier to entry: before you can begin to produce competitive work in an area, it is necessary to not only become familiar with the methods and ideas described in a body of literature but also to have access to a collection of appropriate tools and resources. But the fact that there is a barrier to entry does not excuse poor science.

A danger in an ongoing research program is to fail to update the choice of baseline. In the context of text indexing, for example, early work on signature files compared performance to that of inverted files as reported in papers from before 1980. (One of these papers gave a figure for inverted file size of

50%–300% of the indexed data; simple skeptical considerations suggest that the larger figure does not make sense.) Work on signature files even in the late 1990s continued to quote these baselines, despite dramatic improvements in inverted files and detailed experiments reporting sizes such as 7%–10%. New work in signature files was compared to old work in the same area, but not to relevant work on other pertinent technology.

Some new algorithms solve a novel problem, or solve an existing problem in a novel way that is for some reason not comparable to previous work. There may still be a clear baseline to compare to, however. For example, there may be an obvious algorithm that an intelligent, informed person might use if asked to solve the problem. That is, one potential point of comparison is the first workable option that a reasonable person might suggest.

In the process of developing new algorithms, researchers typically use a data set with which they are familiar as a testbed. If the algorithm is parameterized in some way—by buffer size, say—this testbed can be used for tuning, that is, to identify the parameter values that give the best performance. What this tuning process almost certainly cannot do is identify the best parameters for all data sets, or even identify whether there are stable best parameters to choose. It is for this reason that descriptions of the research cycle strongly distinguish between an observation phase (used to learn about the object under study) and a testing or confirmation phase (used to validate hypotheses). If parameters have been derived by tuning, the only way to establish their validity is to see if they give good behaviour on other data. Choosing parameters to suit data, or choosing data to suit parameters, in all likelihood invalidates the research.

When considering what experiments to try, identify the cases in which the hypothesis is least likely to hold. These are the interesting cases: if they are not tested—if only the cases where the hypothesis is most likely to hold are tested—then the experiments won't prove much at all. The experiment should of course be a test of the hypothesis; you need to verify that what you are testing is what you intended to test, and an experiment should only succeed if the hypothesis is correct.

When checking experimental design or outcomes, consider whether there are other possible interpretations of the results; and if so, design further tests to eliminate these possibilities. Consider for instance the problem of finding whether a file stored on disk contains a given string. One algorithm directly scans the file; another algorithm, which has been found to give faster response, scans a compressed form of the file. Further tests would be needed to identify whether the speed gain was because the second algorithm used fewer machine cycles or because the compressed file was fetched more quickly from disk.

Care is particularly needed when checking the outcome of negative or failed experiments. A reader of the statement "we have shown that it is not possible to make further improvement" may wonder whether what has actually been shown is that the author is not competent to make further improvement. Moreover, the failure of an experiment typically leads to it being redesigned—such failure is as likely to expose problems in the tests as in the hypothesis itself. Design of experiments to demonstrate failure is particularly difficult.

It is also worth considering whether the results obtained are sensible. For example, are there rules of conservation that should apply to this experiment? Sometimes boundary conditions are highly predictable—do the results appear to be right as they approach the boundaries? For a typical case it should be possible to make a rough guess as to expected outcome—is this observed?

Conclusions should be sufficiently supported by the results. Success in a special case does not prove success in general, so be aware of factors in the test that may make it special. A common problem is scale—whether the same result would be observed with a larger data set, for example.

Don't draw undue conclusions or inferences. If, say, one method is faster than another on a large data set, and they are of the same speed on a medium data set, that does not imply that the second is faster on a small data set; it only implies that different costs dominate at different scales. Also, don't overstate your conclusions. For example, if a new algorithm is somewhat worse than an existing one, it is wrong to describe them as equivalent. A reader might infer that they are equivalent if the difference is small, but it is not honest for you to make that claim.

Experiments should as far as possible be independent of the accuracy of measurements or quality of the implementation. Ideally an experiment should be designed to yield a result that is unambiguously either true or false; where this is not possible, another form of confirmation is to demonstrate a trend or pattern of behaviour.

A simple example is the behaviour of query evaluation on a database system with and without indexes. For a small database, the most efficient solution is exhaustive search, because use of an index involves access to auxiliary structures and does not greatly reduce the cost of accessing the data. As database size grows, the cost of data access grows linearly, while index access costs may be more or less fixed. Thus the hypothesis "indexes reduce search cost in large databases" can be confirmed by experiments measuring search costs with and without indexes over a range of database sizes. The trend—that the advantage given by indexes increases with database size—is independent of the machine and data. The exact size at which indexes become beneficial will vary, but this value is not being studied; it is the trend that is being studied.

That is, success or otherwise should be obvious, not subject to interpretation. An example of this principle is the work of Pons and Fleischman on cold fusion. Their claims of success were founded on small discrepancies—only a few percent—between measured input energy and output energy. Admission of only a small experimental error would confound their claims. In contrast, the claims that they had failed were based on the almost complete absence of a particular form of radiation, effectively a straightforward binary test.

Another example of this principle is provided by the various improvements that can be made to the standard quicksort algorithm, such as better choice of pivot and loops that avoid expensive procedure calls. With test data chosen to exercise the various cases—such as initially unsorted, initially sorted, or many repetitions of some values—experiments can show that the improvements do indeed lead to faster sorting. What such experiments cannot show is that quicksort is inherently better than, say, mergesort. While it might, for example, be possible to deduce that the same kinds of improvement do not yield benefits for mergesort, nothing can be deduced about the relative merits of the algorithms because the relative quality of the implementations is unknown, and because the data has not been selected to examine trends such as asymptotic performance.

For speed experiments based on a series of runs, the published results will be either minimum, average, median, or maximum times. Maximum times can include anomalies, such as a run during which a greedy process (a tape dump, for example) shuts out other processes. Minimums can be underestimates, for example when the time slice allocated to a process does not include any clock ticks. But nor are averages always appropriate—outlying points may be the result of system dependencies. Statistical considerations are discussed later.

Results may include some anomalies or peculiarities. These should be explained or at least discussed. Don't discard anomalies unless you are certain they are irrelevant; they may represent problems you haven't considered.

✓ As the graph shows, the algorithm was much slower on two of the data sets. We are still investigating this behaviour.

It is likewise valuable to discuss behaviour at limits and to explain trends.

Measurements and coding

The purpose of experimentation is to take measurements that can be used as evidence. The measurements are intended to be a consequence of some underlying phenomenon that is described by a theory or hypothesis. In this approach to research, phenomena—the eternal truths studied by science—cannot change, but the measurements can, because they depend on the context of the specific experiment.

Measurements can be quantitative, such as number or duration or volume—the speed of a system, say, or an algorithm's efficiency relative to a baseline. They can also be qualitative, such as occurrence or difference—whether an outcome was achieved, or whether particular features were observed. Measurements can be mechanical or human.

In the approach to research planning outlined in Chapters 9 and 10, one of the first steps is deciding what to measure. In computer science research, the sole reason for coding is to build tools and probes for observing and measuring phenomena. Thus the choice of what to measure guides the process of coding and implementation—or, perhaps, indicates what does not have to be coded.

The basic rule is to keep things simple. If efficiency is not being measured, for example, don't waste time squeezing cycles from code. If a database join algorithm is being measured, it is probably not necessary to implement indexes, and it is almost certainly unnecessary to write an SQL interpreter. All too often, computer scientists get distracted from the main task of producing research tools, and instead, for example, develop complete systems. A related principle is that of "one task, one tool". In most cases, integrating the code for every research task into a single piece of software is simply unproductive.

In environments such as the Unix family of operating systems, a program is often tested by being run from the command-line, with output directed to the screen. Parameters may be passed in as arguments, but to simplify coding they may be defined as constants within programs. All too often, though, a researcher discovers that an experiment run in this way cannot be repeated a day or two later.

A more reliable, repeatable approach is to run all experiments from scripts. Parameter settings are captured within the script; the settings used last time can be commented out. Output from the script can be directed to a logfile and kept indefinitely. If the output is well designed, it should include information such as input file names, code versions, parameter values, and date and time.

Using simple Unix tools it is straightforward to take data directly from a log file and produce a graph or other summary of the results. These steps too can be encoded in a script; the process for completing any stages undertaken by hand may well be forgotten if the work is rested for a few months, such as while a paper is under review. A corollary is that the output of your code should be amenable to scripting, with, for example, consideration given to consistent use of fields in each line.

Describing experiments

Your interpretation and understanding of the results is as important as the results themselves. When describing the outcomes of an experiment, don't just compile dry lists of figures or a sequence of graphs. Analyze the results and explain their significance, select typical results and explain why they are typical, theorize about anomalies, show why the results confirm or disprove the hypothesis, and make the results interesting. That is, motivate the work.

Experiments are only valuable if they are carefully described. The description should reflect the care taken—it should be clear to the reader that the possible problems were considered and addressed, and that the experiments do indeed provide confirmation (or otherwise) of the hypothesis. A key principle is that the experiment should be verifiable and reproducible. Results are valueless if they are some kind of singleton event: repetition of the experiment should yield the same outcomes. And results are equally valueless if they cannot be repeated by other researchers. The description, of both hypothesis and experiment, should be in sufficient detail to allow some form of replication by others. The alternative is a result that cannot be trusted.

Researchers must decide which results to report. As discussed earlier, researchers should have logs of experiments recording their history, including design decisions and false trails as well as the results, but such logs usually contain much material of no interest to others. And some results are anomalous—the product of experimental error or freak event—and thus not relevant. But reported results should be a fair reflection of the experiment's outcomes.

If a test fails on some data sets and succeeds on others, it is unethical to conceal the failures, and the existence of failure should be stated as prominently as that of success. Likewise, reporting just one success might lead the reader to wonder whether it was no more than a fluke.

Not all experiments are directly relevant to the hypothesis. An experiment might be used, for example, to make a preliminary choice between possible approaches to a problem; other experiments might be inconclusive or lead to a dead end. It may nonetheless be interesting to the reader to know that these experiments were undertaken—to know why a certain approach was chosen, for example. For such experiments, if the detail is unlikely to be interesting it is usually sufficient to briefly sketch the experiment and the outcome.

The experimental outcomes reported in a paper may represent only a fraction of the work that was undertaken in a research program. There will have been exploratory stages and different kinds of failures, and the reported runs may well be carefully chosen representatives of a broad range of experiments. Thus the published record of the work is highly incomplete.

In other disciplines of science, researchers are expected to keep detailed notebooks recording ideas, methods, experiments, data, participants, outcomes, and so on. These notebooks fill a variety of roles, in particular providing a complete history of the research, allowing the experiments to be reproduced, and proving that the published work took place as described—in labs in the biological sciences, for example, it may be required that a senior scientist sign and date each page.

Notebooks have not acquired these roles in computer science. However, they are invaluable. They can be used to record versions and locations of software, parameters used in a particular experiment, data used as input (or the filenames of the data), logs of output (or the filenames of the logs), interpretations of results, minutes of decisions and agreed actions, and so on. They allow easy reconstruction of old research, and simplify the process of write-up. They are particularly helpful if a paper is accepted after a long reviewing process and experiments have to be freshly run; all too often the code no longer produces anything like the original results, because too many details of the experiments have been lost and the code has been modified. Most of all, notebooks keep researchers honest.

While there are obvious reasons to consider maintaining notebooks electronically, in my experience written notebooks are more effective. In either form, it is good discipline to include dates, never change an entry, and use the notebook as often as possible.

Another strategy that keeps researchers honest, and helps to describe and publicize their work, is to make code and data available online. Doing so shows that you have high confidence in the correctness of your claims. In an informal survey some years ago, several computer scientists commented to me that they would not have made some of the claims in their papers if they had had to publish their code or to run their experiments under external scrutiny. More positively, publishing code reduces the barrier to entry for other researchers, and helps to establish baselines against which new work should be measured.

Variables

The ideal experiment examines the effect of one variable on the behaviour of an object being studied. How does increasing the volume of data affect execution time? Can the vision system track rapidly moving objects? How much compression can be achieved without visibly degrading the image? If no other variables are present, it is easy to be confident that the variable does indeed affect the behaviour in the way observed. The test environment should be designed to minimize the effect of extraneous factors—that is, to unambiguously relate variations in one property to variations in another.[15]

In practice, elimination of variables is remarkably difficult. Even elementary properties can be surprisingly hard to measure: for example, access time to material stored on disk is not just a property of disk hardware, but is affected by access pattern, presence and size of disk cache, and file system design. Tests should be designed to yield results that are independent of properties such as system characteristics or constant-factor overheads that are not part of the hypothesis.

Consider the measurement of performance of two compression techniques. If tested on different data, the results will be incomparable: we have no way of knowing whether the better performance is due to use of a better method, or due to choice of data that is inherently more compressible. Thus one particular component of a test environment is choice of test data. For some experiments standard data is available, such as benchmark problems in machine learning or the corpora used to test compression methods. The use of such standard resources is essential to experimentation on these problems. Where standard data is not available, care should be taken to ensure that the chosen test data is representative.

Another component of many test environments is the hardware. A good option is to describe performance in terms of the characteristics of some commonly available hardware, as for example specified by clock speed, disk access time, and so on. This allows readers to relate published results to observed performance on another system.

In some circumstances it is possible for an experiment to succeed, or at least appear to succeed, by luck; there might be an atypical pattern to the data,

---

[15] In careful research published in 1648, Jan-Baptista van Helmont concluded that plants consist of water:

> That all plants immediately and substantially stem from the element water alone I have learnt from the following experiment. I took an earthen vessel in which I placed two hundred pounds of earth dried in an oven, and watered with rain water. I planted in it the stem of a willow tree weighing five pounds. Five years later it had developed into a tree weighing one hundred and sixty-nine pounds and about three ounces. Nothing but rain (and distilled water) had been added. The large vessel was placed in earth and covered by an iron lid with a tin-surface that was pierced with many holes [to allow the soil to breathe while preventing dust from adding to it –JZ]. I have not weighed the leaves that came off in the four autumn seasons. Finally I dried the earth in the vessel again and found the same two hundred pounds of it diminished by about two ounces. Hence one hundred and sixty-four pounds of wood, bark and roots had come up from water alone.

or variations in system response might favour one run over another. Where such variations are possible, many runs should be made, to reduce the probability of accidental success and (in the statistical sense) to give confidence in the results. This is particularly true for timings, which can be affected by other users, system overheads, inability of most operating systems to accurately allocate clock cycles to processes, and caching effects.

For example, consider the apparently simple experiment of measuring how fast a block can be accessed from a file stored on disk. Under a typical operating system, the first access is slow, because locating the first block of a file requires that header blocks be fetched first; but subsequent accesses to the same block are fast, because in all likelihood it will be cached in memory. Some deviousness is required to ensure that averages over a series of runs are realistic. Now consider a more typical experiment: real time taken to evaluate queries to a database system. If the queries are poorly chosen, the times will vary because of the caching and the complex ways in which the system components interact, and multiple runs will not give realistic figures.

Now consider another elementary experiment—comparing the speed of two algorithms for the same task. The implementations (NEW and OLD) to be used for the experiments take the same input and produce the same output, and thus are externally indistinguishable. The algorithms are run in turn on the same data, and it is observed that NEW is faster than OLD by several percent.

It would be easy to conclude that NEW is the better algorithm. However, on the evidence so far, it would also be possible to conclude that:

- NEW is better implemented than was OLD. After all, NEW is your invention, and it is reasonable to take the care that is necessary to ensure that it runs well. Perhaps the same care was not taken with OLD.
- OLD uses more buffer space than NEW, leading to poor behaviour on this particular computer. The same results might not be observed on another machine.
- OLD uses floating-point operations that are not supported in hardware.
- At compile-time, OLD was accidentally built with debug options enabled, slowing it down.
- Inaccuracies in the timing mechanism randomly favoured NEW. Although, for example, Unix-style timing mechanisms can return values in nanoseconds, their accuracy below tenths of a second is often questionable.
- OLD was run first, and was delayed while the input was copied to memory; NEW accessed the input directly from cache.

- The particular input chosen happened to favour NEW.

Further experiments are required to distinguish which of these conclusions is most likely to be correct.

Some such effects are random, some are systematic—the same wrong measurement is recorded every time the experiment is run. In work on text indexes some years ago, we had some deeply puzzling results. The first stage went exactly as predicted: we built an index for a small text collection (250 megabytes, in an era when the capacity of a typical disk drive was a couple of gigabytes) and tested a heuristic improvement to the query evaluation algorithm. The test showed that the new method was about twice as fast as the old. But how would it scale? My research assistant then built an index for a gigabyte of data, and ran the same queries. The same result was observed, with the new method about twice as fast as the old; but the queries on a gigabyte used only 65% of the time needed for a quarter gigabyte. Considering the detail of the experiment, this result made no sense at all. Two quantities were independent of scale—the number of documents fetched and the total number of disk accesses—but the index size scaled linearly with data volume, and other measurements showed that four times as much index was being processed; yet only two-thirds of the time was required. The explanation, it developed, was that the smaller collection was kept with its index on a single disk drive while, for the larger collection, the index had been placed on a separate drive due to space constraints. In the case of the smaller collection, the accesses to data and index had been interfering with each other, causing disk access delays that were largely absent when two drives were used.

(Problems of this kind, and their solutions, can be highly illuminating. In this case, we discovered that disk seek times were a major component of total costs, accounting for around half of all elapsed time. Had we been explicitly investigating the significance of seek costs, we might not have thought of this experiment. Another aspect of research that this incident illustrates is the need for inventive experiments. Identifying a range of ways to alter the behaviour of a system, then measuring their effect, can lead to unexpected revelations.)

Compilers are a substantial cause of systematic error. Versions of the same compiler can vary dramatically for particular programs, as can system software such as file managers. After an upgrade from one version of Linux to the next release, the time to run an external sort routine we were testing rose from 3500 seconds to 7500 seconds. However, a code profiler showed that some individual routines were running more quickly.

In another experiment, we were troubled by a random error. Sometimes a run completed in around an hour, but often took an hour and a half. Intermediate times were not observed. The experiment involved a complex interaction between stored data, a memory buffer, and temporary files, so some variability was reasonable, but we expected a spread of results—not two widely separated clusters. The explanation was the screen lock; while earlier experiments had been run on a server, we had recently moved to a high-performance desktop PC. The slower runs had been overnight, when the PC was not in use.

Test your intuition on the following example. Suppose you write a program for searching a large file of randomly selected strings. The first stage of the program reads the set of strings into memory, creates an array of pointers (one to the start of each string), then sorts the pointers so that the strings are in lexicographic order. The program then reads a query string and uses binary search in the array to find whether the query is present in the original string set.

1. If two searches in a row are for the same string, do both searches take about the same length of time?
2. Suppose the number of strings in the file is increased by a factor of sixteen. Do searches then take about four times as long?
3. Suppose linear search is used instead of binary search. If the original file is already sorted, are searches the same speed as for an unsorted file? (Recall that the pointers to the strings are sorted after the strings are read in.)

Many programmers answer yes to these questions, but in each case the correct answer is no, largely because of the impact of cache on running time. (1) The first search loads the strings into cache. Memory access costs are a large component of total time, so the second search is much faster. (2) Two factors affect search time as data set size increases. One is that adjacent strings share longer prefixes, so the cost of a string comparison grows, as well as the total number of comparisons. The other is that, at some point, cache becomes ineffective because the volume of data means that there are too many collisions, and memory access costs rise. (3) If the file is sorted, the strings are likely to be sorted in memory, and will be prefetched during the linear search. If the file is not sorted, each string comparison requires a random memory access.

A variable in many studies is the user. Humans need to be involved to resolve many kinds of research question: whether the compressed image is satisfactory, whether the list of responses from the search engine is useful, whether a programming language feature is of value. Design of human studies is treated in detail in research methods texts written for psychology and for business methods. However, far too many human studies in computer science are amateurish and invalid. Instructions to the experimental subjects should be clear; the sample of human subjects should be representative (a class of computer science students may not be typical of users of operating systems); the subjects should be unaware of which of the competing methods under review was proposed by the researcher; anonymity should be preserved; and controls—analogous to placebos in medical trials—should be in place. The ethical guidelines for human studies at most universities are far-reaching, and in all likelihood any investigation involving people evaluating a system needs ethics clearance.

There is no doubt, however, that human studies are an essential element of computer science research. Without a productivity study, for example, it is difficult to see how to support assertions such as that C++ is superior to C. However, human studies of such questions continue to be a rarity. Much of the work in these areas is sound, but it does seem clear that more than a little research in this and a range of other areas is flawed by lack of consideration or measurement of the human element.

One of the longest-running experiments in computer science is the TREC evaluation of information retrieval systems at the U.S. National Institute of Standards and Technology, which has a significant human-factors component. Each year, participants—a large number of research groups from around the world—apply their retrieval systems to standard data and queries. This side of the experiment is *blind*; the researchers do not know which documents are answers and which are noise. The output of the systems is then manually evaluated by human assessors. This side of the experiment is also blind: the outputs are merged prior to inspection and the assessors do not know which system has done what. Another aspect of the TREC work is that the use of standardized resources means that there is direct control of the principal variables, and experiments are comparable between research groups; existing published results provide a baseline against which new results can be directly compared.

By the standards of computer science, the TREC experiment is expensive, with, for example, around a week or two of assessor time required per query per year. However, TREC illustrates that robust experiments can have high impact. When TREC began (in 1992, a couple of years before the web began to be significant), there was a large range of competing theories about the best way to match documents to queries. Weak methods were rapidly culled by TREC, and a great many dramatic improvements in information retrieval were spurred by the opportunity TREC created. The web search engines drew substantial inspiration from the TREC work and, in contrast to some other areas of computer science, the links between academia and commerce remain strong. This impact could not have been achieved without the large-scale involvement of human subjects, or without the commitment to robust experimentation.

Statistics

Much computer science experimentation consists of "doing a run" of some kind and measuring the outcome. From this perspective, in computer science research many people view statistics as no more than reporting of averages and deviations. However, the role of statistics in experimental research is a rich one, and seeking to answer elementary statistical questions can illuminate experimental design. Your research may well benefit from a statistical approach.

An approach to understanding these issues is to explore the meaning of simple statements about the behaviour of a system. When we state, for example, that "algorithm NEW is typically faster than algorithm OLD", it is reasonable to suppose that the intention is to claim that NEW is faster on average. (Such a statement could as easily be made on the basis of a theoretical analysis as on the basis of experiments.) But an average of what? If the intended meaning is only that NEW is faster than OLD on average for the runs undertaken in the experiments, what is it about these runs that makes them representative?

A key concept here is of *population*: the set of all possible runs. If NEW is indeed faster than OLD on average across the whole population, the claim is a reasonable one, but in all likelihood the population is infinite, as it must contain all possible combinations of input data—if the volume of input can be arbitrarily large, even so simple a property as the typical size of an input is ill-defined. As taking the average across such a population is likely to be impossible, it is necessary to resort to taking a *sample*, and to assume that it is representative.

To take a sample, it is necessary to understand what the population consists of. In medicine, to evaluate the benefit of a new antibiotic, the population could be all people, or perhaps all sick people, or possibly just all people for whom other medications have failed. Designing an experiment includes deciding what the possible, or reasonable, inputs are.

Consider how to identify the likely worst case of a particular class of string-hashing functions—that is, to find out how many strings might conceivably hash to the same slot in practice. We faced this problem in work on string hashing, where analysis of the functions would be suspect. (The distribution of characters in words is not uniform, and the distribution varies according to character position within words. Thus an analysis would involve assumptions that could easily be confounded in practice.) Theory tells us that the worst case of all strings hashing to the same slot is ridiculously improbable for an ideal function; the specific question is to identify how close to ideal a randomly chosen member of a class of hash functions is.

In evaluating the properties of string-hashing functions, there are several variables in the population of inputs: the hash table size, the number of input strings, the strings themselves, and a hash function chosen from the class. In this particular class, hash functions are determined by seed value, so the class is finite for an efficient implementation in a language such as C, with say 2^{32} or 2^{64} members. A constraint was that there were theoretical predictions only for some table sizes and load factors. It would be possible to explore other table sizes and input sizes, to seek a wide picture of behaviour, but intuitively it seemed unlikely that different observations would be made. The hash functions were chosen by randomly generating 32-bit seeds. The strings were chosen randomly from about a dozen sources: text, programs, DNA fragments, binary files, and exhaustive sets of strings of some given fixed length.

These strings are clearly not "typical", even assuming we know what "typical" means in such cases; there are many possible sources of strings, and who can say which is most likely to be hashed. Had the behaviour of the functions varied significantly between the different sources of string, it would have been difficult to draw any meaningful conclusion; however, the behaviour for every set was virtually identical, and moreover was indistinguishable from ideal. (Note, too, that this is an example of a multi-variable experiment. The behaviour under each variable can be evaluated by holding the others constant.)

As another example of the pitfalls of sampling and populations, consider natural-language processing, with say the goal of evaluating the accuracy with which a parser can identify nouns. The result depends on the input: perhaps text derived by optical-character recognition from printed material, or randomly chosen web pages, or articles from newspapers. Evaluation of typical accuracy depends on assumptions about the population, and on the sampling process. A truly random sample, if sufficiently large, should have in miniature all of the characteristics of the population it represents.

Given that experiments should be based on explicit assumptions about underlying populations and samples, some interesting consequences follow. Consider a thought experiment: the simple task of measuring the average height of the students at a particular university. Choose a sample of students at random, measure their height, and take the average. It might be found that all the students in the sample, excepting one or two outliers, are between 150 and 200 centimetres, with an average of 172. Now choose one student at random. It should be obvious that the likelihood that this student's height is average, say 172 ± 1 centimetres, is low.

We thus conclude that a randomly chosen individual is likely to be atypical! By the same reasoning, conclusions based on a single input, outcome, or event may well be meaningless.

Whether an average is a reasonable estimate of typical behaviour depends on the kind of event being measured. It makes no sense to report average running time when input size varies, for example. For evaluating the accuracy of noun detection of a sample of documents, average may well be appropriate; but for evaluating typical network delay for a round-trip of a packet, average may well be meaningless. First, some delays are effectively infinite (the packet is lost). Second, the distribution of such delays often consists of a large number of fast responses and a small number of extremely slow responses; the average is therefore somewhat slower than the fast times, but in a range where no values were observed at all. (An analogy is averaging the duration of a plane flight and of a car journey from Paris to Moscow, and stating that this middle value is typical.) In such cases, it may be appropriate to report the fastest time observed, while noting the variance.

Statistical tools that have wide application in computer science research include correlation, regression, and hypothesis testing. Measures of correlation are used to determine whether two variables depend on each other. Regression is used to identify the relationship between two variables. These can be used, for example, to determine whether input size affects speed or whether light intensity affects object recognition.

Hypothesis tests are used to investigate whether improvements are significant. It is often the case that, in a series of comparisons of two techniques for the same task, one is better than the other some but not all of the time. In statistical terms, in such a case the researcher needs to determine whether the two sets of results—two samples—are drawn from the same population.

We may have experimentally determined, for example, that NEW is faster than OLD "on average". That is, perhaps NEW was faster than OLD on balance when measured over a variety of inputs, or was faster in the majority of runs on the same input. In many experiments, execution times can vary substantially from one run to the next, for all the reasons discussed earlier—the layout of a file on disk, for example, could be different each time it is constructed, due to operating system variables.

Whatever the cause of the variability, this experiment is based on two sets of times, one for NEW and one for OLD. But suppose that we have a large population of running times for NEW alone, and we draw two samples from this population. It is unlikely that the two samples will have identical averages. Either we conclude that NEW is faster than itself, or that NEW and OLD might in fact not be meaningfully different. This problem is particularly acute when in some cases OLD is faster (by, say, only a small margin) and in other cases NEW is faster (by a large margin).

The issue can be resolved with a hypothesis test, which compares the distribution of observations. Consider the figures on page 202. Both of the graphs show a pair of normal distributions in which the means are different. In the upper graph, the distributions cover much of the same area; most of the points under one are under the other. Intuitively, it seems quite possible that a single underlying population is involved, and that the differences are due to the randomness of sampling choosing slightly larger instances in one case than in the other. In the lower graph, the distributions barely overlap at all. For the same underlying population to be involved, the sampling process would have had to be highly biased, choosing first a series of small values and then a series of high values. It seems improbable that this could happen by chance, so we conclude that the samples are in all likelihood drawn from separate populations. An example of application of a hypothesis test is shown later.

There is a variety of hypothesis or significance tests. Statistics texts explain this material, as well as related topics such as confidence intervals. Always consider whether your work requires statistics to confirm its validity.

Some researchers are deterred from considering statistics because of the high-powered mathematical analysis that may be involved. However, first, there are packages that do much of the hard work. Second, many statistical problems can be couched in terms of elementary probability and then resolved computationally. For example, consider the problem of identifying the likelihood that a particular tennis player will win a match, given that this player has an independent probability of 60% of winning each point. The rules are: a game is won when either player has at least four points and a two-point advantage; a set is won when either player has at least six games and a two-game advantage; a match is won when either player has a two-set advantage, or by the winner of the fifth set. Determining the probability of a win is non-trivial for the statistically innocent.

However, it is easy to write a program that runs a series of matches with a simple random-number generator for determining who wins each point; over a few thousand matches the average converges on a reliable value. A more computationally sensible option is to run a large series of trials to determine the likelihood of winning a game, then use this value as input to determination of likelihood of winning a set, and so on. It is not difficult to check that such code provides reasonable answers and that the values do indeed converge.[16] Many

[16] A typical guess of the likelihood of the better player winning the match is 90% or 95%; in fact, the likelihood is close to certainty.

When I once suggested to students that they test the code by running it with a probability of 50% of winning each point, several argued strongly that the program wouldn't terminate—which is more or less equivalent to arguing that, when tossing coins, you can't get some given number

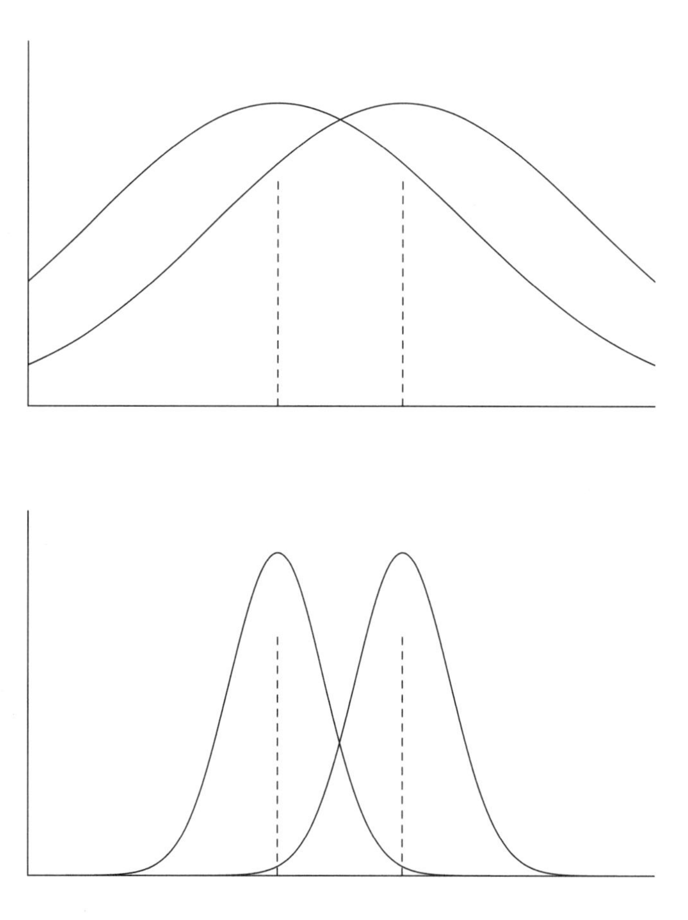

Hypothesis tests. In the upper figure, the means are different, but there is a reasonable likelihood that the samples are drawn from the same population, as the distributions have high overlap. In the lower figure, the means are different, and the distributions are well-separated; a hypothesis test should identify that these samples are drawn from different populations.

statistics can be estimated in this way; it was used, for example, to confirm the outcomes of the string-hashing experiments and to confirm the theoretical predictions for an ideal hash function, where random numbers and 32-bit pieces of pi were used in place of hash values.

Intuition

Intuition is often unreliable in the context of statistics. Perceptual fallacies are well known, such as the elementary mistake that, if the last few coin tosses were heads, then the next is likely to be tails. Coincidences are more memorable than non-coincidences; thus they seem more common than is in fact the case. A long random sequence will have short subsequences that appear non-random. If a selected subsequence has pattern, it is easy to jump to an incorrect conclusion.

A well-known example is the three-box problem. A contestant in a game is told that one of X, Y, or Z contains a prize. The contestant chooses X but does not open it. The host then opens Y and shows that it is empty. Should the contestant change to Z or stay with X? Intuition says that it doesn't matter, as the probability of X containing the prize is 1/2. Careful analysis of the alternatives shows that Z contains the prize with probability 2/3, but when this problem was presented many mathematicians publicly argued that 1/2 was correct.

In a variation of this error, suppose that person P has tossed two coins. Person Q asks if one of them is heads, and P says yes. Then the intuitive estimate of the probability that the other coin is heads is 1/2, on the basis that the status of one coin is independent of the other, but again this is wrong. The correct response is 1/3. The reason is that there are four possible configurations: heads-heads, heads-tails, tails-heads, and tails-tails. Only tails-tails is eliminated by Q's question.

Intuition often seems to fail in the context of randomness and hashing. For example, given a uniform random hash function, the likelihood of a given key hashing to any particular one of 1000 slots in a hash table is 1/1000. However, this does not mean that 1000 random keys will be allocated evenly amongst the slots; the likelihood of this event is an infitesimally low $\prod_{i=1}^{1000} i/1000$. Nor is it feasible for all values to hash to the same slot; the probability of even twenty values hashing to any one slot is absurdly small. On the other hand, simple statistical estimators such as the Poisson distribution can make accurate predictions of values such as the number of empty slots (around 368).

---

of heads in a row. They had confused the short-term variability (any number of consecutive throws of a head will come up eventually) with long-term averages. Such are the pitfalls of intuition.

Observers tend to make unsupported extrapolations from small numbers of events. A sequence of observations can be thought of as a tiny sample drawn from a vast population, and in statistical terms we would not expect a small sample to be representative. However, if a robot successfully traverses a room once, a researcher may well jump to the conclusion that the robot can always do so. The researcher has reasoned that the robot was designed to avoid obstacles; it successfully did so; and therefore the robot was working as intended. But whether this conclusion is reasonable depends on other context. For example, consider a robot that moves entirely at random. It may nonetheless traverse the room without encountering obstacles—sometimes, but not always. If we observed such a robot traversing a room, we could draw the inference that it was doing so by design. The general lesson from such cases is that a cautious researcher should consider whether any assumptions are statistically reasonable.

An experimentation checklist

- What is to be measured? How is it be evaluated?
- What code has to be obtained? What data has to be gathered? What has to be implemented?
- Should the experimental results correspond to predictions made by a model?
- What enduring properties might be observed by other people attempting to validate the work with different hardware, data, and implementation?
- Have appropriate baselines been identified?
- Do the results make sense? Are they consistent with any obvious points of comparison?
- Is the code going to be made publicly available? If not, why not?
- What variables might influence the results? How do the experiments distinguish between the effects of the variables?
- Are statistical methods necessary for validation of the results?
- What is the population? How is a sample to be taken?
- Are notebooks being kept? What is being recorded in the notebooks?
- Is ethics clearance required?

12 Refereeing

And diff'ring judgements serve but to declare,
That truth lies somewhere, if we knew but where.

William Cowper
Hope

Refereeing is a central part of the scientific process. Criticism and analysis of papers written by other scientists is the main mechanism for identifying good research and eliminating bad, and is arguably as important an activity as research itself. This chapter is written for referees, to help guide reviewing, and for authors, to explain the standards expected of a submitted paper.

Every new scientist eventually faces the task of refereeing a paper. Many find it intimidating, bringing as it does the possibility of wrongly criticizing somebody else's hard work, or of recommending that some irretrievably flawed research be published. Often the work to be refereed is unfamiliar and outside the referee's domain of expertise, yet a review must be written. Learning to referee is part of the apprenticeship of being a research student, and even mature researchers do not always referee well. It is easy to fall into a habit of careless or superficial refereeing—most researchers have stories to tell of good work rejected with only a few hasty words of explanation, or (if they are honest) of the most glaring errors going unnoticed by every member of a team of referees.

Refereeing can be a chore, but deserves the same effort, care, and ethical standards as any other research activity. Careful refereeing has its rewards, and not just the gratitude of editors and authors. It can lead you to look at your own work from a fresh perspective. It can stretch you and so improve your capacity for productive and interesting research. And it exposes you to different kinds of error or failure in research; the typical standard of work submitted for publication is well below that of work that gets published.

Responsibilities

When an author completes a paper, it is submitted to the editor of a journal (or the program chair of a conference) for publication. The editor sends the paper to referees, who evaluate the paper and return assessments. The editor then uses these assessments to decide whether the paper should be accepted, or, in the case of a journal paper, whether further refereeing or revision is required.

Authors are expected to be honest, ethical, careful, and thorough in their preparation of papers. It is ultimately the responsibility of the author—not of the journal, the editor, or the referees—to ensure that the contents of a paper are correct. It is also the author's responsibility to ensure that the presentation is at an appropriate standard and that it is their own work unless otherwise stated.

Referees should be fair, objective, maintain confidentiality, and avoid conflict of interest. In addition, they should complete reviews reasonably quickly (since delay can hurt an author's career), declare their limitations as reviewers, take proper care in evaluating the paper, and only recommend acceptance when confident that the paper is of adequate standard. Although referees can usually assume that authors have behaved ethically, many weak or flawed papers are submitted, and a disproportionate amount of refereeing is spent on such papers because they are often resubmitted after rejection. Moreover, it would be negligent of a referee to assume that a paper is correct and interesting for superficial reasons such as good writing, impressive mathematics, or author prestige. Referees must also ensure that their reports are accurate and of an appropriate standard.

The editor's responsibilities are to choose referees appropriately, ensure that the refereeing is completed promptly and to an adequate standard, arbitrate when the referees' evaluations differ or when the authors argue that a referee's evaluation is incorrect, and use the reports to decide whether the paper should be accepted.

Contribution

Contribution is the main criterion for judging a paper. However, there is no single, straightforward definition of what a contribution is. It is primarily defined by the peer review process—if you like, by the opinions of referees. In broad terms, however, a paper is a contribution if it has two properties: originality and validity.

The originality of a paper is the degree to which the ideas presented are significant, new, and interesting. Most papers are to some degree extensions or variations of previously published work; really groundbreaking ideas are rare. Nonetheless, interesting or important ideas are more valuable than trivial increments to existing work. Deciding whether there is sufficient originality to warrant publication is the main task of the referee. Only a truly excellent presentation, thorough and written well, can save a paper with marginal new ideas, while a revolutionary paper must be appalling in some respect to be rejected.

When evaluating the significance of a contribution, it is helpful to consider its effect: to judge how much change would follow from the paper being published and widely read. If the only likely effect is passing interest from a few specialists in the area, the paper is minor. If, on the other hand, the likely effect is a widespread change of practice or a flow of interesting new results from other researchers, the paper is indeed groundbreaking.

That some ideas appear obvious does not detract from their originality. Many excellent ideas are obvious in retrospect. Moreover, the ideas in a well-presented paper often seem less sophisticated than those in a poorly presented paper, simply because authors of the former have a better knack for explanation. Obviousness is not grounds for rejecting a paper. The real achievement may have been to ask the right question in the first place or to ask it in the right way, that is, to notice that the problem even existed. Organization of existing ideas in a new way or within an alternative framework can also be an original contribution, as can reevaluation of existing ideas or methods.

The validity of a paper is the degree to which the ideas have been shown to be sound. A paper that does no more than claim from intuition that the proposal should hold is not valid. Good science requires a demonstration of correctness, in a form that allows verification by other scientists. As discussed in Chapter 10 such a demonstration is usually by proof or analysis, modelling, simulation, or experiment, or preferably several of these methods together, and is likely to involve some kind of comparison to existing ideas.

In the area of algorithms, proof and analysis are the accepted means of showing that a proposal is worthwhile. The use of theory and mathematical analysis is one of the cornerstones of computer science: computer technology is ephemeral but theoretical results are timeless. Their very durability, however, creates a need for certainty: an untrustworthy analysis is not valuable. Thus a paper reporting experimental work can be a contribution. The experiment, to be of sufficient interest, should test behaviour that had not previously been examined empirically, or contradict "known" results.

Demonstrations of validity, whether by theory or experiment, should be rigorous: carefully described, thorough, and verifiable. Experiments for assessment of algorithms should be based on a good implementation; experiments based on statistical tests of subjects should use sufficiently large samples and appropriate controls. Comparison to existing work is an important part of demonstration of validity. A new algorithm that is inferior to existing alternatives is unlikely to be significant.

Evaluation of papers

The process of evaluating a paper involves answering questions such as:

- Is there a contribution? Is it significant?
- Is the contribution of interest?
- Is the contribution timely or only of historical interest?
- Is the topic relevant to the likely readership?
- Are the results correct?
- Are the proposals and results critically analyzed?
- Are appropriate conclusions drawn from the results, or are there other possible interpretations?
- Are all the technical details correct? Are they sensible?
- Could the results be verified?
- Are there any serious ambiguities or inconsistencies?
- What is missing? What would complete the presentation? Is any of the material unnecessary?
- How broad is the likely readership?
- Can the paper be understood? Is it clearly written? Is the presentation at an adequate standard?
- Does the content justify the length?

Of these, contribution is the single most important component, and requires a value judgement. It is not uncommon to have to referee a string of poor papers, but try to retain a long-term perspective.

The presence of a critical analysis is also important: authors should correctly identify the strengths, weaknesses, and implications of their work, and not ignore problems or shortcomings. It is easier to trust results when they are described fairly.

Most papers have an explicit or implicit hypothesis—some assertion that is claimed to be true—and a proposal or innovation. Try to identify what the hypothesis is: if you can't identify it, there is probably something wrong, and if you can, it helps you to recognize whether all of the paper is pertinent to the hypothesis, and whether important material is missing.

The quality of a paper can be reflected in its bibliography. For example, how many references are there? This is a crude rule-of-thumb, but often effective. For some research problems there are only a few relevant papers, but such cases are the exception. Giving only a few references may be evidence of bad scholarship. Also, some authors cite a reasonable number of papers without actually citing related literature, thus disguising a core bibliography that is far too short. If many of the references are by the author, it may be that some of them are redundant. If only a couple of the references are recent, how sure can you be that the paper is valid? The author doesn't appear to be familiar with other research. Similarly, be suspicious of papers with no references to the major journals or conferences in the area. Also, some references age more quickly than others. Most technical reports describe work in preparation and are not refereed, and thus readers have less confidence that their contents are correct. Once the technical report has been accepted for publication somewhere, it is the refereed version that should be cited. A corollary is that, often, old technical reports are papers of dubious merit that have been persistently rejected, and shouldn't be cited.

Occasionally an author submits a paper that is seriously incomplete. No effort has been made to find relevant literature, or the proofs are only sketched, or the paper has quite obviously never been proofread, or, in an extreme case, the paper does little more than outline the basic idea. With such papers the author is possibly just kite-flying, with no real expectation that the paper be accepted. Such authors perhaps want to establish that an idea is theirs, without going to the trouble of demonstrating its correctness, or are simply tired of the work and hope referees will supply details they haven't bothered to obtain themselves. Such papers don't deserve a thorough evaluation. However, don't be too quick to judge a paper as being in this category.

Referees should undertake at least elementary nitpicking, to search for errors that don't affect the quality of the work but should be corrected before going into print. These include spelling and syntax, written expression, errors in the bibliography, whether all concepts and terms have been defined or explained, errors in any formulas or mathematics, and inconsistency in just about anything from variable names to table layout to formatting of the bibliography.

Nitpicking errors can become more serious defects that might make the paper unacceptable. A few typographic errors in the mathematics are to be expected, for example, but if the subscripts are often mixed up or the notation keeps changing case then it is quite likely that the author has not checked the results with sufficient care.

Similar arguments apply to the presentation: to a certain extent poorly written papers must be accepted (however reluctantly), but real incompetence in the presentation is grounds for rejection, because a paper is of no value if it cannot be read. But note that the converse does not apply: excellence in presentation does not justify acceptance. Occasionally a referee receives a paper that is well written and shows real care in the development of the results, but which does no more than reproduce existing work. Such papers must, regrettably, be rejected.

A difficult issue for some papers is whether to recommend outright rejection or to recommend resubmission after major changes. The latter means that, with no more than a reasonable amount of additional work, the paper could be of acceptable standard. This recommendation should not be used as a form of "soft reject", to spare the author's feelings or some such, while asking for changes that are in practice impossible; eventual acceptance, perhaps after several more rounds of refereeing, is the usual final result of such a recommendation. If getting the work to an acceptable standard will involve substantial additional research and writing, rejection is appropriate. This verdict can be softened in other ways, such as suggesting that the paper be resubmitted once the problems have been addressed.

As a consequence of the peer review system, active researchers should expect to referee about two to three times as many papers as they submit (or somewhat less if their papers are usually co-authored) and only decline to referee a paper with good reason. For many papers, there may be no potential reviewer who is truly expert in the area, so be prepared to referee even when not confident in your judgement of the paper. Always state your limitations as a reviewer—that you are unfamiliar with the literature in the area, for example, or were not able to check that certain proofs were correct. That is, you need to admit your ignorance.

A referee should not recommend acceptance if the paper is not of adequate standard in some respect—the onus is on the referee to fully evaluate the paper. Referees who are unable to assure the quality of the paper should not recommend acceptance without an appropriate caveat.

Referees' reports

Refereeing of papers serves two purposes. The explicit purpose is that it is the mechanism used by editors to decide whether papers should be accepted for publication. The implicit purpose—equally important, and often overlooked—

is that it is a means of sharing expertise between scientists, via comments for the authors. Reviews usually include other things besides written comments (such as scores on certain criteria, used to determine whether the paper should be accepted), but it is the comments that authors find valuable. The report should make some kind of case about the paper: whether it is of an adequate standard and what its flaws are. That is, it is an analysis of the paper, explaining why it is or is not suitable for publication.

There are two main criteria for measuring referees' reports.

- Is the case for or against the paper convincing?

  When recommending that a paper be accepted, the editor must be persuaded that it is of an adequate standard. Brief, superficial comments with no discussion of the detail of the paper provoke the suspicion that the paper has not been carefully refereed. A positive report should not just be a summary of the paper; it should contain a clear statement of what you believe the contribution to be.

  When recommending that a paper be rejected, a clear explanation of the faults should be provided. It is not acceptable, for example, to simply claim without references and explanation that the work is not original or that it has been done before—why should the author believe such a claim if no evidence is given? Having gone to considerable lengths to conduct and present their work, few authors will be persuaded to discard it by a couple of dismissive comments, and will instead resubmit elsewhere without making changes.

- Is there adequate guidance for the authors?

  When recommending that a paper be accepted, referees should describe any changes required to fix residual faults or to improve the paper in any way—technically, stylistically, whatever. If the referee doesn't suggest such changes, they won't get made.

  When recommending that a paper be rejected, a referee should consider what the authors might do next—how they can proceed from the rejection to good research. There are two cases. One is that the paper has some worthwhile core that, with further work, will be acceptable. A referee should highlight that core and explain at least in general terms how the authors should alter and improve their work. The other case is that nothing of the work is worthwhile, in which event the referee should explain to the author how to come to the same conclusion. Sometimes the referee just cannot tell whether there is worthwhile material because of defects in the presentation. It is helpful to explain to the authors how they might judge the significance of their work for themselves by, for example, sketching questions the authors should consider.

There are many reasons why these criteria should be observed. The scientific community prides itself on its spirit of collaboration, and it is in that spirit that referees should help others to improve their work. Poor reviews, although saving the referee effort, make more work for the research community as a whole: if a paper's shortcomings are not adequately explained, they will still be present if the paper is resubmitted. Most of all, poor refereeing is self-reinforcing and is bad for scientific standards. It creates a culture of lacklustre checking of other people's work and ultimately saps confidence in published research.

In a review recommending acceptance, there is no further chance to correct mistakes—the referee is the last expert who will carefully examine the paper prior to its going into print. Only obvious errors such as spelling and punctuation may be caught later. The referee is obliged to carefully check that the paper is substantially correct: no obvious mathematical errors, no logical errors in proofs, no improbable experimental results, no problems in the bibliography, no bogus or inflated claims, and no serious omission of vital information or inclusion of irrelevant text.

In reviews that recommend rejection or substantial revision, such fine-grain checking is not as important, since (presumably) the paper contains gross errors of some kind. Nonetheless some level of care is essential, if only to prevent a cycle of correction and resubmission with a few points addressed each time. Specific, clear guidance on improving the paper is always welcome.

First impressions of papers can be misleading. My refereeing process is to read the paper and make marginal notes, then decide whether the paper should be accepted, then write the comments to the authors. But often, even in that last stage, my opinion of a paper changes, sometimes dramatically. Perhaps what seemed a minor problem is revealed as a major defect, or perhaps the depth of the paper becomes more evident, so that it has greater significance than had seemed to be the case. The lesson is that referees should always be prepared to change their minds, and not get committed to one point of view.

Another lesson is that positives are as important as negatives: reviews should be constructive. For example, in the refereeing process it is sometimes possible to strengthen the paper anonymously on behalf of the author. The refereeing process can all too easily consist of fault-finding, but it is valuable for authors to learn which aspects of their papers are good as well as which aspects are bad. The good aspects will form the basis of any reworking of the material and should thus be highlighted in a review. Even in the case of a paper that a referee believes to be totally without contribution, it is helpful to explain how the author might verify for themselves whether this evaluation is correct.

Some referees construct flaws in papers where none exist. For example, an assessment may include generic statements that could be made almost regardless of relevance to the paper's topic, such as "the authors have not considered parallel architectures" on a paper about document processing. Other examples are vague complaints such as "the problem could have been investigated more deeply" or "aspects of the problem were not considered". Comments of this kind suggest that the referee is not concerned with making a fair evaluation. If there is a genuine problem, then describe it, preferably with examples; otherwise say nothing.

Referees should offer obvious or essential references that have been overlooked (if they are reasonably accessible), but should not send authors hunting for papers unnecessarily, and should refrain from pointing to inaccessible references such as their own technical reports. A referee who recommends acceptance requires at least a passing familiarity with the literature—enough to have reasonable confidence that the work is new and to recommend references as required.

Reviewers need to be at least reasonably polite. It can be tempting to break this rule (particularly when evaluating an especially frustrating or ill-considered paper) and be patronizing, sarcastic, or downright insulting, but such comments are not acceptable.

Some review processes allow for confidential remarks that are not seen by the author. You can use these remarks to emphasize particular aspects of your report or, if the editor requested a score rather than a recommendation to accept or reject, to state explicitly whether the paper should be accepted. However, since authors have no opportunity to defend themselves against comments they cannot see, it is not appropriate to make criticisms in addition to those visible to the author.

A refereeing checklist

When you recommend that a paper be accepted, you should do the following:

- Convince yourself that it has no serious defects.
- Convince the editor that it is of an acceptable standard, by explaining why it is original, valid, and clear.
- List the changes, major and minor, that should be made before it appears in print, and where possible help the author by indicating not just what to

change but what to change it to (but if there are excessive numbers of errors of some kind, you may instead want to give a few examples and recommend that the paper be proofread).

- Take reasonable care in checking details such as mathematics, formulas, and the bibliography.

When you recommend that a paper be rejected, or recommend that it be resubmitted after major changes, you should do the following:

- Give a clear explanation of the faults and, where possible, discuss how they could be rectified.
- Indicate which parts of the work are of value and which should be discarded, that is, discuss what you believe the contribution to be.
- Check the paper to a reasonable level of detail, unless it is unusually sloppy or ill-thought.

In either case you should do the following:

- Provide good references with which the authors should be familiar.
- Ask yourself whether your comments are fair, specific, and polite.
- Be honest about your limitations as a referee of that paper.
- Check your review as carefully as you would check one of your own papers prior to submission.

13 Ethics

People will work every bit as hard to fool
themselves as they will to fool others.

Robert Park
Voodoo Science

The Piltdown hoax ... seriously delayed and distorted the urgent work of science ... Young scientists and old alike wasted untold thousands of hours on the Piltdown phenomenon ... [*It*] *was nothing short of despicable, an ugly trick played by a warped and unscrupulous mind on unsuspecting scholars.*

John Evangelist Walsh
Unravelling Piltdown

These words hereafter thy tormentors be!

William Shakespeare
Richard II

Science is built on trust. Researchers are expected to be honest and research is assumed to have been undertaken ethically. For example, referees assess whether results are significant but rarely investigate whether the reported experiments actually took place, because it is assumed that the authors have not lied about their work.

The major societies of science have codes of conduct that scientists are expected to adhere to. Breaches of these codes are regarded as extremely serious;

even the most senior academics have been sacked for offences committed many years earlier. Familiarity with these codes and their implications for day-to-day work is essential for a practicing scientist. In brief, the scientific community expects published research to be new, objective, and fair; researchers should not present opinion as fact, distort truths, plagiarize others, or imply that previously published results are original.

The most conspicuous form of unethical behaviour is plagiarism, because it steals work from other scientists and the hurt to others is obvious. (Also, it is relatively easy to detect.) However, other forms of misconduct are arguably as pervasive. One is abuse of power, such as when senior academics insist on being listed as authors of papers they have not contributed to. Another is fraud, in which claimed results were not in fact observed. In medicine, fraud is viewed as serious because of issues such as the potential consequences—deaths and vast financial liabilities—and because of high-profile cases in which fraud has been detected. In computer science, there is also the potential for such issues. The safety, reliability, and security of computer systems is increasingly a central element of our social infrastructure. Researchers who make grandiose claims based on poor evidence and whose work is subsequently acted on are creating risks, and may be held responsible for the consequences. For example, in some cases the software replaced due to concerns raised by the Y2K "bug" was in fact perfectly reliable; some software replacement may have increased risk rather than otherwise.

Issues of ethical concern for science include misrepresentation, plagiarism and self-plagiarism, authorship, confidentiality and conflict of interest, harrassment and abuse of power, and use of human subjects. The ethics of studies of human subjects are complex, and are beyond the scope of this book. The other issues are discussed in this chapter.

It would be satisfying to be able to give a formula for handling ethical issues. However, the two principal pieces of advice on this topic contradict each other. One is that problems that at first sight seem to be intractable ethical conflicts often turn out to be more superficial; it is sensible to wait and reflect before pursuing action. The other piece of advice is that unresolved tensions can fester, with the potential to permanently damage a relationship; it is sensible to take steps before too much harm is done.

A difficulty in resolving such issues is the imbalance between advisor and student, or between senior and junior academics. If you believe that there is an issue to resolve that cannot be resolved fairly by a direct approach, you need to seek confidential advice and support, preferably from a senior academic who knows the individuals involved and who can understand the issues. It can be difficult to take this step, but it is essential. Keep in mind that public accusation, justified or otherwise, can end a career. Mishandled, a genuine grievance can become a scandal in which any of the participants is a potential victim. Moreover, while issues such as whistleblowing and breaches of research ethics can be highly politicized, and it can be intimidating to approach a senior figure with accusations about a colleague, academics are in the main highly principled people who can be relied on to be fair.

Plagiarism

A central element of the process of science is that each paper is an original contribution of new work. Scientists' reputations are built primarily on their papers: both the work and how it is reported.

Plagiarism is re-use in one paper of material that has appeared in another, without appropriate acknowledgement. The theft may involve ideas, illustrations, results, text, or even whole papers; and includes, not just copying from published papers, but from material in electronic form, such as web pages, news articles, or email. By plagiarizing, a researcher hopes to obtain credit for work that has already been published, and not necessarily by someone else (the issue of self-plagiarism is discussed in the next section). However, while some people do make a deliberate decision to steal and there is a complex range of factors that lead people to plagiarize, one cause of plagiarism seems particularly common: misjudgement by an inexperienced researcher.

Such misjudgements can arise when a research student is unaware of appropriate academic style. For example, a researcher investigating B-trees may find an elegant illustration in a textbook and decide that it is perfect for a forthcoming paper; but copying this illustration (either by scanning it or drawing an imitation of it) is plagiarism. Similarly, a researcher describing B-trees may feel that a paragraph in a reference cannot be improved on; but copying it verbatim is plagiarism. Even a close paraphrase of it is likely to be plagiarism.

Another form of misjudgement is inappropriate or inadequate citation. Suppose that Barlman and Trey (2001) wrote the following:

> The impact of viruses has become a major issue in many large organizations, but most still rely on individual users maintaining virus definitions, with no internal firewalls to protect one user from another. However, any structure is only as strong as its weakest link; these organizations are highly vulnerable.

It would then be considered plagiarism to write the following:

✗ Viruses have become a major issue in many large organizations, but most organizations still rely on users maintaining virus definitions on their individual computers, with no internal firewalls to protect one computer from another. However, any structure is only as strong as its weakest link; these organizations are highly vulnerable to infection (Barlman and Trey 2001).

In this example, a citation is given, but it isn't clear that it refers to the whole block of text. Also, there is nothing to indicate that the wording is unoriginal—despite a few small changes, the text is copied. If the wording or the sense of the original text is required, it would instead be appropriate to write something like the following:

✓ As discussed by Barlman and Trey (2001), who investigated the impact of viruses in large organizations, "most still rely on individual users maintaining virus definitions, with no internal firewalls to protect one user from another. However, any structure is only as strong as its weakest link; these organizations are highly vulnerable."

Alternatively, the essence of the original can be concisely summarized, with clear attribution:

✓ Barlman and Trey (2001) investigated the impact of viruses in large organizations. They found that organizations are vulnerable if individuals fail to keep virus definitions up to date, as internal firewalls are rare.

The lesson of this example is that citation by itself is not sufficient. It is necessary to indicate exactly what material is taken from the reference, and to identify that material as a quote.

The following is adapted (to protect the guilty) from a real example:

✗ This distribution of costs follows a power law [2] in which only a few tasks have high impact. The form of the law is [13] for fixed cost C given by $P(x > C) \sim 2^{-\alpha}k$ where $\alpha > 1$ and $k > 1$. The parameter α describes user behaviour. Determination of k for a specific application can be achieved through modelling as a Poisson distribution.

In this example, everything but the citations are copied from the reference "[2]", including the erroneous misplacement of k, which should be a superscript.

Paraphrase of the structure of a paper is also plagiarism. If one paper follows another to the extent that they use the same headings, have tables of the same layout, cite much the same background literature, describe the literature with respect to the same criteria, and have similarly designed experiments with similar data exploring the same properties, then the second paper is plagiarized.

These kinds of plagiarism can arise when trying to start a paper (or impress an advisor). An author might, for example, copy the background of a paper with the intention of replacing it later on; or an advisor might give a student an existing paper to use as a model, and the student might then keep some of the text; or any of a range of such scenarios. Without adequate guidance about plagiarism, it is understandable that inexperienced scientists make mistakes, especially when other similar mistakes are in published papers.

It is easy to avoid plagiarism. When writing fresh text, avoid using other text as a guide, even if you are discussing outcomes reported by someone else. Cite other text, and be explicit about which material in your work is derived from elsewhere: mark where the cited material begins and where it ends. Use quotation marks for borrowed text. Construct reference lists by enumerating the papers you have read, not by copying the lists in other papers. And design all your own pictures.

For advisors, a lesson is that naïve students may copy, unintentionally or otherwise. Advisors need to ensure that their students understand what plagiarism is and that their material is original. All of the authors are culpable if published material turns out to be plagiarized.

Self-plagiarism

Authors who re-use their own text may well be plagiarizing. Using the same text in two papers is a step in the direction of publishing the same work twice.

Some scientists feel that it is acceptable to re-use their own background material from paper to paper. A series of papers may be based on the same ideas or previous work, and—it might be argued—rewriting the background each time is pointless. However, there are both ideological and pragmatic arguments against this practice. First, if an author is in the habit of copying the background in each paper, the material is likely to rapidly become stale, and authors who adopt this practice often seem unwilling to adapt the material even for papers on a different topic; in contrast, the discipline of writing new text each time helps to keep the material fresh. Second, a high-quality discussion of background material or of competing proposals adds weight to a paper, and increases the chance of it being accepted; by copying, the author is obtaining credit for old work. Third, some scientists view any significant re-use as improper, and authors presumably do not wish even a minority of their colleagues to view them as lazy or unethical. Fourth, most researchers work in teams of shifting membership. The authors of a paper collectively own its text; for some of the authors to take text and re-use it is inappropriate. The safe approach is to write fresh text for each new paper.

Publication of more than one paper based on the same results is prohibited under the standard scientific codes of conduct. An exception is when there is explicit cross-referencing, such as by reference to a preliminary publication from a more complete article that is a later outcome of the same research. (This is the one instance in which significant re-use of text can be acceptable.) Simultaneous submission to more than one journal or conference of papers based on the same results should be disclosed at the time of submission; the usual response to such a disclosure is to ask you to withdraw the paper. In this context, "the same results" does not necessarily mean a particular experimental run; if an experiment has been tried on some data, running the same experiment on other data is not new work unless it leads to new conclusions.

In the context of plagiarism and self-plagiarism, remember that publications are a permanent record. It may well be that a researcher successfully publishes the same results twice, or publishes a series of papers with figures and text in common, and in so doing rapidly develops an impressive publication list. But as time passes it is increasingly likely that such abuses of the system will be noticed, and there is no statute of limitations on plagiarism. The zeal of young researchers to publish should not blind them to the possibility of disciplinary action years or decades in the future. (In 2002, the Vice Chancellor of the largest Australian university had to resign when it was discovered that he had plagiarized as a junior academic.)

Self-plagiarism can also be considered from the point of view of copyright. In most instances, when you publish a research paper the copyright is assigned to the publisher, who thus owns, not the ideas, but your expression of them. The publisher also owns the paper's illustrations. The issue of re-use of material is then one of property. Technically, an author who re-uses more than a couple of paragraphs or a figure requires the publisher's permission. Although it is improbable that a publisher would be concerned by a minor breach, copyright law does establish an alternative benchmark for what is acceptable. Moreover, although some academics regard copyright law as excessively restrictive of free speech and would prefer to see alternative forms of refereed publication, this does not mean that these academics approve of self-plagiarism.

Many authors make their papers available via the web. Such informal publication opens the issue of copyright: editors of journals or conferences might regard a paper that has been made available in this way as already published, and decline to consider it for formal publication. However, publishers increasingly accept that authors use the web in this way, while, for example, requiring that an appropriate copyright notice be inserted.

Misrepresentation

Misrepresentation is when a paper does not accurately reflect the outcomes that were observed or the contribution of previous research. (Misrepresentation in the context of pseudoscience was discussed on page 178.) When presenting results, researchers are expected to ensure that they are accurate, describe any experimental issues or limitations that could have affected the outcome, provide enough detail to enable reproduction or verification, be fair in description of other work, report negative as well as positive results, not state falsehoods, and take the effort to ensure that statements are complete and accurate. However, an honest mistake is not misconduct.

In its clearest form, misrepresentation is fraud: the making of claims that are outright false. Other forms of misrepresentation are more subtle. A behaviour that is far too common and, arguably, is fraud is to understate other people's work. It can be tempting for authors to exaggerate the significance and originality of their results, and to diminish the status of previous results in the field, to increase the likelihood of their work being published. If you would be uncomfortable defending what you have written about other people's work, then your text should probably be changed.

Another form of misrepresentation is when authors imply that they have high confidence in their results when in fact the experiments were preliminary or were limited in some way. For example, reported running times may be based on a small number of runs with high variance, or there may be uncertainties about the quality of the implementation. Even more dubious are cases where the efficiency of a method being tested is based on some parameters, and the reported times are those achieved by tuning the parameters to the input data. Failure to report relevant unsuccessful experiments is explicitly condemned in the academic codes of conduct.

The issue of misrepresentation arises with online publication. When an author discovers an error in an online paper it is all to easy to correct it silently, with no explicit indication that the paper has changed. (Such changes can be made to a printed technical report, but the continued existence of the original version means that there is a fixed document to refer to.) Modifications to online papers should always be made explicit, by use of a version number and date of publication; and the original version should continue to be available, as others may have referred to it. Retrospective alteration of a document is not something that should be done lightly.

It is because of the possibility of misrepresentation that codes of conduct require that scientists and departments retain their research data. A typical requirement is that the data must be held for five years from the date of publication and must be accessible to other researchers. In computer science, a reasonable interpretation of this guideline is that it is necessary to keep notebooks, software, results, and descriptions of inputs—the material that establishes that the research took place with the claimed outcomes. In computer science, implementation of such guidelines is at best inconsistent, but a central lesson is that it is reasonable for other scientists to seek to view your experimental setup as reported in a paper.

Authorship

Deciding who has merited authorship of a paper can be a difficult and emotional issue. A broadly accepted view is that each author must have made some significant contribution to the intellectual content of the paper. Thus directed activities such as programming do not usually merit authorship, nor does proofreading. An author should have participated in the conception, execution, or interpretation of the results, and usually an author should have participated to some degree in all of these activities. The point at which a contribution becomes "significant" is impossible to define, and every case is different, but neither code-cutting under the direction of a researcher nor management roles such as obtaining funding justify authorship. Nor is it appropriate to give authorship as a reward or favour.

A researcher who has contributed to the research must be given an opportunity to be included as an author, but authors should not be listed without their permission. On the other hand, involvement in an extended project does not guarantee authorship on every paper that results from the project. Contributors who are not authors should be acknowledged in some way.

Papers that are generated during the course of a student's research program are often jointly attributed to both student and advisor. Usually the student has undertaken the bulk of the task: capturing some idea in writing, running experiments, and locating background literature, for example. However, often the work would not have reached a reportable outcome without the involvement of the advisor. When students work independently, the research is theirs alone, but a student who has put in the majority of the effort while working under supervision should remember that it is intellectual input that determines authorship.

An advantage to inclusion of the advisor as an author is that the advisor is committing to responsibility for the quality and originality of the work.

It is not appropriate for an advisor to publish the work of a student without the student's permission; if the student has completed a thesis reporting some research results, then the student has earned authorship on papers derived from these results. Nor is it appropriate for the student to publish without the permission of the advisor.

A related issue is that of author order, since readers may assume that the first author is the main contributor. A researcher who is clearly the main contributor should be listed first—don't believe Alfred Aaby when he tells you that alphabetic ordering is the norm.

Confidentiality and conflict of interest

Researchers need to respect each other's privacy. Sharing of a computer system with other people does not mean that one has the right to use their data without permission, for example, or to disclose their results to other people. Code or executables may be made available under terms such as commercial-in-confidence, and the fact that many people use software they haven't paid for does not mean that it is appropriate for researchers to do so.

Commercial relationships may need to be disclosed to editors or in the text of a submitted paper. Researchers who are publishing work on products or technologies should not conceal their involvement with the companies that own these products.

Another area where there is potential for conflict of interest is in refereeing of papers and grant proposals, and examination of theses. Researchers should not referee a paper where there is a possible conflict of interest, or where there is some reasonable likelihood that it will be difficult for the referee to maintain objectivity; or even where others might reasonably suspect that the referee would be unable to maintain objectivity. Examples include papers by a recent advisor, student, or co-author of the referee, or an author with whom the referee recently had close interaction, including not only personal or employment relationships but also situations such as competition for an appointment. In such cases, the referee should return the paper to the editor (and explain why).

It can be difficult to maintain objectivity if the author's opinions strongly conflict with your own. Make every effort to be fair, or seek an alternative referee. Also, your evaluation should be based on the paper alone; don't be swayed by the stature of the author or institution. Perhaps the trickiest case is that of a paper replicating your current work, or worse, is a faulty version of work you are currently doing but illustrates that you have made mistakes too. Probably the only solution is to contact the editor, state the case, and seek guidance. Whatever you do, act quickly; delay hurts the author.

A related issue is of confidentiality: papers are submitted in confidence and are not in the public domain. Papers you are reviewing should not be shown to colleagues, except as part of the refereeing process; nor should they be used as a basis for the your own research. In practice there is something of a grey area—it is impossible not to learn from papers you are refereeing, or to ignore the impact of their contents on your own work. Nonetheless, the confidentiality of papers should be respected.

An ethics checklist

- Is all the text yours?
- Are you the copyright holder for all figures and illustrations?
- Have any authors been listed without their knowledge?
- Have other potential authors been omitted? Do they know that publication is proceeding without them?
- Is any of the material confidential?
- Was clearance obtained for any human studies?
- Is the scope of citation and attribution clear? Is there a clear distinction between new work and previous knowledge?
- Has other work with similar results been appropriately cited and discussed?
- If any material is shared with another paper, has the sharing been explained to the reader? Has it been explained to the editor?
- Does the paper include material recycled from your earlier work?
- Are other papers accurately described?
- Do you know which version of the code was used to run the experiments? Could you run the experiments again and get the same outcome?
- Are there any weaknesses or limitations in the experiments that need to be described? Would you be prepared to show other researchers the raw experimental materials?
- Are any claims overstated?

14 Giving presentations

Members [use] a close, naked, natural way of speaking; natural expressions; positive expressions; clear senses; a native easiness: bringing all things as near the Mathematical plainness, as they can.

Bishop Thomas Sprat
History of the Royal Society

You, having a large and fruitful mind, should not so much labour what to speak as to find what to leave unspoken. Rich soils are often to be weeded.

Francis Bacon
Letter to Coke

Scientists often have to talk about their work in front of an audience. The success of a talk depends on factors such as the skill of the speaker and the audience's interest in the topic. There are many common problems in presentation of talks that can be addressed by careful preparation and familiarity with the possible pitfalls. Only practice can turn a nervous researcher into an accomplished public speaker, but with the right preparation even a first talk can be successful.

In contrast to a paper, a talk leaves no permanent record for the audience to dissect at leisure. The purpose of a talk is to introduce a research program and persuade the audience that the work is significant and interesting. There can be inaccuracies or generalizations that would be unacceptable in a paper, while obvious mistakes—or even correct statements that have not yet been justified—may be criticized immediately. Detail that is essential to a paper is often of little value in a talk. The principles of organization and presentation for a talk are quite different to those of a write-up.

Presentations (half-hour or one-hour explanations of research) are the topic of this chapter. Some issues, such as speaking skills and good design of slides, are applicable to any form of presentation. Others are primarily of relevance to brief research talks. For example, in contrast to the task of giving lectures, in talks it is more important to get the timing right, while detailed explanations may be unimportant, and the audience management skills may be very different. Experience with any kind of audience is of value, but may be only a partial preparation for learning to talk about research.

Content

The first step in preparation of a research talk is deciding what to cover. Such talks are usually based on a paper or thesis, or on work in preparation, but most papers have far more detail than can be conveyed in half an hour. Problems of this kind are highlighted in the experiences of research students. The initial reaction of a typical student preparing a talk is concern that there isn't enough to say, but the initial reaction of an advisor is, often, that the student's draft talk is far too long. Thus the content must be selected carefully.

What and how much to select depends not only on the time available but also on the expertise of the audience. A workshop attended by specialists in a narrow topic would suggest a different talk to one to be given to researchers in your department. Papers are usually specialized, but a diverse audience may be unfamiliar with even the area of your research, so it may be necessary to introduce basic concepts before proceeding to the results. For any audience, there is no need for a talk to be an overview of the paper; it is an introduction to the ideas and research results described in the paper, and many paths can lead to that same outcome of teaching the audience about your work.

When constructing a talk, begin by choosing the single main goal, that is, the particular idea or result the audience should learn. Then work out what information is required before the result can be understood. Often this information is in effect a tree whose branches are chains of concepts leading to the result at the root. Much of the hard work of assembling the talk is pruning the tree, both to suit the audience and to strip the talk down to essential points that listeners should remember.

An approach to gathering material for a talk is "uncritical brainstorming, critical selection" (which can also be applied to writing). In the first phase, jot down every idea or point that might be of value to the audience, that is, list the topics you might conceivably have to cover. Imagine yourself chatting with someone about your work, and note down the things you might say. During this first phase it is helpful to not judge each point, because questioning as you write tends to stall the brainstorming process. It can be helpful to set a time limit on this phase of no more than twenty minutes.

In the second phase, assemble the talk by critically selecting the important points and ordering them into sequence. During the second phase you should judge harshly because otherwise the talk will contain too much material; be lean and leisurely, not crowded and hasty.

A talk should be straightforward, although it can be used to convey complex ideas. Rather than asking yourself what you want to tell the audience—the interesting little issues explored, the technical problems confronted, the failings of the previous research—consider what the audience needs to know to understand the main result. Remember that a talk is a discussion with peers, not a sales pitch or a political speech. There should be a logical reason for the inclusion of each part of the talk. Provide the minimum of detail that allows the audience to understand the result, while being inclusive. If the audience believes that they have learnt enough to confidently discuss the work with someone else, they will feel that the talk was of value. Think of the talk as a demonstration that the work is of value and, in particular, that your papers are worth reading.

Context can be as important as the ideas themselves. Take the time to explain why a problem is important, where it arises, or why previous approaches are unsatisfactory. Motivate the listeners so that they want to hear how a problem was solved. Use repetition to emphasize major points; present a second example, or explain the impact of the work in several contexts. And use key examples: show how it works, why it works, or problems it solves.

Complex issues should be presented slowly and in stages; avoid detail that the audience is unlikely to follow. Once listeners do not understand the flow of the discussion, they are lost and will remain that way. Material that some speakers present but shouldn't includes messy details such as the internals of a system, a proof of a theorem (attempting to walk the audience through a long series of logical steps is a particularly bad idea), the elements of an architecture, technicalities, or arcane information that is only of interest to a few specialists. There are of course cases in which such material is necessary—the proof might be the main idea to be conveyed, for example, or the theorem so unlikely that the proof, or its outline, is required to convince likely skeptics—but as a rule the audience is more satisfied if not exposed to intricate material that is unnecessary to understanding of the overall result.

Some material, particularly abstract theory, is dry and difficult to present in an interesting way. However, there are alternatives to using the presentation to work through the details of a theory. Rather than just discuss the research, explain the relationship of the results to the broader research area. Explain why the project was worth investigating or consider the effect of the results on related research. Listeners who are interested in the theory itself can speak to you privately or read the paper afterwards.

A talk is an opportunity to discuss problems. A speaker who is not frank about shortcomings or difficulties, but is then exposed during questioning, can look foolish. Obstacles are part of doing research and, not only can they add interest to a talk, but just possibly the audience may offer solutions.

Never have too much material for the alloted time. Either you hurry through your talk, not explaining the ideas well and getting flustered, or you run over time, the audience is irritated, and the time for subsequent speakers is cut—not something for which they will thank you.

Organization

A crucial difference between a talk and a paper is that talks are inherently linear. A reader can move back and forth in a paper and has the leisure of putting the paper aside for a time; but in a talk the audience must learn at the speaker's pace and cannot refer to material that was presented earlier on. Talks must be designed within this constraint. A standard structure is of a sequence of steps leading the audience to the single main point. Broadly, the structure might be: the topic of the talk, any necessary background, the experiments or results, and the conclusions and implications of the results.

This structure is not without potential pitfalls. In particular, take care to ensure that the relevance of the background is obvious. You will lose the audience's attention if they are wondering why you are discussing an apparently unrelated topic. Whatever the structure, ensure that all topics are relevant and follow an obvious sequence.

For the audience to follow the flow of argument in a talk, they need to understand its logical structure. The preview-do-review strategy is highly effective. Use backward and forward references ("I previously showed you that ...", "I will shortly demonstrate that ... , but first I must explain ...") to show how the current topic relates to rest of the talk. At changes of topic, summarize what should have been learnt by the audience and explain the role of the new topic in the talk overall. Distinguish between material that the audience must know to understand the main point and material that is minor or incidental. If you skip important detail, say so.

Getting the timing right, particularly for a short talk, can be difficult. Somehow the pace is never quite as you expect. It helps if your talk is designed so that there is material towards the end that can be skipped without breaking continuity, or included seamlessly if time permits.

The introduction

Begin well. The audience's opinion of you and of the topic will form quickly and a bad first impression is hard to erase. The first few sentences should show that the talk will be interesting—make a surprising claim, argue that some familiar or intuitive solution is incorrect, or show why the problem to be solved is of practical consequence.

Many speakers begin with an outline that lists the topics to be covered. At the beginning of the talk, however, the audience may not even understand the terminology, and such outlines are quickly forgotten because they have no context. Outline the talk's structure if you want to, but not on the first slide. Before you reach the outline, make sure that the goal of the talk is clear. That is, explain where you are going before explaining how you will get there.

✗ "This talk is about new graph data structures. I'll begin by explaining graph theory and show some data structures for representing graphs. Then I'll talk about existing algorithms for graphs, then I'll show my new algorithms. I'll show experimental results on our cluster machine and then show why the algorithms are useful for some practical graph traversal problems."

Not only is this a poor introduction, but the outlined structure is poor too. (But note that the speaking style in this example is fine; it is my impression of a typical fluent speaker, punctuated for readability.) A better introduction is as follows, of a talk in which interesting material is discussed much earlier on.

✓ "My talk today is about new graph data structures. There are many practical problems that can be solved by graph methods, such as the travelling salesman problem, where good solutions can be found with reasonable complexity so long as an optimal solution isn't needed. But even these solutions are slow if the wrong data structures are used. I'll begin by explaining approximate solutions to the salesman problem and showing why existing data structures aren't ideal, then I'll explain my new data structures and show how to use them to speed up the travelling salesman algorithms. I conclude with examples of where the new method makes a real difference."

The speaker should then continue on the topic of why the algorithm is useful, and, once the main concepts have been introduced, present the outline of the main part of the talk.

Some talks can be introduced with a tale or anecdote, to motivate the need for a solution to the problem or to illustrate what would happen if the problem were not solved. For example, a talk on automatic generation of acceptable timetables began with an account of the timetabling problems at a certain large university; the speaker made a good story of the estimate that, without computer support, the timetabling of a new degree utilizing existing subjects from several faculties would require 200 years. But in no circumstances should you try to tell a funny story unless you are an experienced speaker and are *certain* it will be funny.

All talks need a few words of preamble and warm-up. A surprisingly frequent omission is that speakers forget to say who they are! Begin with the title of the talk, your name, the names of any co-authors, and your affiliation. If there are several authors, make sure the audience knows which one is you.

The conclusion

End the talk cleanly; don't let it just fade away.

✗ "So the output of the algorithm is always positive. Yes, that's about all I wanted to say, except that there is an implementation but it's not currently working. That's all."

Clearly signal the end. Use the last few moments to revise the main points and ideas you want the audience to remember, and you may also want to outline future work or work in progress. Consider saying something emphatic—predict something, or recommend a change of practice, or make a judgement. Such statements should of course be a logical consequence of the talk.

Preparation

As a research student I was advised that the best way to prepare for a talk was to write it out in full so that (supposedly) if I froze I could just start reading from my notes. This was terrible advice. Text that is fluid when spoken is an art few people master. Written English sounds stilted, most speakers cannot scan far enough ahead to predict the right intonation and emphasis, and the act of reading prevents you from looking at the audience. Even the vocabulary of written and spoken English differ; for example, written English has "do not", "will", and "that" where spoken English has "don't", "shall", and "which".

Supporting notes can be helpful, if they are treated as prompts for issues to discuss rather than a script. Write notes as points of a few words each, in a large print that is easy to read while you are standing at a podium and doing things such as operating a computer.

Rehearse the talk often enough and the right words will come at the right time. You want to appear spontaneous, but this takes practice. A casual style is *not* the product of casual preparation. You will only be relaxed and deliver well if you have prepared thoroughly and are confident that you have prepared thoroughly. However, don't memorize your talk as a speech; decide what you want to say but not every word of how you will say it. Recitation sounds as stilted as reading and you are likely to freeze when trying to remember an exact phrasing.

Time the talk and note what stage you expect to reach at 5 minutes, 10 minutes, and so on, to help you finish on time. An effective exercise is to rehearse in front of a mirror or onto tape. Rehearse while standing, because that is how you will deliver. Think about possible questions. Familiarize yourself with equipment: for example, find out how to start up the computer, connect it to the projector, and run the presentation software. Last, get someone to give you feedback, and make use of it. If one person dislikes something it is likely that others will too.

Delivery

Assembly of the material is one aspect of a successful talk. Another aspect is creation of a cohesive sequence of slides, as discussed later. The other main aspect is presentation: speaking well, making good use of slides, and relating to the audience.

An obvious point is that you must speak clearly: develop sufficient volume and project your voice without shouting. Use a natural tone of voice. Breathe deeply, not by gulping air like a swimmer but by inhaling slowly to the bottom of your chest. Speak a little slower than you would in normal conversation; around 400–500 words per three minutes is right for most people. Slightly overemphasize consonants, a habit that is particularly helpful to the 10% or so of your audience who are at least a little deaf. Keep your head up, thus deconstricting your throat. And face the audience.

Consider your style of speech. Avoid monotony, both in pace and tone. Pause occasionally, particularly when you have given the audience something to think about, and pause in preference to filling gaps with noise such as "um" or "I mean". Pause to collect your thoughts before speaking rather than pausing mid-sentence.

Also consider the personality you present. As a speaker you want to be taken seriously, but this does not mean that you cannot be relaxed, vivid, even amusing. Show your enthusiasm. Avoid sudden movements or distracting mannerisms such as pacing, bouncing, or gesticulating, but don't freeze; gestures should be natural. Vary what you are doing: move away from the computer to talk to the audience directly, for example, spend a couple of minutes with a non-technical slide after working through complex material. Make frequent eye contact with the audience; find some friendly faces to check with every now and again. Above all, be yourself—don't adopt a false persona and don't show off. The right note to hit is of a conversation with friends.

Showing off, swagger, or vanity of any kind, is if anything worse in a talk than in a paper. Be modest. Don't talk down to the audience or make aggrieved statements such as "people all said it couldn't work, but my work proves them wrong". Maybe the work is indeed remarkable, but that doesn't mean that the speaker is too; keep the distinction between presentation and presenter clear.

At the same time, you shouldn't diminish your achievements. Avoid excess humility, don't suggest that the outcomes are unimportant or uninteresting, and don't begin by saying that the talk will be dull or that you are nervous. Too many talks begin with a disclaimer such as "the talk was only written last night" or "I haven't had time to prepare". The intention is to lower the audience's expectations and thus mute any possible criticism, but the effect is to diminish their interest; and, if the talk turns out to be excellent, the disclaimer is then an unfortunate boast.

Beware of irritating habits. "Umming", pacing, and gesticulating were mentioned above. Consider taking off your watch; if it is on your wrist you cannot check the time inconspicuously. Only drink if you absolutely have to; if you have to drink, don't gulp. Don't read directly from slides or written notes, or stand behind the projector so that your face can't be seen and you cast a shadow on the screen. When referring to the screen, use a stick or laser pointer rather than the computer's mouse. Don't overact, use slang, or laugh at your own jokes. Don't act nervous, mumble, look at your feet, face the wrong way, scratch, fiddle, or fidget. If you think you might be tempted to rattle the coins in your pocket, put them somewhere else. If you are using an overhead projector, don't use sheets of paper (or worse, your hands) to mask off parts of slides, particularly in darkened theatres, because masking the projector varies the ambient light level. And don't change slides before the audience has had a chance to read them.

Handle distractions tactfully. If someone persistently interrupts, or excludes the rest of the audience by asking too many questions, offer to talk to them afterwards.

Expect to be nervous—adrenaline helps you to talk well. Even experienced speakers can be highly agitated, despite their cool calm on the podium. The best cure for serious attacks of fright is to give a preparatory talk or two, so if possible practice before a friendly (but critical) audience. A constructive attitude is to view each talk you give as training for the next one. Don't be too ambitious; master the basics of getting a clear message across before, for example, attempting to tell jokes or make advanced use of presentation tools.

Standing in front of an audience of your peers or superiors can be intimidating, particularly if the audience is silent. But silence is a good sign; it means people are paying attention. Even yawning isn't necessarily a disaster; lecture halls are often stuffy, and nobody stays focused indefinitely. A typical listener's attention drifts away momentarily now and again, no matter how good the speaker is.

Most importantly, remember that the audience wants to enjoy your talk—their attitude is positive. People don't attend talks with the intention of being bored, and welcome any sign that the talk is interesting. The need to build on this initial goodwill is why opening well is so important.

Question time

Question time at the end of a talk is used to clarify misunderstandings and to amplify any points that listeners want discussed in more detail. Five or ten minutes is too brief for serious discussion: you need to keep answers short and avoid debating with an audience member, because it is unedifying for everyone else. Some questions can't be answered on the spot: they are too complex, or the questioner has misunderstood a fundamental issue, or you simply don't know the answer.

Involve the audience in question time. Repeat the question in your own words and talk to the whole audience, not just the questioner, in your reply. Respond positively and honestly to all questions. Never try to bluff when you don't know—doing so inevitably looks stupid. It is far better to be frank and admit ignorance. It is equally important to never be rude to audience members or dismissive of their questions. Questions can be misguided, irrelevant, or amazingly inane, but more than one audience member may think such a question to be reasonable, and the only appropriate response is to answer as politely and accurately as the question permits.

Slides

Slides (or overheads, transparencies, or foils) are a point of focus for the attention of the audience. The traditional technology for slides is to use an overhead projector, but these are increasingly rare, and the great majority of talks in computer science use software and a projection system. A typical slide consists either of text or of a figure with a few words of explanation. Text slides are a visual guide to what the speaker is saying. Figures—graphs, images, diagrams, or tables—show results or illustrate a point.

However, keep in mind that the focus of the talk is you, not the slides. What you are saying, rather than the sketchy content of a slide, should be the centre of attention. Don't use slides as a way of avoiding contact with the audience.

Each slide should have a heading and be fairly self-contained; don't rely on the audience remembering complex details or notation introduced elsewhere. Aim for about one slide per minute or so—too few is dull and too many is bewildering. It is a mistake to design a talk so that rapid back-and-forth switching between slides is required. Consider instead repeating crucial information. For instance, show a whole algorithm, then on successive slides show each step with an example. Some example slides are at the end of this chapter.

Slide tools

The tools for making and presenting slides continue to develop. Those in wide use—currently, Microsoft® PowerPoint and LaTeX—provide an excellent environment for writing slides, and both include a range of elaborate features. Even the most inexperienced speaker can use these tools to produce a professional-looking talk, and they protect novices from some of the mistakes that can seem particularly amateurish, such as the difficulties of managing a pile of printed overheads in the confined space next to an overhead projector.

However, the fact that a tool provides features does not mean that the features have to be used—ease of use and necessity of use are not the same thing.

The principles of a good presentation have not changed since the era of hand-written overheads: legibility, simplicity, and relevance. In far too many talks, the speaker has decided to use some element of the software that neither entertains the audience nor helps them to learn. The goal of a well-written talk is for the audience to listen to the speaker; distractions, no matter how nifty, should be eliminated. Another perspective is that a simple, elegant slide design may be less dramatic than the alternatives, but does not annoy; and people are not impressed by the ability to use the latest software.

Slide layout is a basic issue. To begin with, dark backgrounds do not work. In a dimly lit auditorium, if the projected image is dark the atmosphere is unpleasant. Light fonts on dark background do not display as well as dark fonts on white. Variable-brightness backgrounds are even worse—text that is legible in some areas is inscrutable in others. The use of logos and images should be limited to borders. If you have something to communicate to the audience, screen area is precious; don't waste it on meaningless graphics.

Animation is entertaining at most once. Animated entry and exit amuses small children; use it for that age group, if at all.

A specific form of animation is point-at-a-time display. There are several reasons why such display works against the success of a typical presentation. One is that it is a constraint on the speaker, who must keep to a rigid script and remember several times a minute to click a button to get the next point displayed. (All too often the speaker does not remember, and then has to click-click-click to catch up.) In contrast, if a whole slide is displayed, the speaker can focus on talking to the audience and can improvise more easily. Another reason is that audiences want to know where the speaker is going; typically a listener reads a slide, then waits to hear the speaker explain it. Point-at-a-time display makes it harder for the listener to focus.

Some speakers decide to use the computer to draw during a talk, using the mouse as a pencil, but even in ideal conditions such drawings are dreadful. If you need to draw, use a whiteboard, but it is preferable to avoid drawing altogether, as doing so may involve fiddling with lights and projection gear. Many projection systems allow you to add music or noises to individual slides. Don't do it. Most of the audience shares neither your taste in music nor your sense of humour.

This is not an exhaustive list, so use it to guide your own sense of what is appropriate; some other issues are considered below in the context of particular kinds of slides.

Text slides

Text slides provide structure and context. They are usually written in point form, and should be brief summaries in short sentences of the information you want to convey. The audience will expect you to discuss every point listed on each slide, or, rather, expect that by the time you switch to the next slide every point will have been covered. Never read your slides to the audience—they can read faster than you can speak. Each point should be a topic to discuss, not necessarily a complete statement in itself. A slide may be a series of points, but that doesn't mean that the points need to be numbered or even bulleted. Some people argue that bullets add interest. Slide after slide of slabs of text can be dull, but bullets, which are greatly overused, do not make much difference.

Some speakers use a kind of pidgin-English for their slides.

✗ Coding technique log-based, integer codes.

Be brief, but not meaningless.

✓ The coding technique is logarithmic but yields integer codes.

Another example is on pages 245–246.

Explain all variables and where possible simplify formulas. In papers it is helpful to state types of variables when they are used; in talks it is crucial. Minimize the volume of information, especially detail of any kind, that the audience must remember from previous slides.

Overheads should not be crowded with text; see page 246 for a slide with a reasonable maximum of text and page 242 for a slide that is unacceptable. Never display a page from a paper: even a well-designed page is almost certainly unreadable in the context of a presentation. Don't break words between lines; instead, have an uneven right margin. Keep the layout simple—minimize clutter such as frames, shading, cross-hatching, shadows, and artwork.

Use a font of reasonable size and have plenty of white space. Huge or small fonts look ridiculous (see the examples). Explore the available fonts, but don't worry too much: while to some people sans serif may look cleaner than the alternatives, for example, any modern font is fine. Be consistent, however; one talk needs no more than three fonts and a couple of font sizes.

Strings of exclamation marks and text in uppercase do not add a sense of excitement. They add a sense of ineptitude.

Figures

Good figures and graphs can make ideas much easier to understand. Figures should be simple, illustrating a concept or result with minimum fuss; messy or crowded figures have no impact. Don't use a table unless it is necessary—they can be hard to digest.

An illustration from a paper may not be appropriate for a talk. Smaller details may not be clearly visible. In a paper, the reader can consider the figure at leisure, but in a talk it is only shown for a limited time, and the freedom of the presenter to point to the parts of a figure and to add to it incrementally means that it may be appropriate to organize the figure rather differently. Perhaps most significantly, in a talk a figure can be coloured. For example, text can be in different colours to show an ordering of events; different kinds of entities can have different colours; or colouring can be used to show how routes through a process relate to outcomes. If the slides are to be printed, note that differences between shades of grey can be lost in reproduction.

Figures in slides, as in papers, should focus on the technical content. Distracting elements should be removed. Present the bars of a histograms in three dimensions only if the third dimension carries some information. Keep all objects to a reasonable size—why include a gigantic block-coloured arrow when a simple line will do? Include an image or movie only if there is a need to do so. Animate only if necessary, such as when explaining a data structure.

Clip art, especially of stylised people, can inspire hilarity and is often ugly. It does not add class. Use it only when necessary, and select the simplest picture that suits the need.

Label everything, or at least every kind of thing. The labels should be meaningful to the audience—if you have omitted material from the talk, omit corresponding material from the figure. When checking a figure, ask yourself: Does it illustrate a major point? Does it illustrate the point unambiguously? Is it self-contained? Is it uncluttered? Is all of the text legible? Is all of the text (other than axes of graphs) horizontal?

A presentations checklist

- What is the key thing the audience should remember?
- Is there enough background material for the intended audience?
- Is any material unnecessary?
- Could some of the material be left for people to read about later?

- Is the talk self-contained?
- Does the talk have a motivating preamble?
- Have complex issues been explained in gentle stages?
- Are the results explained?
- Are the numbers necessary?
- Are more diagrams needed?
- Are the slides simple? Do they have unnecessary ornamentation or distracting use of colour?
- Is there any unnecessary animation?
- Are the font sizes reasonable?
- Are there enough examples?
- Have you rehearsed the talk?
- Have you prepared something to say about each slide?
- What were the limitations of the research?
- Do you explain why the research is interesting or important?
- Is there a clear conclusion?
- Have you memorized the talk?
- If you are asked a question you can't answer, how will you respond?
- Have you rehearsed your manner? Will your enthusiasm show?
- Do you know how to use the equipment?

Examples of slides

Examples of problems in slides are shown on the following pages. These illustrate some common mistakes, but are not intended to be a comprehensive introduction to the design of slides. Indeed, they are all in much the same layout, so that design changes don't distract from the content issues being discussed, and cover only a few of the aspects of style for presentations.

Optimizing skip length

How long should a skip be?

With a length p vector and skips of length j, suppose there are b accumulators $\Rightarrow$ searching for b values.

Average cost (at one per skip) is $\frac{b}{j} + \frac{bj}{2}$. Differentiating gives $-\frac{p}{j^2} + \frac{b}{2}$.

Thus $j = \sqrt{\frac{2p}{b}}$.

Example: $b = 2,000$ and $p = 100,000 \Rightarrow j = 10$ and the cost is $20,000$, or 20% of base.

X This is not an effective slide. The division of text into points is untidy. Terminology is not carefully used—words such as "accumulators" have been introduced unnecessarily. Average cost of what? What does "one per skip" mean? What is the "base"?

A slide is unlikely to be entirely self-contained; the audience expects it to be explained by the speaker and to be based on material introduced earlier. But some effort should be taken to make the slide self-explanatory. This slide is puzzling.

Optimizing skip length

Skip length j can be optimized for vector length p.

Assume that we are searching for b entries in a vector where $b \ll p$. Without skips, the decoding cost is $c = p$.

With skips, the average decoding cost is $c' = p/j + bj/2$.

The cost is minimized when $j = \sqrt{2p/b}$.

Example: $b = 2{,}000$, $p = 100{,}000$.

Then $j = 10$ and the cost is $c' = 20{,}000$.

✓ A possible revision of the slide on page 239. This is a minimalist revision—a better result might be achieved by starting from scratch.

The slide style here is extremely plain. In practice it would be common to include a logo and the speaker's name somewhere, and the text and background might be coloured. Such details are enough to give the slide some interest; more ornamentation is unnecessary.

Optimizing skip length

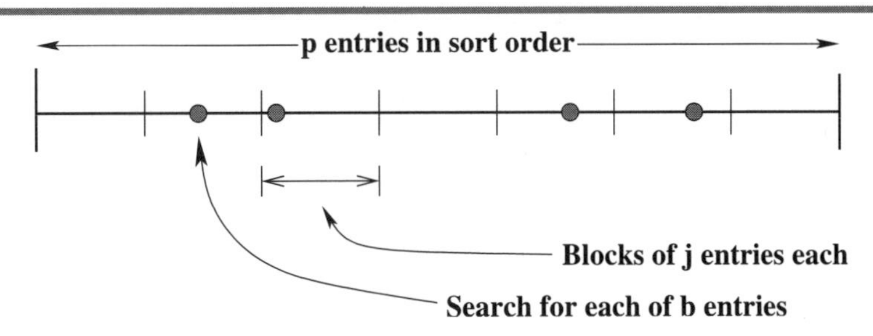

Without skips, the decoding cost is $c = p$.

With skips, the average decoding cost is $c' = p/j + bj/2$.

The cost is minimized when $j = \sqrt{2p/b}$.

If $b = 2{,}000$ and $p = 100{,}000$ then $j = 10$ and the cost is $c' = 20{,}000$.

✓ Another possible revision of the slide on page 239. This version is more dependent on the speaker explaining the task (choice of j for indexed search through a sorted array), but the picture makes the task easier to explain.

The picture itself is extremely simple, and required only a few minutes with a simple drawing tool (`xfig`). However, the picture makes a considerable difference both to the appearance of the slide and the way the material might be delivered.

Approximating number sets

One technique for coding a b-bit approximation of a set of numbers is as follows. Each number x is such that $L \leq x < U$ for some positive lower bound L and upper bound U. In practice $U = Max + \varepsilon$ for some small ε.
For a base

$$B = (U/L)^{2^{-b}} \text{ where } \log_B(U/L) = 2^b \tag{1}$$

$$f(x) = \lfloor \log_B(x/L) \rfloor \tag{2}$$

is integral in the range $0 \leq f(x) < 2^b$ and will require only b bits as a binary code. If x is represented by code c, that is, $f(x) = c$, an approximation $\hat{x}$ to x can be computed as $\hat{x} = g(c + 0.5)$ where g is the inverse function

$$g(c) = L \times B^c \tag{3}$$

Each code value c corresponds to a range of values x such that $g(c) \leq x < g(c+1)$.

X Another poor effort. The font is too small. There is too much text; so much that the speaker is almost irrelevant. There is also too much detail. The equation numbers aren't valuable, since, to refer the equations later on, the speaker must display them again.

Approximating number sets

Assume that each number x is such that $0 < L \leq x < U$.

In practice $U = Max + \varepsilon$ for some small ε.

Consider a base $B = (U/L)^{2^{-b}}$.

Then $c = f(x) = \lfloor \log_B(x/L) \rfloor$ is an integer where $0 \leq c < 2^b$.

The inverse function is $g(c) = L \times B^c$.

$c = f(x)$ corresponds to a range of x values:

$$g(c) \leq x < g(c+1)$$

✓ A revision of the slide on page 242. Some detail has been removed and the terminology has been made more accessible.

Proof of injectivity

Let $\Sigma = \{a, s\}$, where a is a constant symbol and s has arity 1.

Let $G = \{x \to a,\ x \to sx',\ x' \to sx,\ y \to a,\ y \to sy',\ y' \to sy'',\ y'' \to sy\}$.

That is, $[x]_G = \{\, s^{2n}a | n \geq 0\}$ and $[y]_G = \{s^{3n}a | n \geq 0\}$.

$$\begin{aligned}
&x \cap y \;\to\; (a \cup sx') \cap (a \cup sy') \;\to\; (a \cap a) \cup (a \cap sy') \cup (sx' \cap a) \cup (sx' \cap sy') \\
&x' \cap y' \;\to\; sx \cap sy'' \;\to\; s(x \cap y'') \\
&x \cap y'' \;\to\; (a \cup sx') \cap sy \;\to\; (a \cap sy) \cup (sx' \cap sy) \;\to\; s(x' \cap y) \\
&x' \cap y \;\to\; sx \cap (a \cup sy') \;\to\; (sx \cap a) \cup (sx \cap sy') \;\to\; s(x \cap y') \\
&x \cap y' \;\to\; (a \cup sx') \cap sy'' \;\to\; (a \cap sy'') \cup (sc' \cap sy'') \;\to\; s(x' \cap y'') \\
&x' \cap y'' \;\to\; sx \cap sy \;\to\; s(x \cap y)
\end{aligned}$$

$G' = G \cup \{x \cap y \to a,\ x \cap y \to s(x' \cap y'),\ \ldots,\ x' \cap y'' \to s(x \cap y)\}$ and
$V' = \{x \cap y,\ x' \cap y',\ \ldots,\ x' \cap y''\}$.

It follows that $[x \cap y]_{G'} = \{\, s^{6n}a | n \geq 0\}$.

X Only the most specialized audience could reasonably be expected to make an attempt to understand this. There is nothing wrong with the math itself—and it is carefully typeset although woefully underexplained—but a talk is the wrong environment for trying to convey material of this kind. Explain what the math is for; the math itself belongs in your paper.

Total access costs

Inverted file vocabulary disk-resident.

Small ($\approx$ 50 Kb) memory-resident index.

One access per term.

In total two per query term, two per answer.

Ordered disk accesses $\Rightarrow$ lower average cost.

✗ Too cryptic; it gives so little support to the speaker that it is almost irrelevant. The text is difficult to parse because the form of the sentences is too far removed from that of ordinary text.

Total access costs

The vocabulary of the inverted file is on disk.

A small ($\approx$ 50 Kb) index to the vocabulary is in memory.

Only one disk access to the vocabulary is required, followed by one further access to fetch the inverted list.

- Two accesses in total per query term, two per answer.

If the accesses to the vocabulary, lists, and answers are ordered, then average costs are reduced.

✓ A revision of the slide on page 245. The statements have been fleshed out into complete sentences and a little information has been added. This is about the maximum amount of text that is reasonable for a slide.

The single bullet adds emphasis, identifying the key conclusion the audience should be aware of.

Total access costs

- The vocabulary of the inverted file is on disk
- A small ($\approx$ 50 Kb) index to the vocabulary is in memory
- The accesses are
    - One disk access to the vocabulary
    - One further access to fetch the inverted list
    - Thus the accesses in total are
        - two per query term
        - two per answer
- If all of the accesses are ordered
    - Average costs are reduced

✕ A bulleted version of the slide on page 246. The use of bullets encourages speakers to add more structure to slides; the structure can be useful, but it can also be noise. There is something slightly patronizing about reducing each point to an elementary statement. Sometimes bullets are valuable, but in this instance they have been overused.

If you do use bullets, make them inconspicuous: small, grey or pastel rather than bright, and simple rather than elaborate. Two levels of bullets is sufficient.

Total access costs

- **The vocabulary of the inverted file is on disk**
- **A small ($\approx$ 50 Kb) vocabulary index is in memory**
- **The accesses are**
    - One disk access to the vocabulary
    - One further access to fetch the inverted list
    - Thus the accesses in total are
        - *two per query term*
        - *two per answer*
- **If all of the accesses are ordered**
    - Average costs are reduced

X Variation in font and font size almost never works. Use one or at most two fonts and sizes.

Afterword

Ready, set, go.

Schoolyard expression

The only way to produce a well-written paper is to start early and revise often. Write about what you plan to do, or what the project will be, or related literature, or anything of relevance. A researcher who argues that it is not yet time to start writing is mistaken: once you have a topic, you are ready to go.

Every stage of research benefits from writing. Once you have described your project, it is easier to ask skeptical questions about the direction and aims. Describing a project forces you to analyze it, and fruitful research directions may suggest themselves. Sketching an algorithm can highlight the fact that you do not yet understand some of its properties. A description of experiments allows examination of whether they are consistent and complete.

Procrastination is the enemy of good writing. There are always plenty of things you *might* do first—whether they are sufficiently important is another question. To do good science, it is necessary to write. Start now.

Bibliography

The following is a list of books and papers that I found valuable in the course of writing this book. Most of them have contributed to my own writing as a practising scientist. Not all of the entries are on style; some are about the process of science. These books and others are discussed at `www.justinzobel.com`.

D. F. Beer (ed.), *Writing and Speaking in the Technology Professions: A Practical Guide*, IEEE Press, New Jersey, 1992.

G. Blake and R. W. Bly, *The Elements of Technical Writing*, Macmillan, New York, 1993.

W. C. Booth, G. G. Colomb, and J. M. Williams, *The Craft of Research*, Second edition University of Chicago Press, Chicago, 2003.

A. F. Chalmers, *What Is This Thing Called Science?* Third edition, University of Queensland Press, Brisbane, 1999.

P. R. Cohen, *Empirical Methods for Artificial Intelligence*, MIT Press, Cambridge, Massachusetts, 1995.

B. M. Cooper, *Writing Technical Reports*, Penguin, London, 1964.

A. Eisenberg, *Guide to Technical Editing*, Oxford University Press, Oxford, 1992.

D. Evans and P. Gruba, *How to Write a Better Thesis*, Second edition, Melbourne University Press, Melbourne, 2002.

H. W. Fowler, *Modern English Usage*, Second edition, Oxford University Press, Oxford, 1965.

L. Gillman, *Writing Mathematics Well*, Mathematics Association of America, Washington DC, 1987.

E. Gowers, *The Complete Plain Words*, Third edition, Penguin, London, 1986.

D. E. Knuth, T. Larrabee, and P. M. Roberts, "Mathematical Writing", Mathematics Association of America, Washington DC, 1989.

M.-C. van Leunen, *A Handbook for Scholars*, Knopf, New York, 1985.

P. B. Medawar, *Advice to a Young Scientist*, Pan, London, 1981.

M. O'Connor, *Writing Successfully in Science*, Chapman & Hall, London, 1991.

A. O'Hear, *An Introduction to the Philosophy of Science*, Oxford University Press, Oxford, 1990.

I. Parberry, "A guide for new referees in theoretical computer science", *ACM SIGACT News*, 20(4):92–109, 1989.

R. Park, *Voodoo Science: The Road from Foolishness to Fraud*, Oxford University Press, Oxford, 2001.

E. Partridge, *Usage and Abusage*, Penguin, London, 1973.

W. Poundstone, *Labyrinths of Reason: Paradox, Puzzles and the Frailty of Knowledge*, Penguin, London, 1988.

B. Ross-Larson, *Edit Yourself*, Norton, New York, 1996.

A. J. Smith, "The task of the referee", *IEEE Computer*, 23(4):65–71, 1990.

W. Strunk and E. B. White, *The Elements of Style*, Third edition, Macmillan, New York, 1979.

E. Thiroux, *Thinking and Researching in a Virtual Society*, Prentice-Hall, New Jersey, 1999.

W. F. Tichy, "Should computer scientists experiment more? 16 reasons to avoid experimentation", *IEEE Computer*, 31(5), May 1998, 32–40.

E. R. Tufte, *The Visual Display of Quantitative Information*, Graphics Press, Cheshire, Connecticut, 1983.

E. R. Tufte, *Visual Explanations*, Graphics Press, Cheshire, Connecticut, 1997.

W. Zinsser, *On Writing Well*, Sixth edition, Harper, New York, 1998.

Exercises

The skill of good writing is acquired through practice. Pushing yourself, deliberately testing your ability to write new kinds of material and to write faster and better, can make a remarkable difference to the ease with which you can create polished text. Below is a series of exercises, intended not just for novice writers but also to help more experienced writers test and maintain their skills.

Some of these exercises are self-contained; others will be most helpful if adapted to your area of research, in particular by involving papers or passages that are relevant to your work. Educators may wish to choose standard papers and passages to be used by their students.

These exercises require substantial effort to complete—don't expect to run through one or two in a few spare minutes. Set aside a block of time that will be free of interruptions, say two hours, and in that time aim to do one exercise well. The exercises are loosely ordered by the kind of activity they involve, so if you only do a few, choose them carefully.

1. Choose a paper from your research area and write a brief answer to each of the following questions.

   (a) What are the researchers trying to find out?

   (b) Why is the research important?

   (c) What things were measured?

   (d) What were the results?

   (e) What do the authors conclude and to what factors do they attribute their findings?

   (f) Can you accept the findings as true? Discuss any failings or shortcomings of the method used to support the findings.

   (These questions are not just an exercise: to some degree you should ask them for every paper you read.)

   Justify your opinions as carefully as you can. As part of the answers to these questions you should summarize the proposed method and the results achieved. The answers should be substantially your own writing, not quotes, paraphrases, or illustrations from the paper.

   Alternatively, use the questions on pages 167 and 208 to assess the paper.

2. Choose a paper, perhaps the same paper as for Exercise 1, and criticize the structure and presentation.

   (a) Is the ordering (of sections and within sections) reasonable?

   (b) Are sections linked together?

   (c) Does the paper flow? Are important elements appropriately motivated and introduced?

   (d) Where is the survey?

   (e) Is there a non-technical introduction?

   (f) How carefully has the paper been edited?

   (g) Are there aspects of the presentation that could be improved?

   Based on your criticism, write a referee's report for the paper, including a recommendation as to whether to accept or reject. Take care to discuss all of the paper's major problems.

   Now read your review as if you were the paper's author. Is the review fair or harsh?

3. Some journals have special issues of a series of papers on a related topic. Choose two (or more) papers presenting a similar kind of result and compare them. Have the authors designed and organized the papers in the same way? Where the design choices differ, is one of the alternatives preferable?

4. Various services provide abstracts online. In an area where you have some technical knowledge, choose an abstract, but do not look at the paper. Using only the abstract and your experience to guide you, suggest section headings and sketch likely content for each section. Draft the first few paragraphs of the introduction. How do these compare to the actual paper? What strengths and weaknesses does your version have?

5. Some of the papers in the *Communications of the ACM* argue for a point of view rather than present technical results; for example, there are often papers on legal or ethical issues or about computing practice. Choose such a paper and answer the questions in Exercise 1. Carefully analyze the argument used to defend the author's opinion, identifying the major steps in the reasoning. Are the conclusions sufficiently justified?

6. Choose a paper with substantial technical content from *ACM Computing Surveys*. In many such papers the authors are placing their own work in the context of other research results in the area. Do you regard the survey as fair? That is, is the survey an unbiased reflection of the relative strengths of the work in the area?

7. Choose a journal paper presenting new technical results. (Journal papers are usually more carefully written and revised than are conference papers.) Based on the content of the introduction—you should not read the rest of the paper—do the following tasks.

   (a) Identify the hypothesis.
   (b) Suggest a suitable methodology for testing the hypothesis.
   (c) Suggest an organization for the paper, with headings and specific suggestions for the content of each section.

   Now compare your proposals to the body of the paper. Where there are differences, decide which alternative is better. The authors had much more time to think about the paper than you did, but are there any problems with the original organization?

8. Summarize a passage, perhaps the introduction of a paper, by jotting down the important points. These notes should be as brief as possible. Now write

your own version of the passage using only your notes, without reference to the original. (Mary-Claire van Leunen attributes this exercise to Benjamin Franklin.)

9. Choose a popular article about computer science (from *Scientific American*, say) and summarize it in 500 words. Put the summary aside for a day or two, then review it. Did you include all the important details? Have you represented the article fairly? Would a reader of the summary arrive at the same conclusions about the work as a reader of the original article?

10. Iteratively edit a passage to reduce its length. Start with a passage of, say 300 words, then reduce it in length by 10%, that is, about 30 words; then reduce by a further 30 words; and so on, for at least seven iterations. (To make this exercise more challenging, reduce by *exactly* 30 words at each step.) The aim at each step is to preserve the information content but not necessarily the original wording.

    Consider the resulting sequence of versions. With this exercise it is not uncommon for the passage to improve during the first couple of iterations, then become cryptic or incomplete as the text becomes too short for the content. Rate the versions: Which is best? Which is worst?

11. Rewrite the following passage to make it easier to understand. You may find it helpful to introduce mathematical symbols.

    > The cross-reference algorithm has two data structures: an array of documents, each of which is a linked list of words; and a binary tree of distinct words, each node of which contains a linked list of pointers to documents. When a document is added its linked list of words is traversed, and for each word in the list a pointer to the document is added to the word's linked list of documents. An order-one expansion of a document is achieved by pooling the linked lists of document pointers for each word in the document's linked list of words.

12. Choose a passage of 1,000 words or so, either a piece of your own work or any passage that you understand well. Revise it to improve the writing—that is, edit for flow, expression, clarity, and so on. Make the changes on paper, then type up the result, retaining the paper copy as a record.

    Put the revised passage aside for a few days, then repeat the exercise. Aim to make significant further improvements. (Did you undo any of the previous changes?) Revise again after a break of a few days; and continue until you have five revisions in total. Such revision is the best way to learn how to produce really good text, and many of the best writers revise this thoroughly.

13. The following fragments are flawed. They are ambiguous, or inelegant, or do not parse, or do not make sense. For each fragment, identify the problems—many of them have multiple shortcomings—and suggest revisions. If you need to make assumptions, state them clearly. (Most of these examples are from papers.)

    (a) As search engine systems emerge as the principle information finding tool within commercial enterprises due to the enormous popularity of WWW technology, the lack of options for integrating text and relational data on the web is becoming crucial.

    (b) Information retrieval systems appear in the Web with the purpose of managing, retrieving and filtering the information available there.

    (c) The first approach is not practical. Thus the changes to the architecture of the system, including threads for the dictionary and client response components.

    (d) Concerning answer locality, usual tools tolerate lower first guess accuracy by returning multiple responses and allow the user to interact with the system to localize answers.

    (e) The difference in the previous results and the results from this study can be an artifact of the different collections that are being used in the two studies.

    (f) Authority work, the need to discover and reconcile variant forms of the same record will become more critical in the future.

    (g) The age of the mobile internet is dawning rapidly day by day and will demand more and more efficient solutions as disparate online resources are integrated in numbers of new ways.

    (h) There are increasingly more online databases in the current climate of electronic publishing.

    (i) There are several challenges to be associated with the data management of this information because the associated databases are highly multidimensional and dynamic.

    (j) Ambiguity resolution was investigated by Klein [4]. Reverse parsing was shown in [4] to be a better method.

    (k) Costing was performed on each option.

(l) The method, to be chosen is active mapping, as it is definitely superior in each experiment.

(m) One of these tools is one which automatically creates a short version which contains as much of the content as possible as the original.

(n) To compute whether the expected performance is achieved in a way that is automatic the only difficulty is to have a definition of similarity that is consistent with the user's perception.

(o) An effective alignment method that employs dynamic programming is presented to locate optimal points of match between the original text and the optically recognized version provided.

(p) An important phase of any system development process is the evaluation phase.

(q) It is also of interest how well the terms reflect the content of the indexed document as it is well known that assessing the quality of manual keywords is difficult, due to the fact that there is no general correct set of keywords for any given document and the preferred terms may vary from task to task, user to user, and even system to system, depending on the factors to be considered such as retrieval mechanism and search context.

(r) There are some audio-visual speech recognition systems that processes both the audio and visual channels, and complete recognition in real-time.

(s) The sudden growth of the WWW observed over recent times has triggered a lot of research fields to occur, web services being only one of them.

(t) Association rules are rules that identify associations between items in transactions.

(u) A number of software packages exist, which are capable of designing relational models online.

(v) Most of today's complex systems are based on a hardware architecture that makes a physical separation of memory and processing and a software architecture that divides functionality into a hierarchy.

(w) The rest of this paper is organized, as follows.

(x) Given a range of options usually people are more interested in the extremes than in the middle part of the range since the two ends are more distinctive.

(y) Given a set of reference points, or cluster centroids, for a vector space and a quantization rule that provides a mapping to no more than 2^b distinct values then a filtering method consists of no more than building an injection from each site in the vector space to a binary signature which is just the concatenation of the binary expression of the quantized values.

(z) There are many applications, however, whose needs relational database systems do not meet, including diverse applications such as geographical information systems, CAD/CAM systems, expert systems, and the new kid on the block, text retrieval systems. And although not common today, text retrieval systems will undoubtably propagate as paper technologies such as offices and libraries are automated and the volume of text available in electronic form to the average user grows far beyond what it is today, already much more than it was in the recent past. Text retrieval is not well served by the current generation of database systems, despite the improvements they represent over earlier network, hierarchical, and file systems. Ironically, relational systems have only superficially incorporated text support, while the many purpose-built text retrieval systems usually don't support other kinds of data, or even complex forms of text, that might well be useful and important in some applications.

14. Typeset the following mathematical expressions.

(a) $\hat{\beta}_0 = \frac{\sum y_i - \hat{\beta}_1 \cdot \sum x_i}{m}$

(b) $y = \beta_0 + \beta_1 \cdot x$

(c) $\sum_{j=1}^{k-1} v_j < x \leq \sum_{j=1}^{k} v_j$

(d) $b = \left\lceil \frac{\log(2-p)}{-\log(1-p)} \right\rceil$

(e) $f(x) = e^{2^{g(x)}}$ where $g(x) = -\frac{b}{a} x \sqrt{1 - \frac{a^2}{x^2}}$

(f) $\hat{\beta}_0 \pm t_{\omega/2,m-2} \cdot \hat{\sigma} \cdot \sqrt{\left\{ \frac{1}{m} + \left(\frac{\sum x_i}{m} \right)^2 \cdot \frac{1}{\sum x_i^2 - (\sum x_i)^2/m} \right\}}$

15. Revise a mathematical argument to use less mathematics and more explanation. In a paper with a long proof or mathematical argument, identify the pivotal points of the argument. Is the argument complete? Are too many or too few details provided?

16. Choose a simple algorithm and a standard description of it, such as linear search in a sorted array. Rewrite the algorithm in prosecode. Repeat the exercise with a more interesting algorithm, such as heapsort. Now choose an algorithm with a complexity analysis. Rewrite the algorithm as literate code, incorporating the important elements of the analysis into the algorithm's description.

17. Design an experiment to compare two well-known algorithms for solving some problem. An elementary example is binary search in an array versus a hash table with separate chaining, but a more sophisticated example such as a comparison of sorting algorithms will make the exercise more interesting.

    (a) What outcome do you expect—that is, what is the hypothesis?

    (b) Will successful results confirm a complexity analysis?

    (c) What resources should be measured? How should they be measured?

    (d) What are appropriate sources of test data?

    (e) To what extent are the results likely to be dependent on characteristics or peculiarities of the data?

    (f) What properties would the test data have to have to confound your hypothesis?

    (g) Is quality of implementation likely to affect the results?

    (h) In the light of these issues, do you expect the experiment to yield unambiguous results?

18. Write a program to find out how likely a tennis player is to win a match. (See page 201.) How many matches are needed to converge on the result to a reasonable level of accuracy?

    Suppose a tennis tournament is to be played under the usual rules: players who lose a match are immediately eliminated, producing rounds in which the number of surviving players is successively halved, starting initially with 128 participants. Suppose all the players are equally good, with one exception, the champ, who wins 60% of the points. What is the likelihood that the champ wins the tournament?

    Suppose instead that the players are ranked from 1 to 128, and that player n wins 51% of the points against player $n+1$. Can the probability of the top-ranked player winning the tournament be investigated with the same method? Explain.

19. Choose a well-known researcher and identify the area in which the researcher is expert. Using the web, identify other researchers in the same area. Which of these researchers might be regarded as authorities? Which are the key papers in the area? What evidence did you use to make these judgements?

20. The following bibliography has several faults and inconsistencies. Identify them.

    T. Cornish and J. Warren, "Networks without wires", 16(3):11–17, 2001.

    Frank Dean, "Wireless transaction resolution with do-nothing devices", *International Journal of Portable Computing*, 2(1):75–81, 2003.

    L .T. Lee, B. Clarke, and C. C. Cheng, "Systems analysis and systems design in Mobile Databases", *Jour. Portable Computing*, vol. 2, pp. 72–74, May 2003.

    Macic, V., et al., "Connectedness in low-bandwith local area networks", *Proc. International Mobile and Wireless Computing Conference*, Toby Thomas (ed.), ICM, June 2002, pp. 166–176.

Index

An entry in an upright font refers to discussion of a concept; for example, pages listed under "abstract" consider abstracts. An entry in italics concerns word usage; for example, the page listed under "*also*" considers the word "also".